GET YOUR SHIT TOGETHER

DAVID SHRIGLEY

CHRONICLE CHROMA

TABLE OF CONTENTS

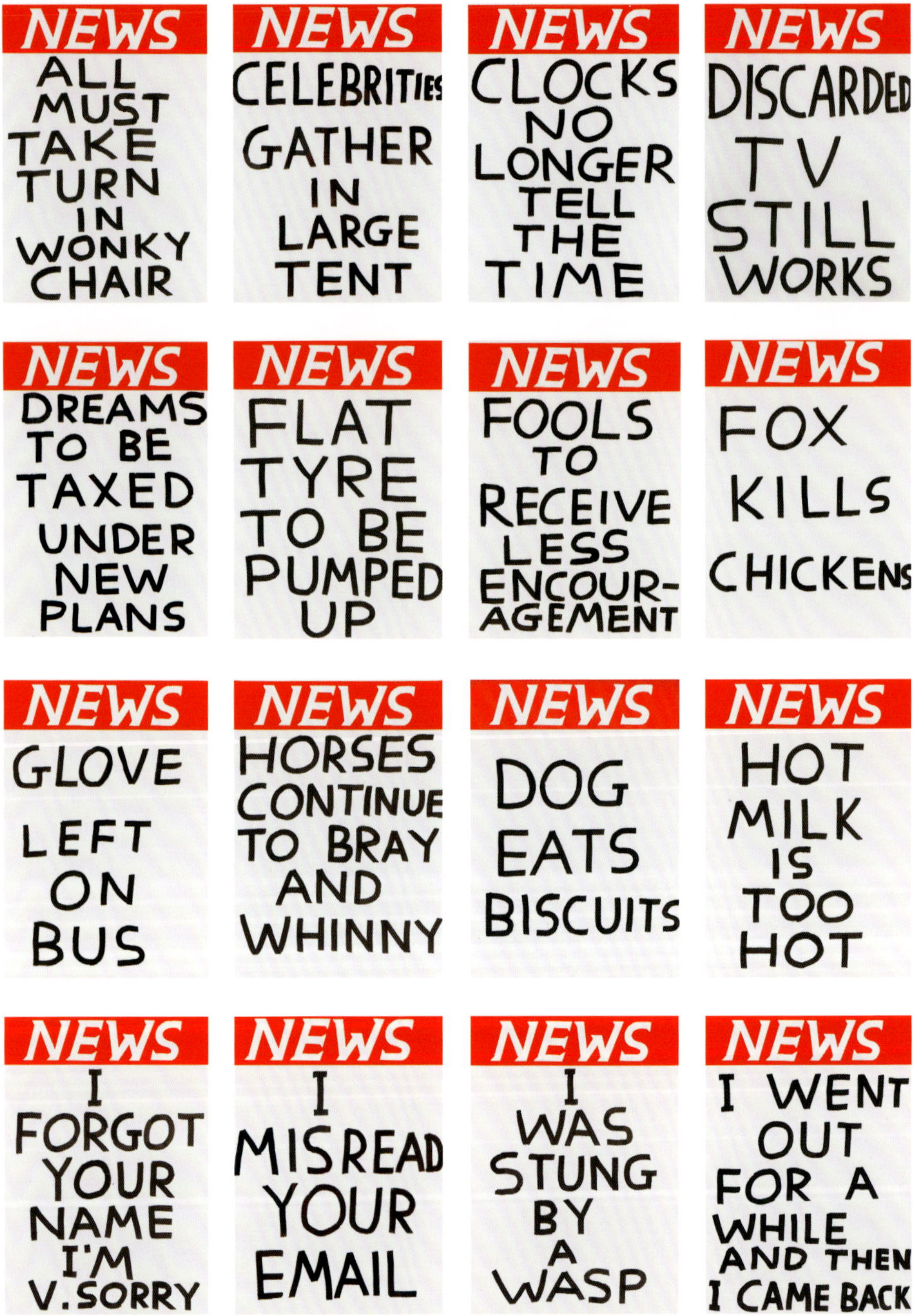

NEWS

ALL MUST TAKE TURN IN WONKY CHAIR

NEWS

CELEBRITIES GATHER IN LARGE TENT

NEWS

CLOCKS NO LONGER TELL THE TIME

NEWS

DISCARDED TV STILL WORKS

NEWS

DREAMS TO BE TAXED UNDER NEW PLANS

NEWS

FLAT TYRE TO BE PUMPED UP

NEWS

FOOLS TO RECEIVE LESS ENCOUR-AGEMENT

NEWS

FOX KILLS CHICKENS

NEWS

GLOVE LEFT ON BUS

NEWS

HORSES CONTINUE TO BRAY AND WHINNY

NEWS

DOG EATS BISCUITS

NEWS

HOT MILK IS TOO HOT

NEWS

I FORGOT YOUR NAME I'M V. SORRY

NEWS

I MISREAD YOUR EMAIL

NEWS

I WAS STUNG BY A WASP

NEWS

I WENT OUT FOR A WHILE AND THEN I CAME BACK

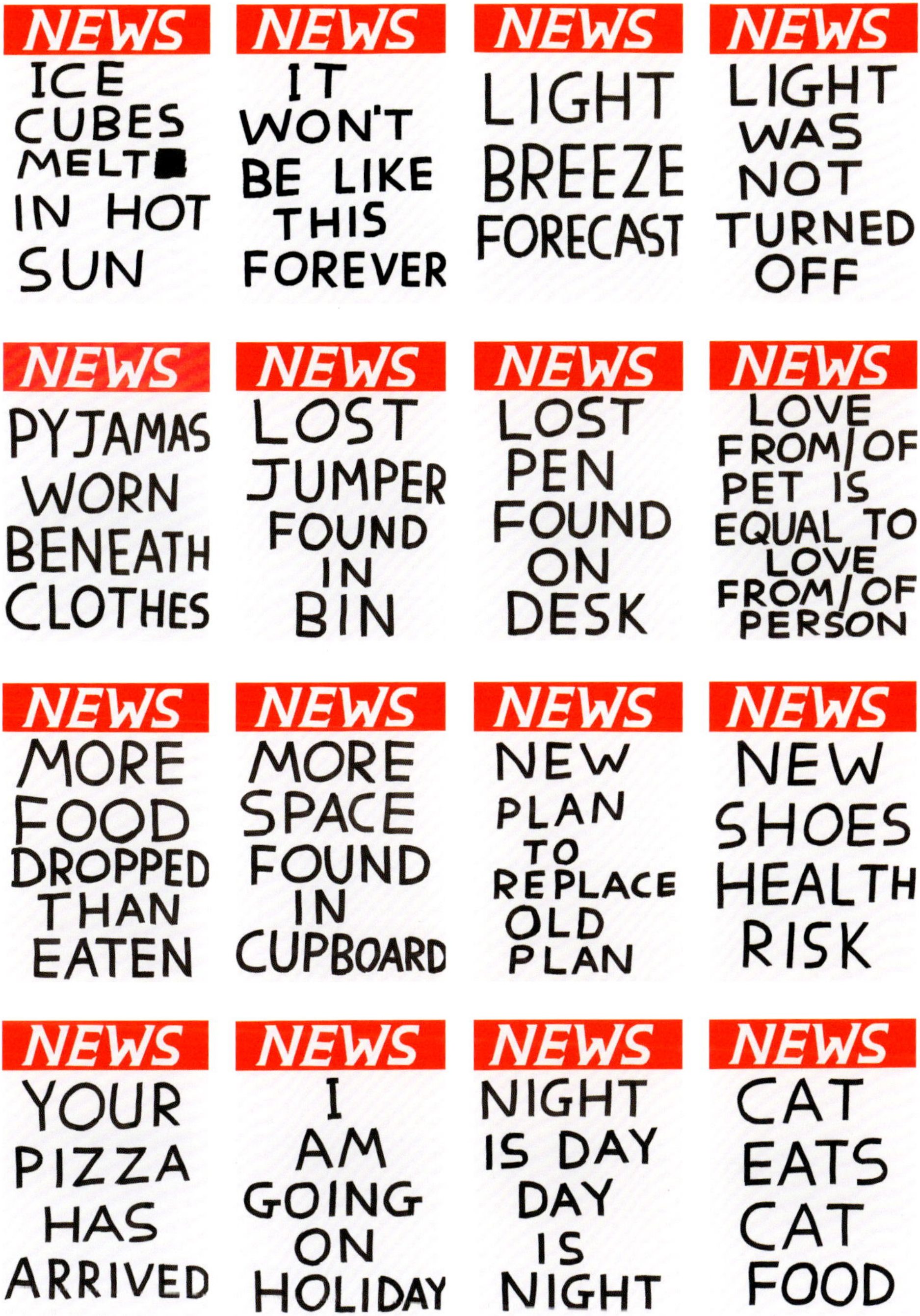

NEWS

ICE
CUBES
MELT
IN HOT
SUN

NEWS

IT
WON'T
BE LIKE
THIS
FOREVER

NEWS

LIGHT
BREEZE
FORECAST

NEWS

LIGHT
WAS
NOT
TURNED
OFF

NEWS

PYJAMAS
WORN
BENEATH
CLOTHES

NEWS

LOST
JUMPER
FOUND
IN
BIN

NEWS

LOST
PEN
FOUND
ON
DESK

NEWS

LOVE
FROM/OF
PET IS
EQUAL TO
LOVE
FROM/OF
PERSON

NEWS

MORE
FOOD
DROPPED
THAN
EATEN

NEWS

MORE
SPACE
FOUND
IN
CUPBOARD

NEWS

NEW
PLAN
TO
REPLACE
OLD
PLAN

NEWS

NEW
SHOES
HEALTH
RISK

NEWS

YOUR
PIZZA
HAS
ARRIVED

NEWS

I
AM
GOING
ON
HOLIDAY

NEWS

NIGHT
IS DAY
DAY
IS
NIGHT

NEWS

CAT
EATS
CAT
FOOD

BLANK PAGE

I WAS READING A BOOK
AND I GOT TO A BLANK PAGE
I WAS ANGRY
I TOOK THE BOOK BACK TO THE SHOP
I DEMANDED MY MONEY BACK
THEY SAID THAT IT WAS NOT A
MISTAKE
THEY SAID THE BLANK PAGE WAS
SUPPOSED
TO BE THERE
I SAID IT WAS RIDICULOUS
THEY GAVE ME MY MONEY BACK

I CAN'T READ

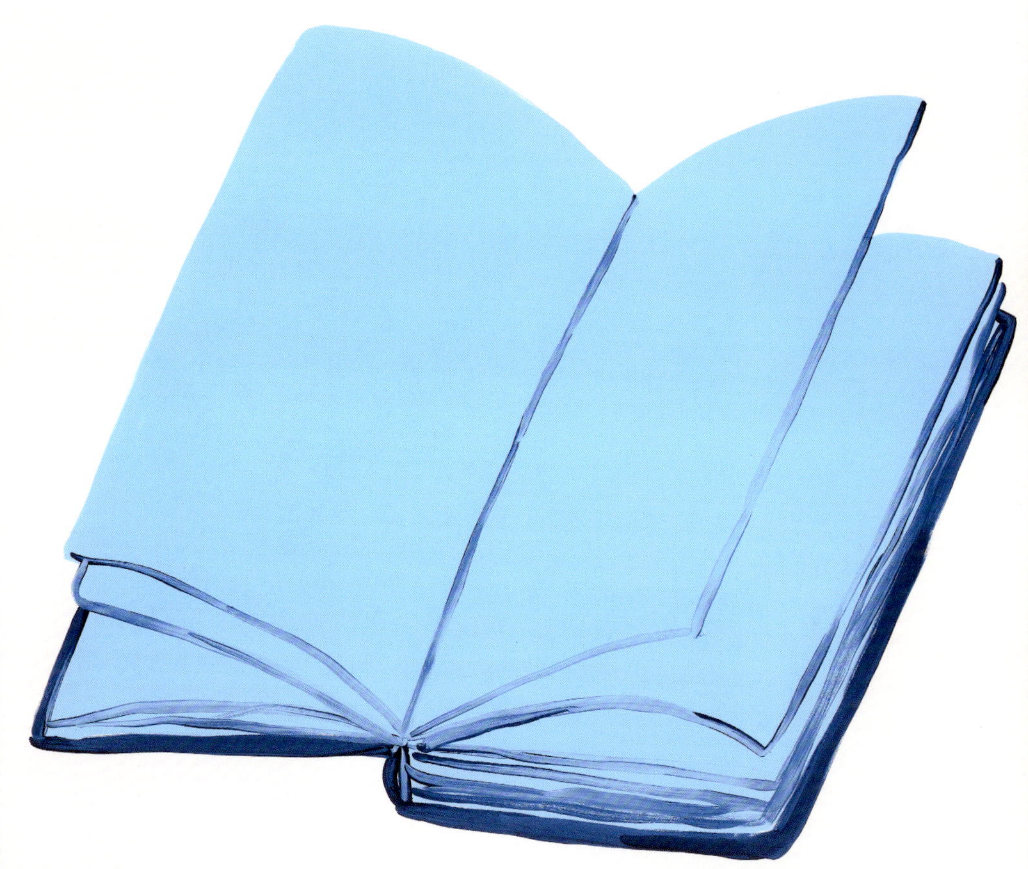

AND I'M TOO BUSY TO LEARN

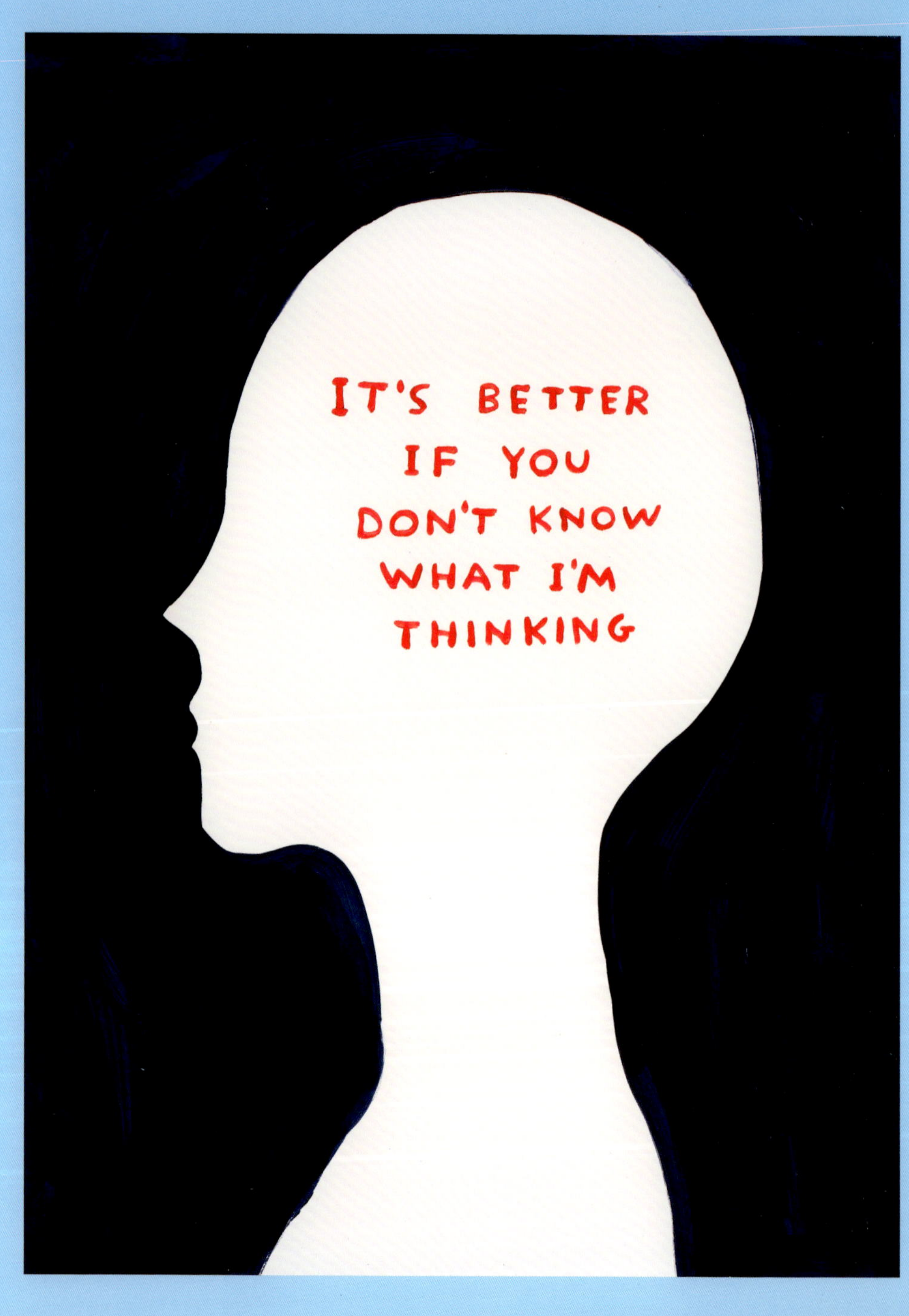
IT'S BETTER
IF YOU
DON'T KNOW
WHAT I'M
THINKING

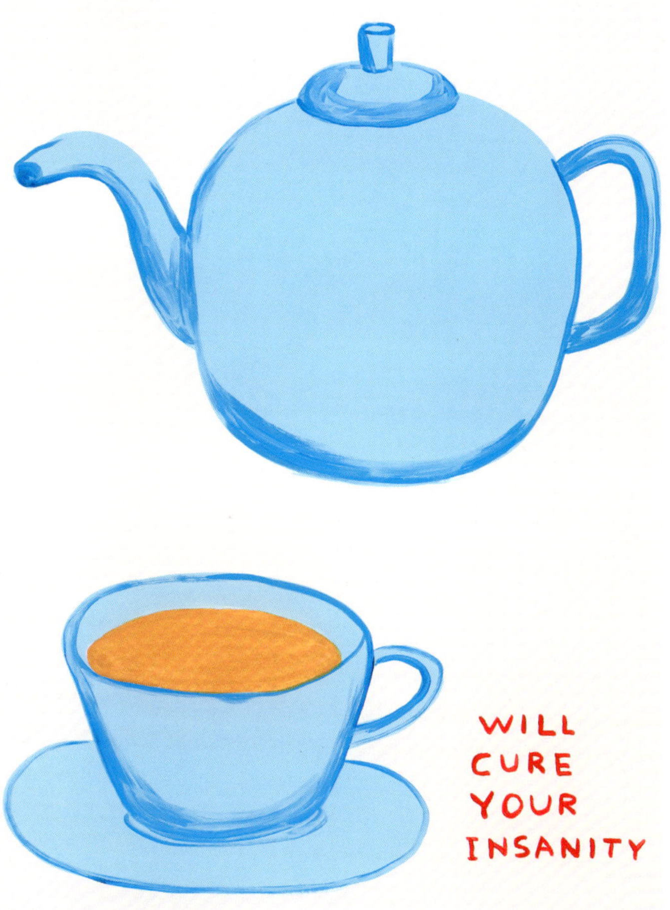
A CUP OF TEA
WILL
CURE
YOUR
INSANITY

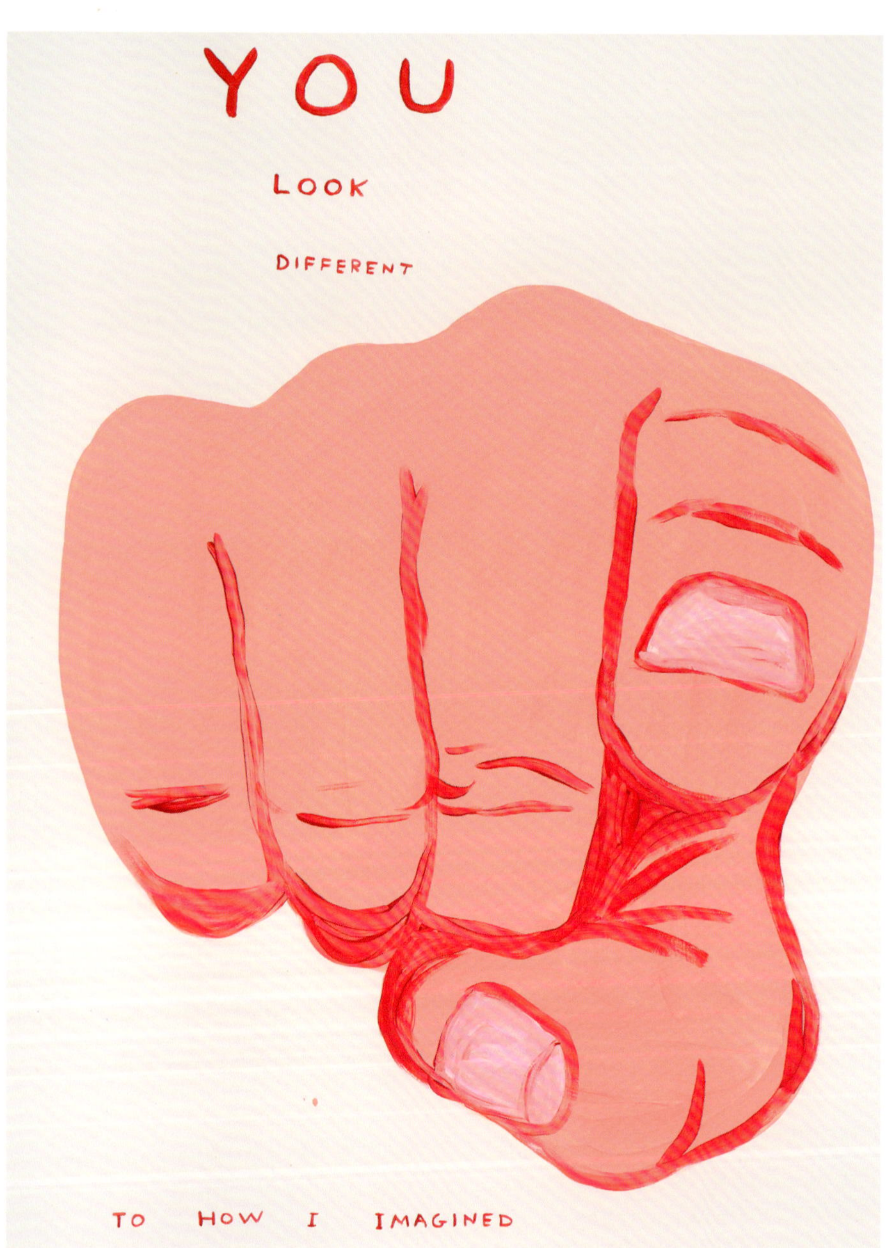
YOU
LOOK
DIFFERENT
TO HOW I IMAGINED

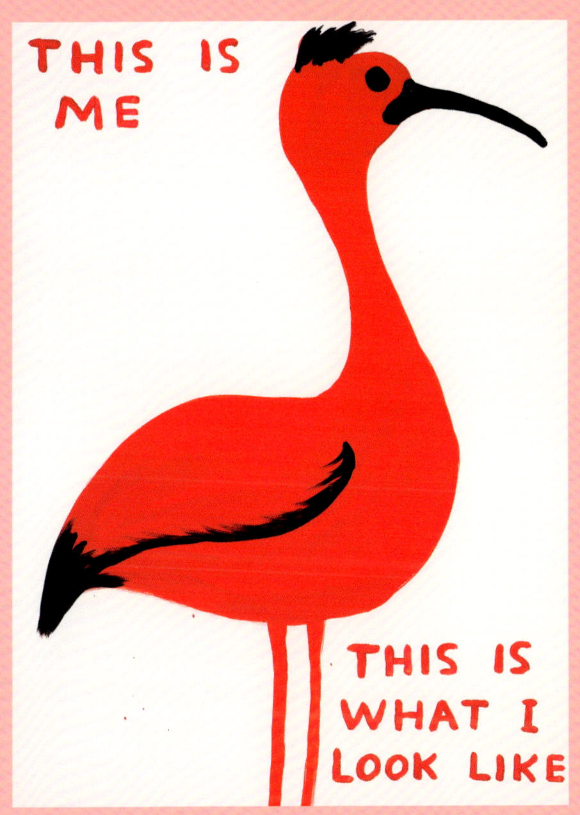
THIS IS
ME
THIS IS
WHAT I
LOOK LIKE

ME / YOU

I AM ME
YOU ARE YOU
IT IS OK

YOU MUST STAY AS YOU
YOU CANNOT BE ME
THAT WOULD NOT BE OK

I DO NOT WANT TO BE YOU
I WILL NOT ALLOW IT
IT WILL NOT HAPPEN

LATER

IT NOW APPEARS THAT I AM YOU
AND YOU ARE ME
IT IS NOT OK
BUT I MUST ACCEPT IT

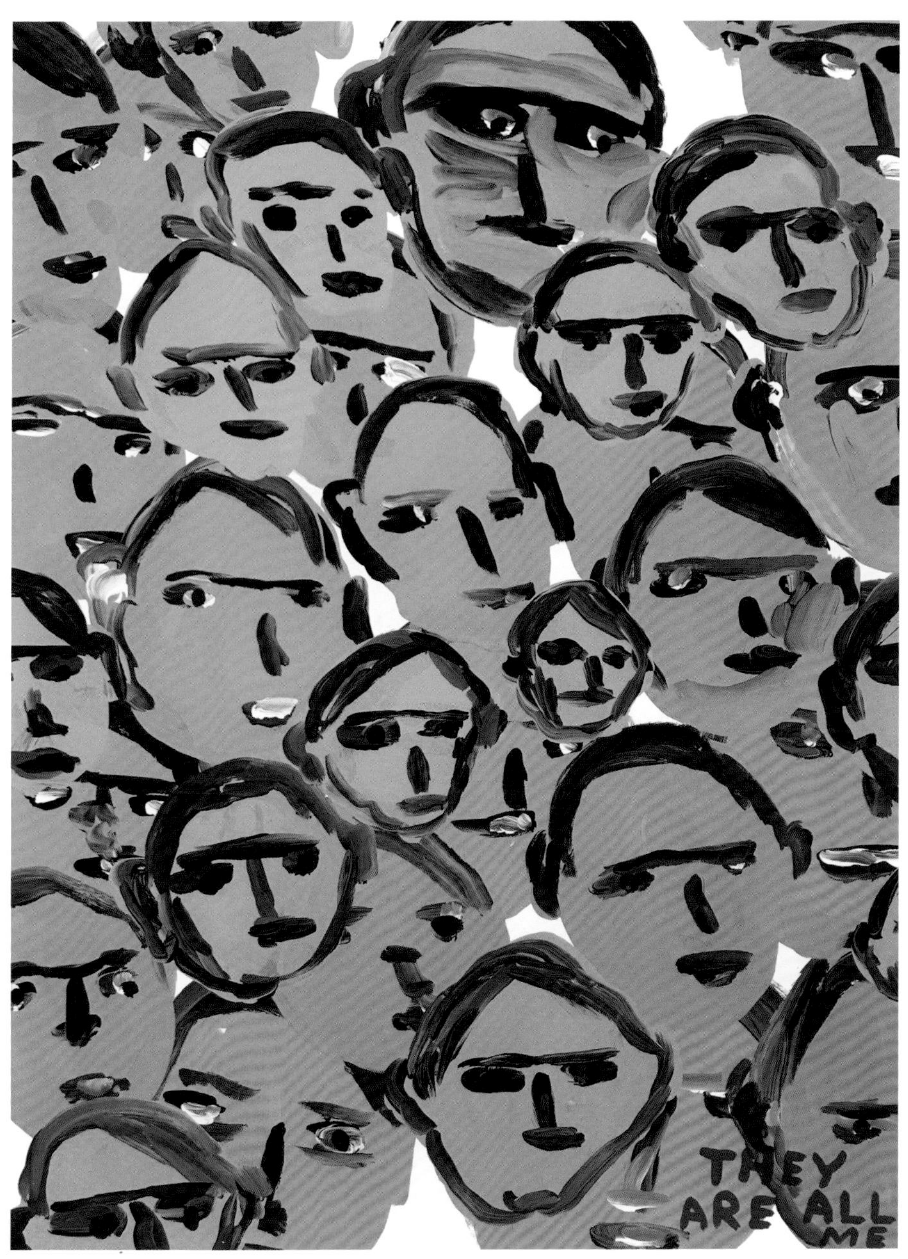
THEY ARE ALL ME

I
LIKE
EXIST
-ING

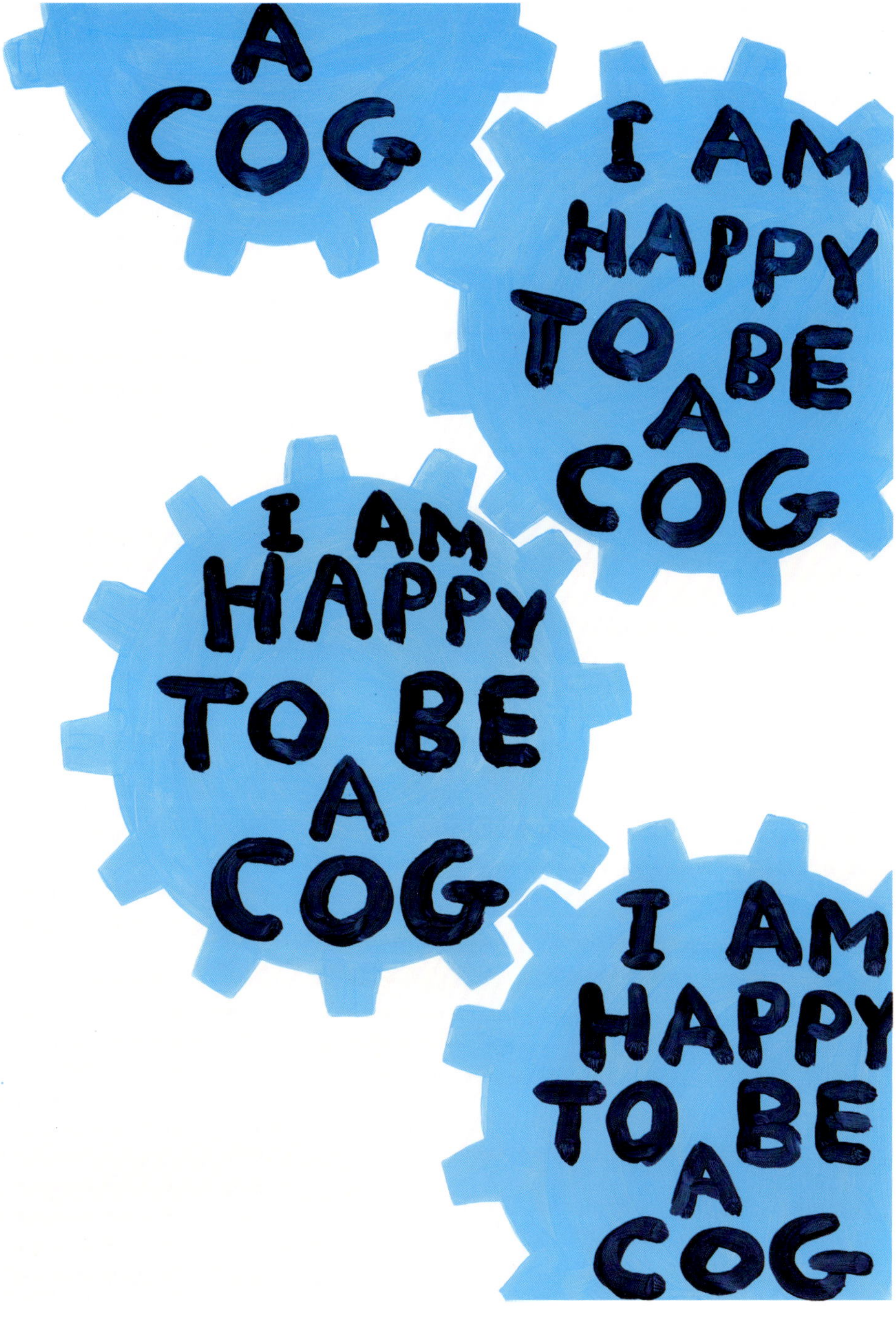

A
COG

I AM
HAPPY
TO BE
A
COG

I AM
HAPPY
TO BE
A
COG

I AM
HAPPY
TO BE
A
COG

SUN

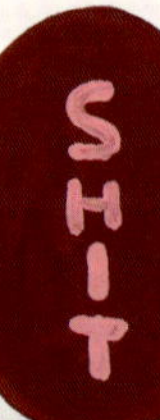

EARTH

MY
WHOLE
LIFE

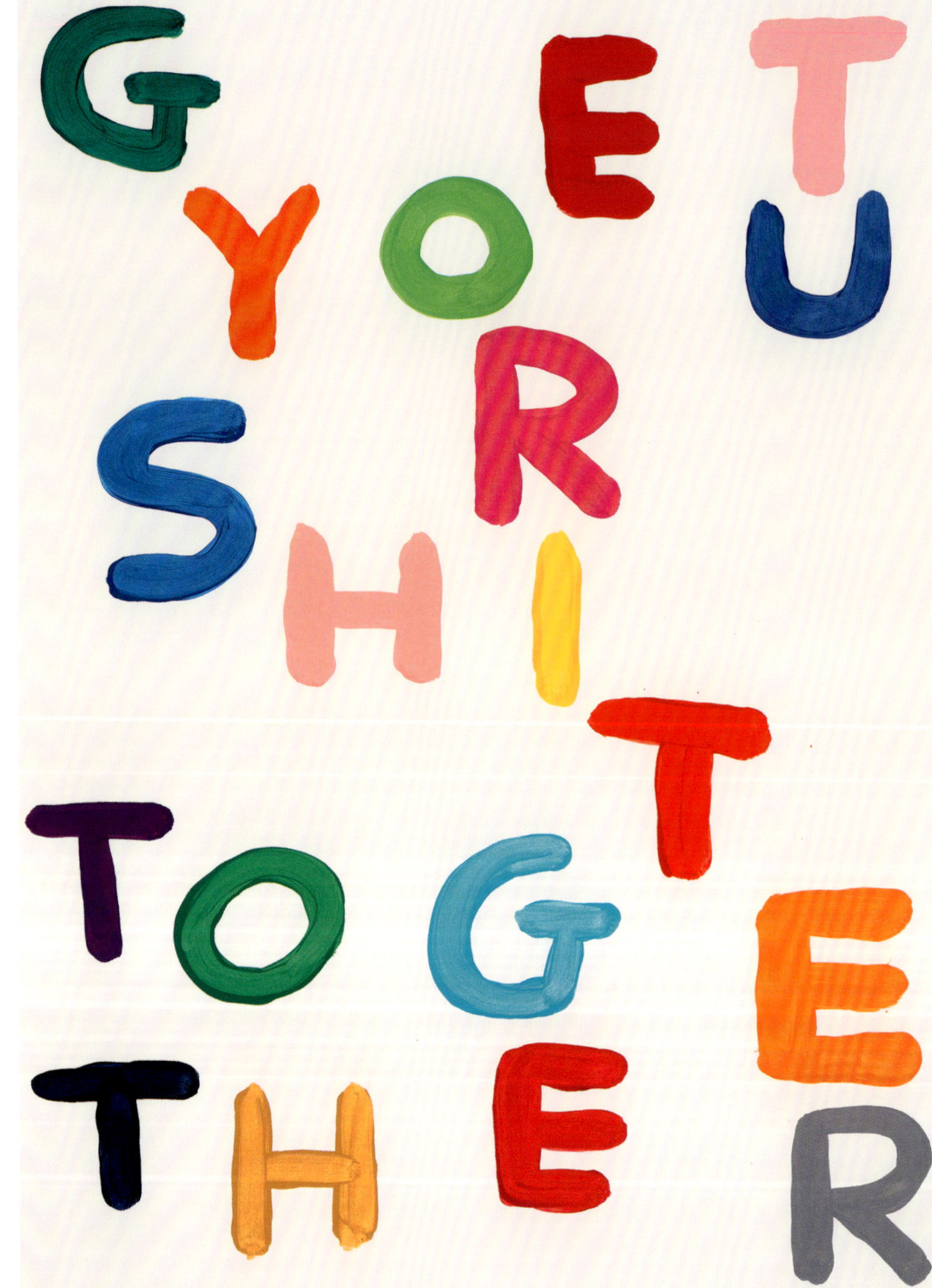
GET YOUR SHIT TOGETHER

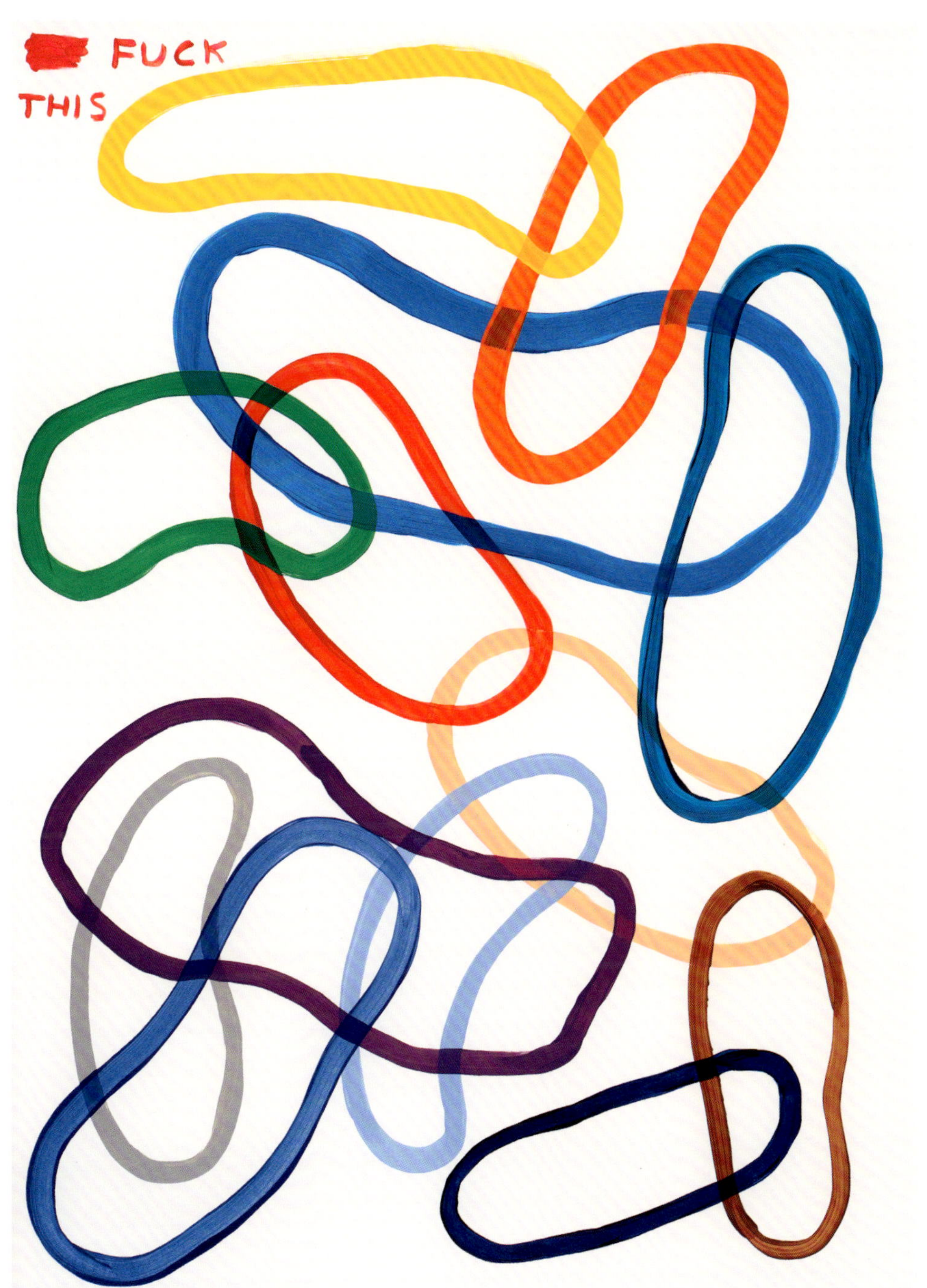
FUCK
THIS

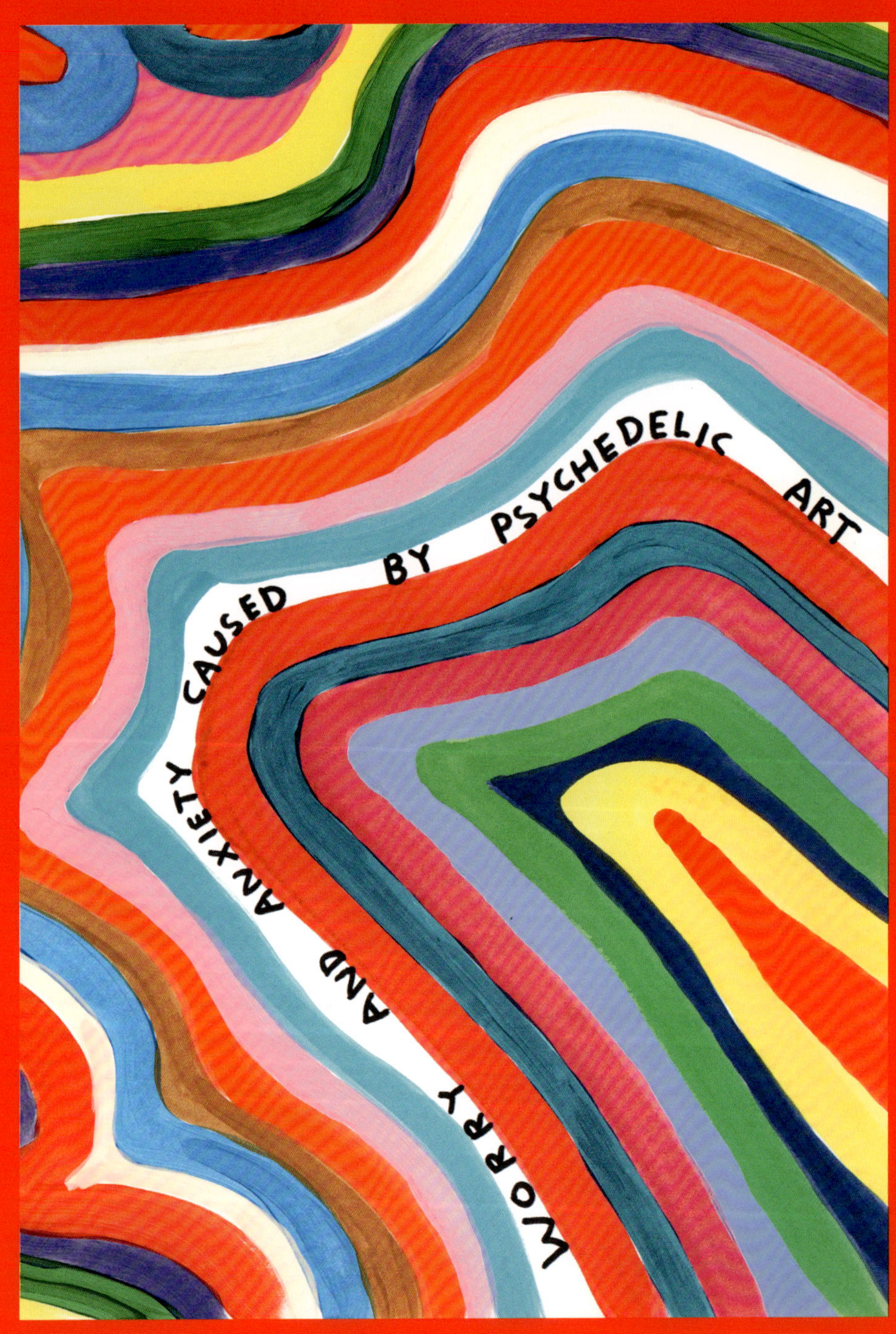
WORRY AND ANXIETY CAUSED BY PSYCHEDELIC ART

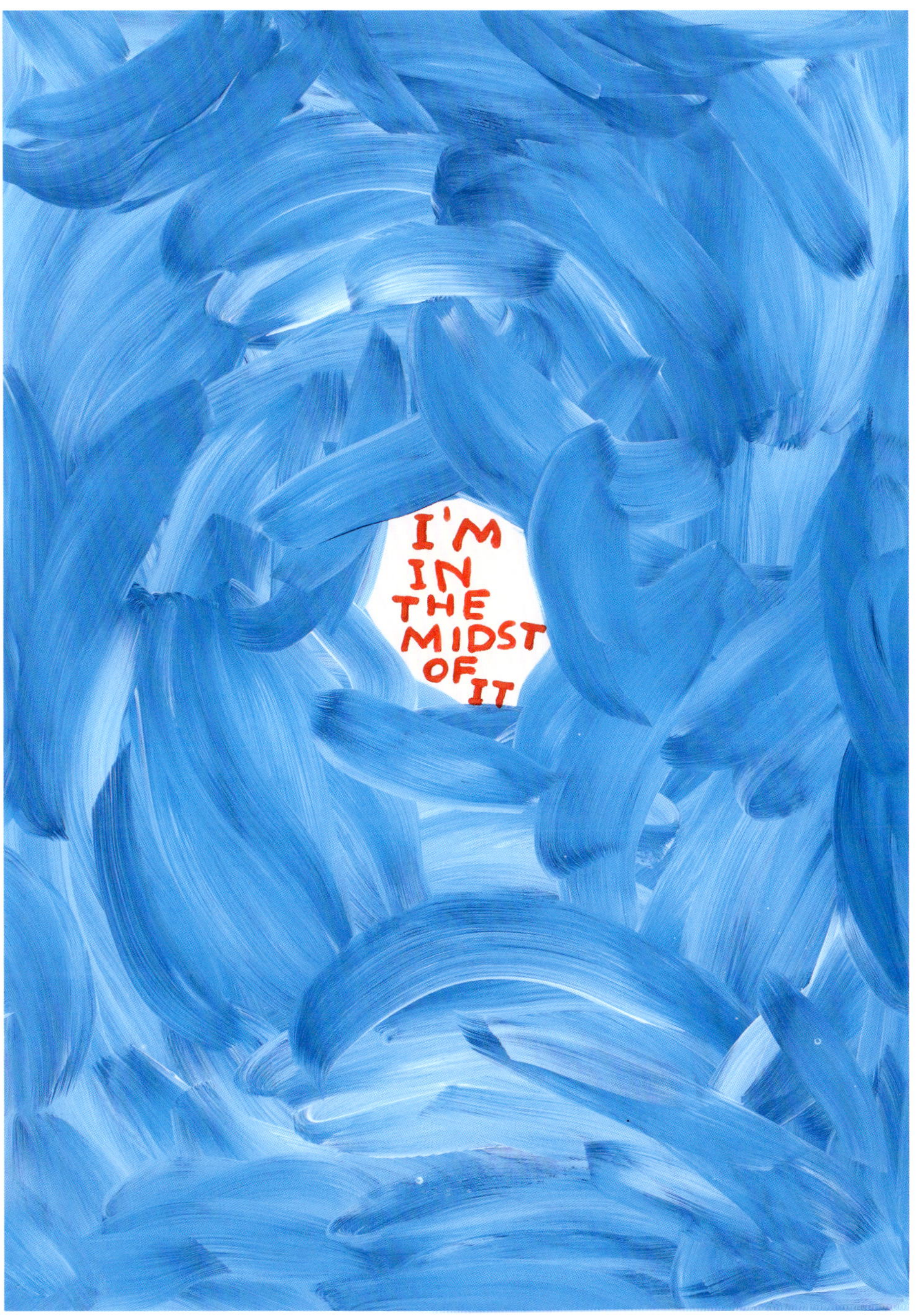
I'M
IN
THE
MIDST
OF
IT

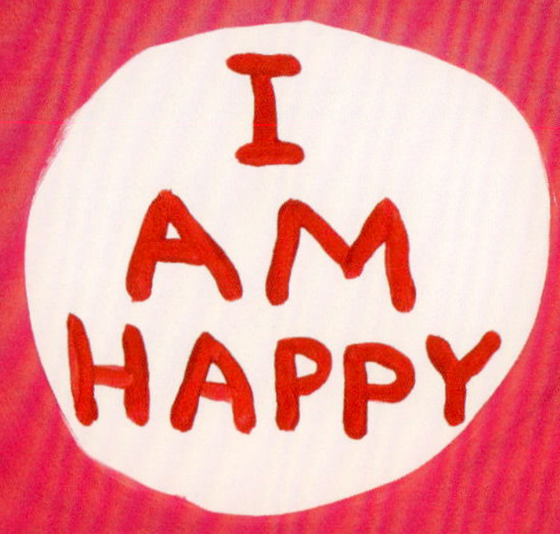

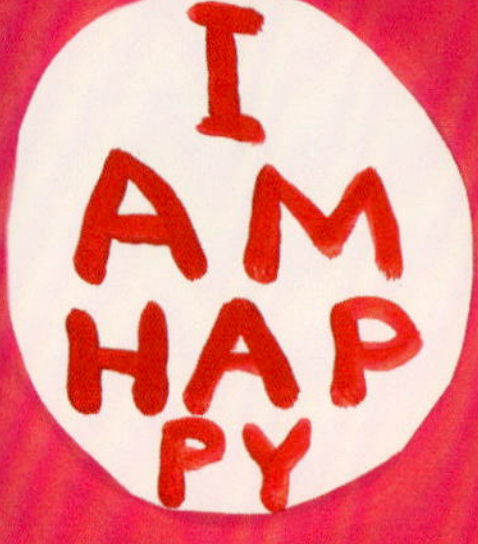

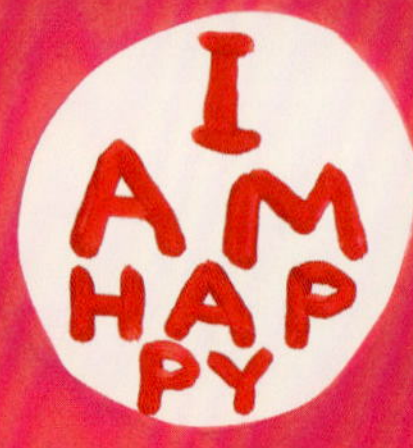

I
AM
HAPPY

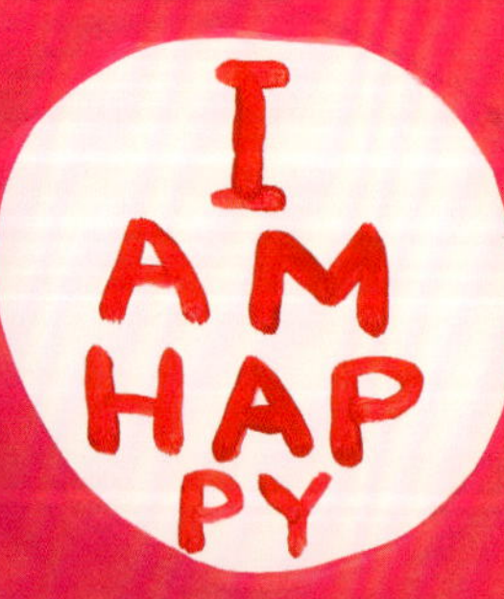

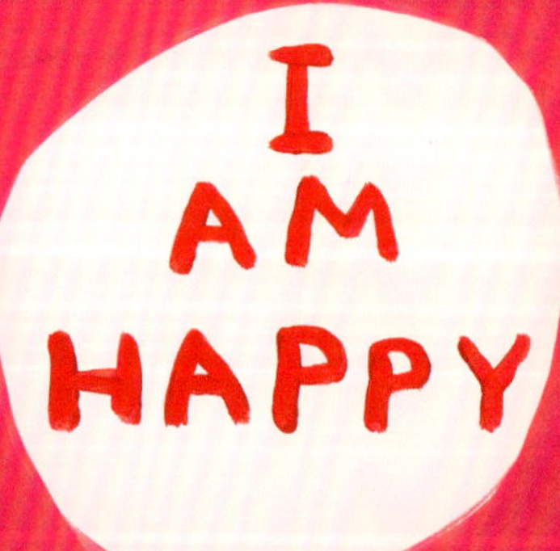

BEFORE YOU CAN ENTERTAIN OTHERS

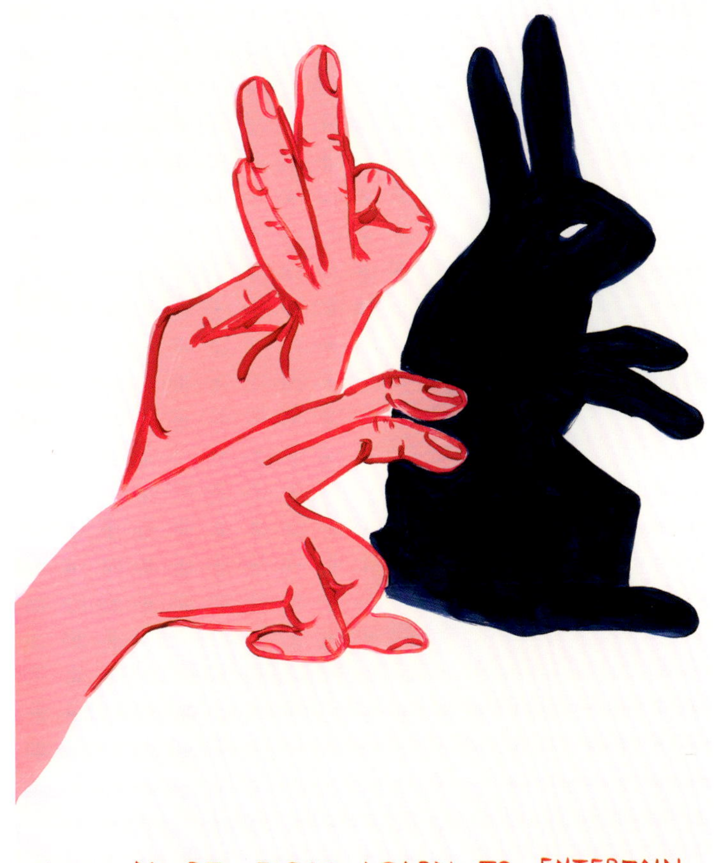

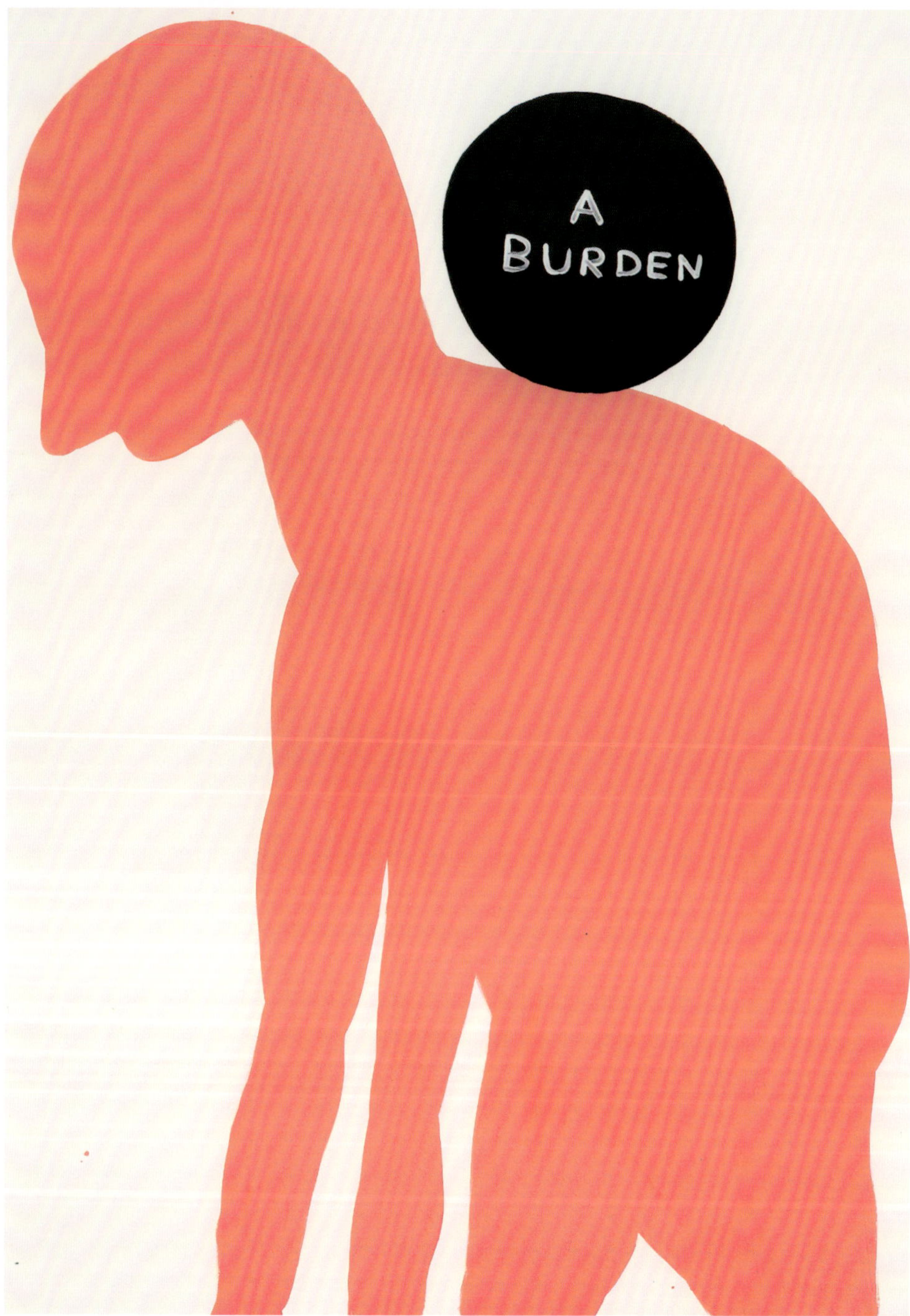
A
BURDEN

DON'T FLUSH YOURSELF

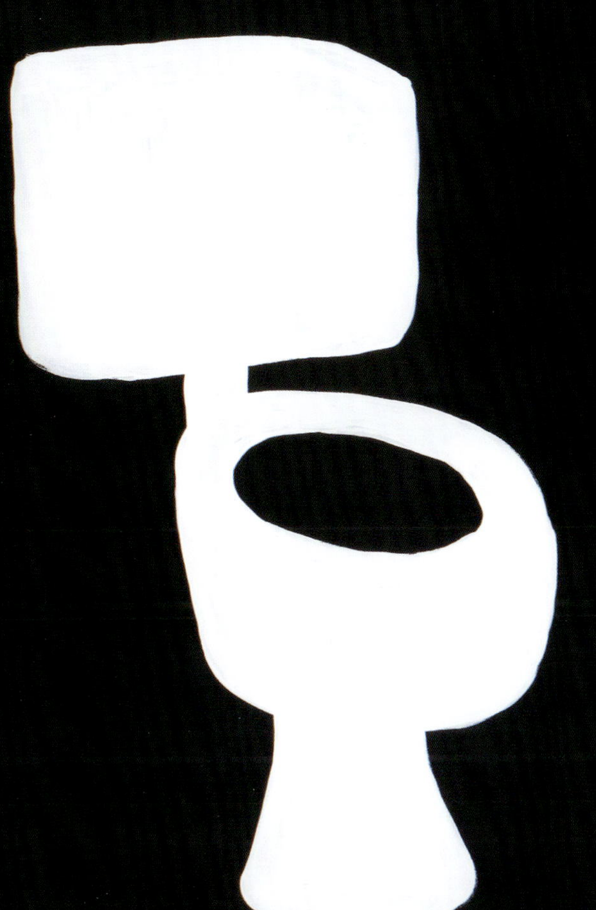

DOWN THE TOILET

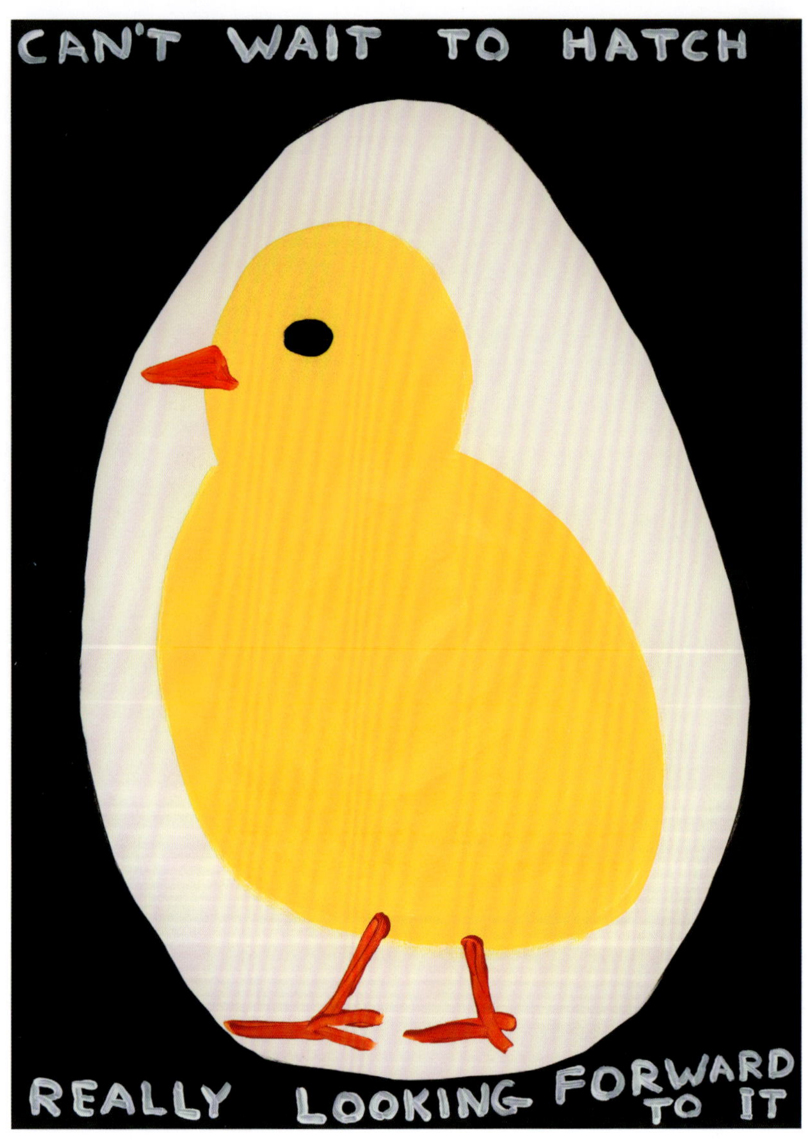
CAN'T WAIT TO HATCH
REALLY LOOKING FORWARD TO IT

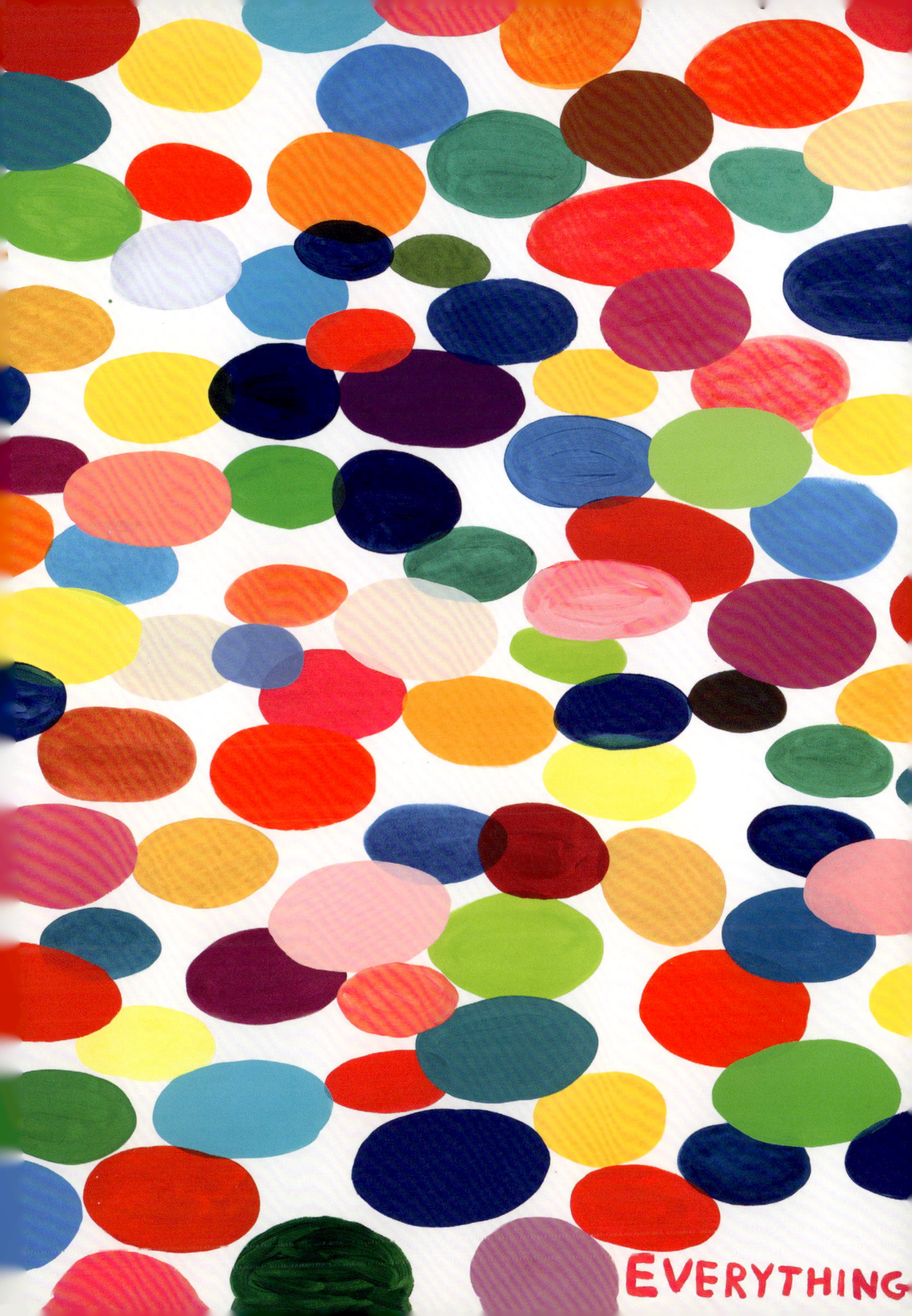
EVERYTHING

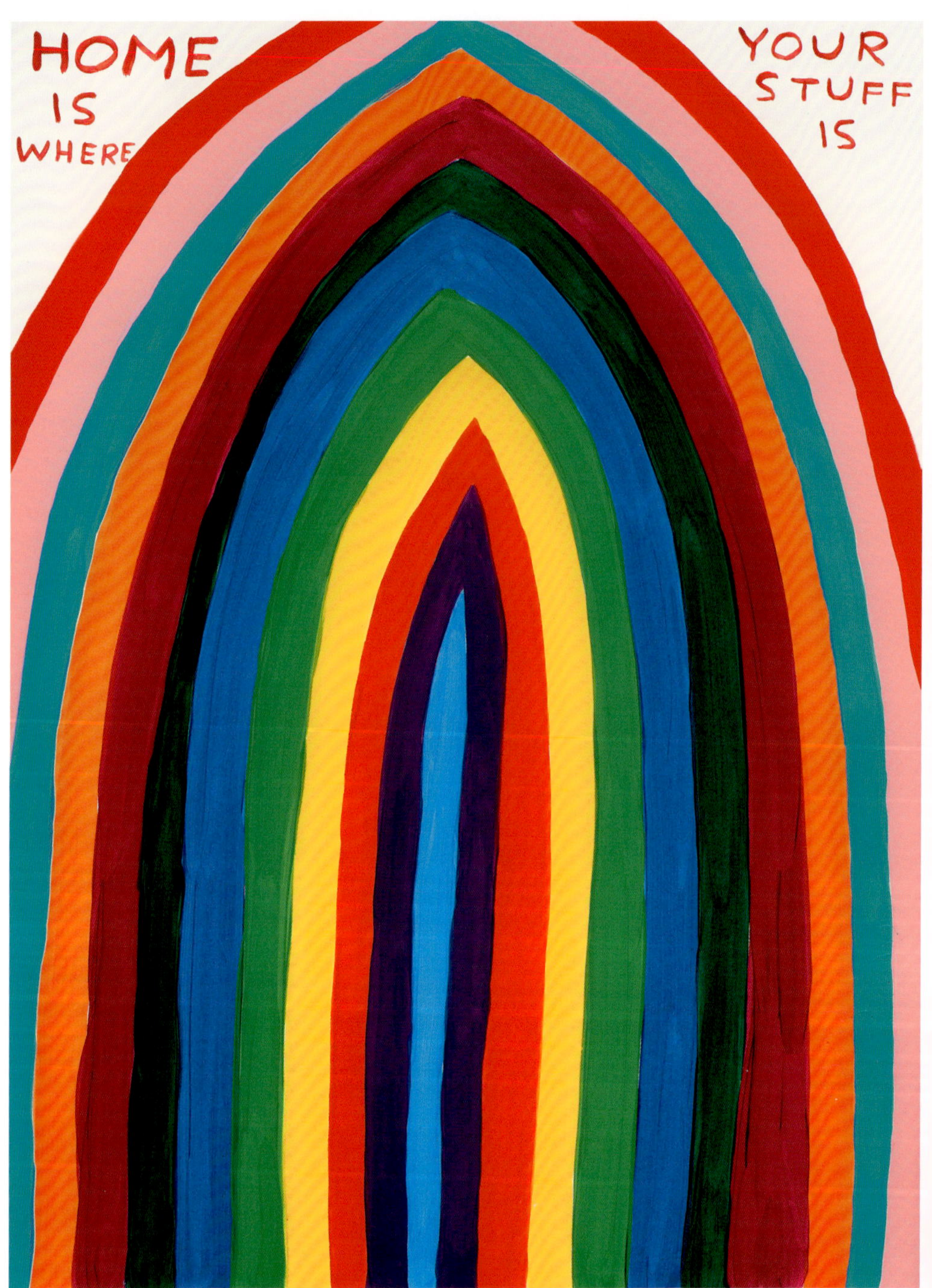
HOME
IS
WHERE
YOUR
STUFF
IS

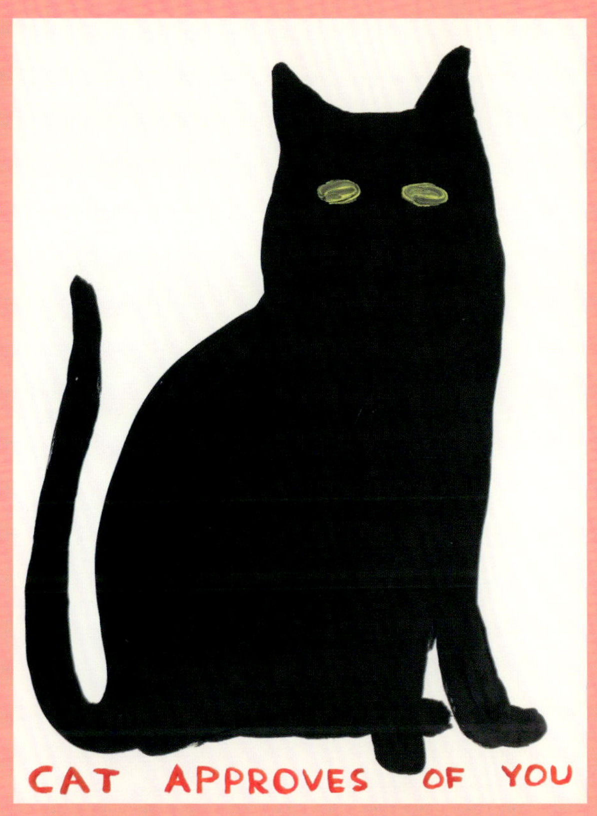
CAT APPROVES OF YOU

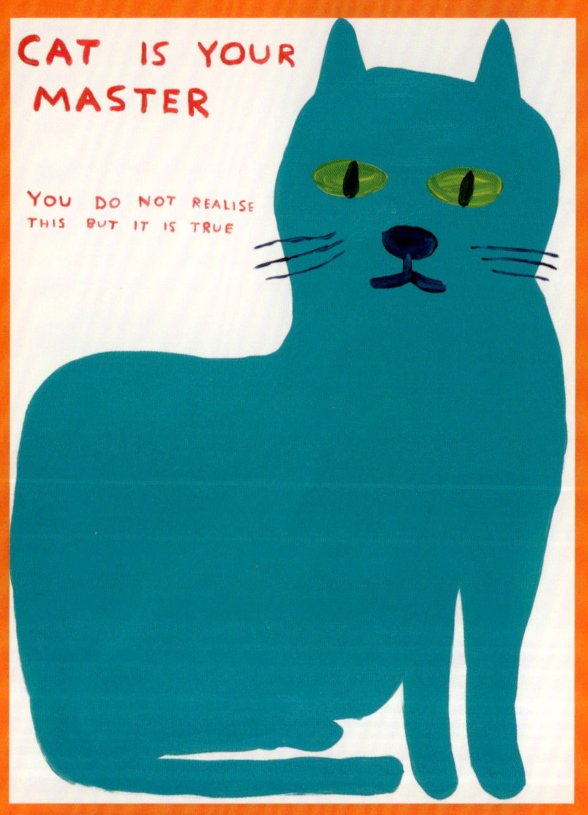
CAT IS YOUR MASTER
YOU DO NOT REALISE THIS BUT IT IS TRUE

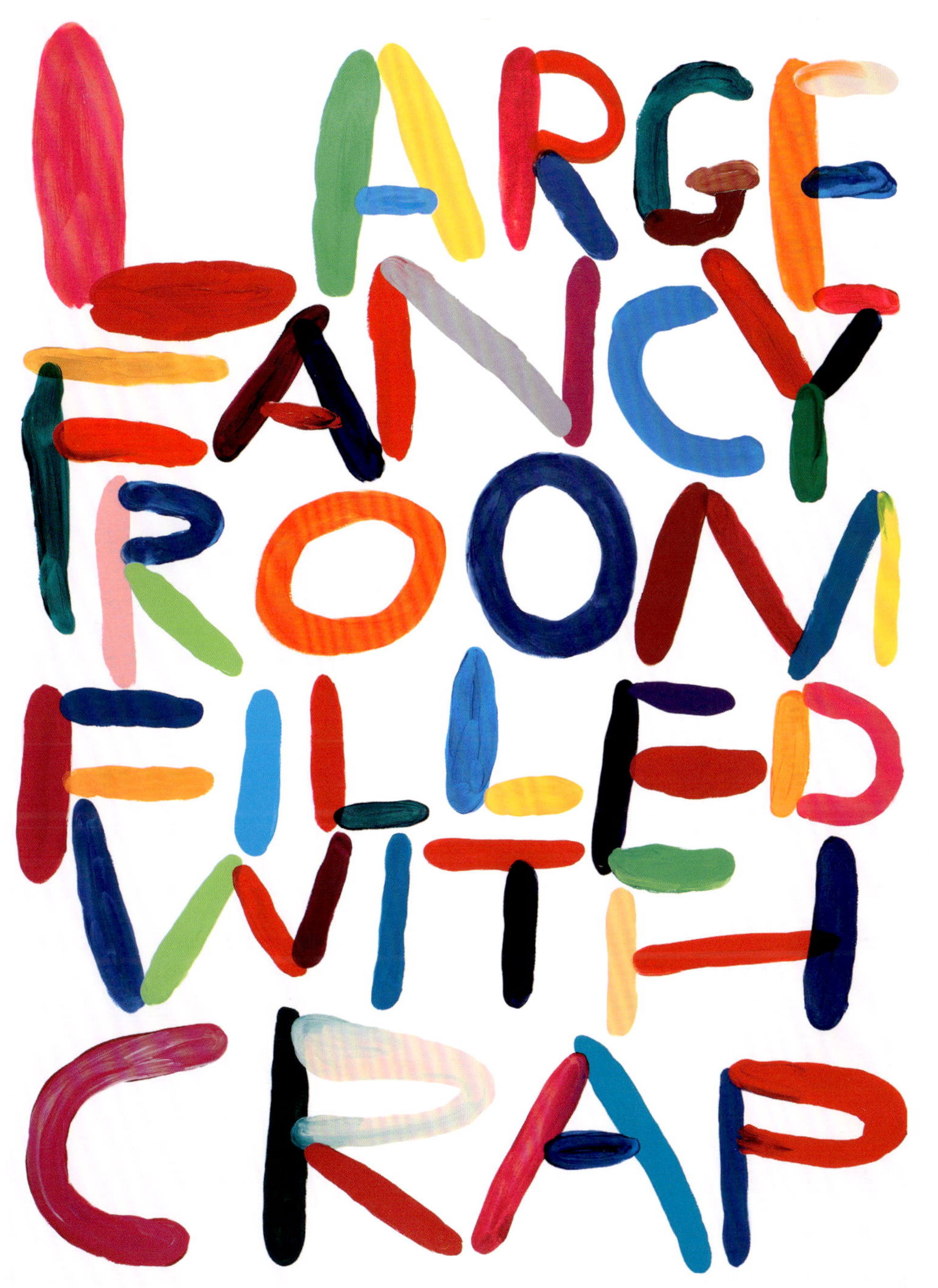
LARGE
FANCY
ROOM
FILLED
WITH
CRAP

THE PAST

THE PAST IS GONE
IF YOU LIKED THE PAST
THEN HARD LUCK
IT'S GONE
AND YOU HAD BETTER GET USED
TO IT

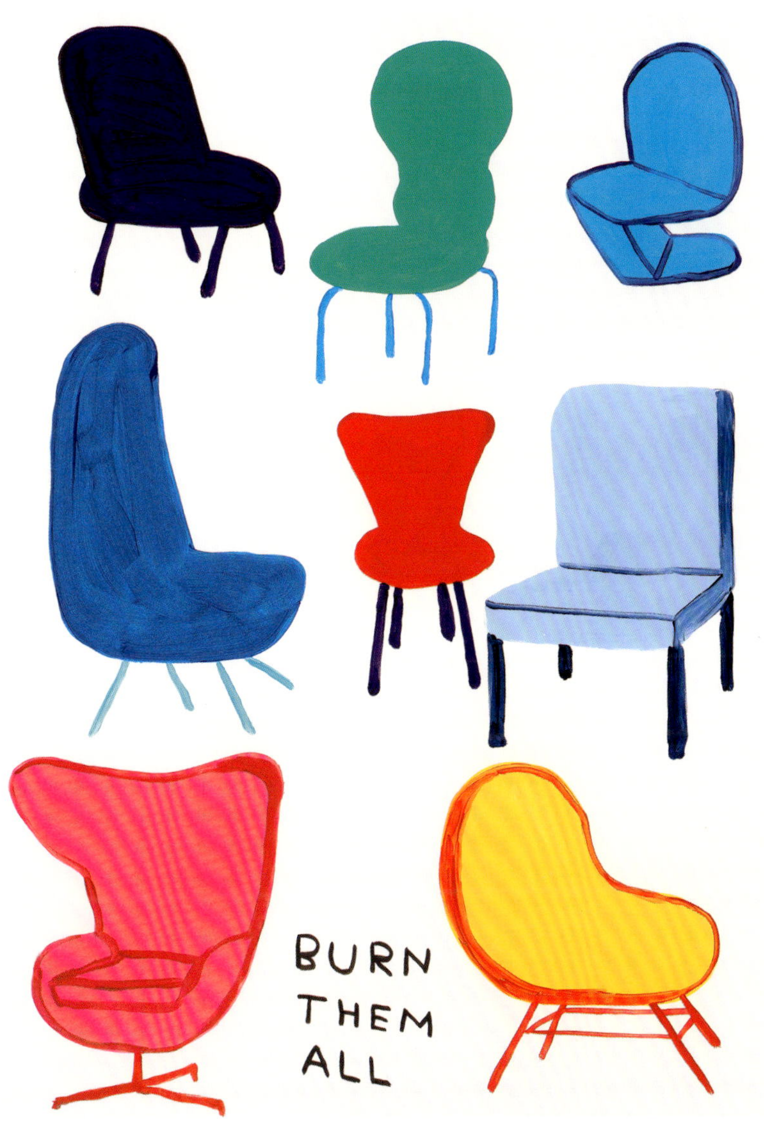
BURN
THEM
ALL

STUPID

I'M NOT STUPID
I AM PRETENDING TO BE STUPID
IN ORDER TO GAIN AN ADVANTAGE
IF YOU KNOW WHAT I MEAN

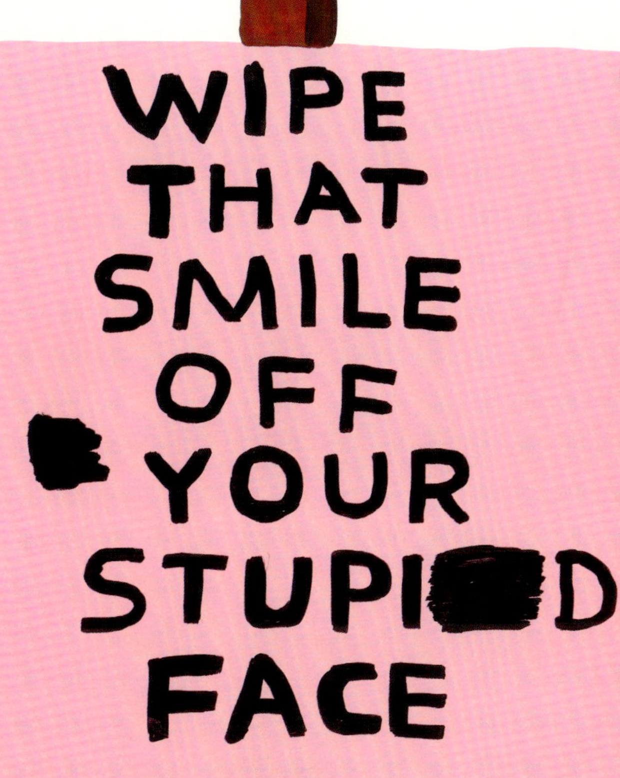
WIPE
THAT
SMILE
OFF
YOUR
STUPID
FACE

FASHION

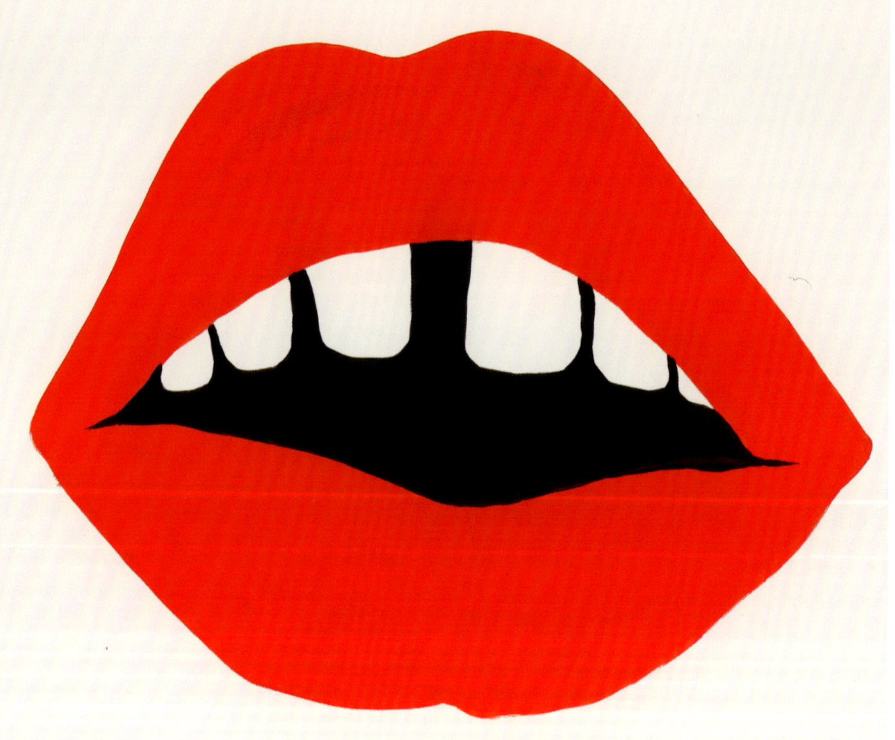

IS
STUPID

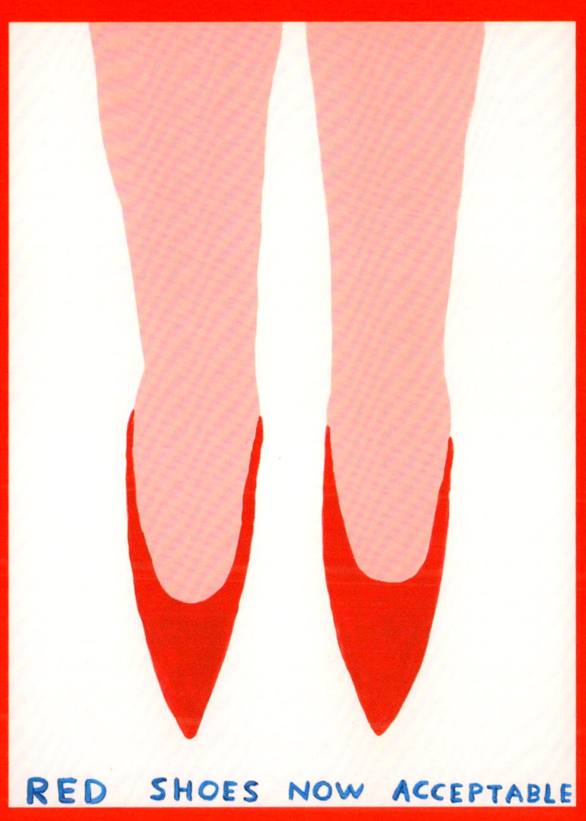
RED SHOES NOW ACCEPTABLE

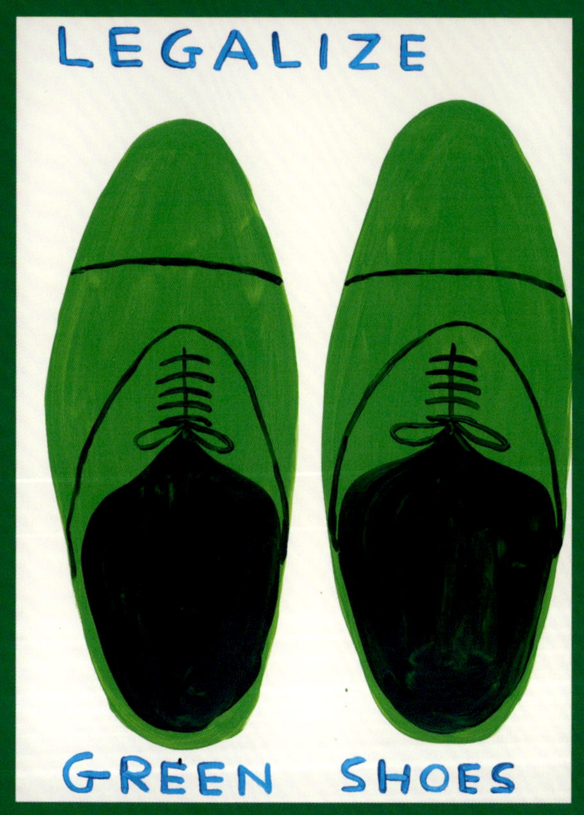
LEGALIZE
GREEN SHOES

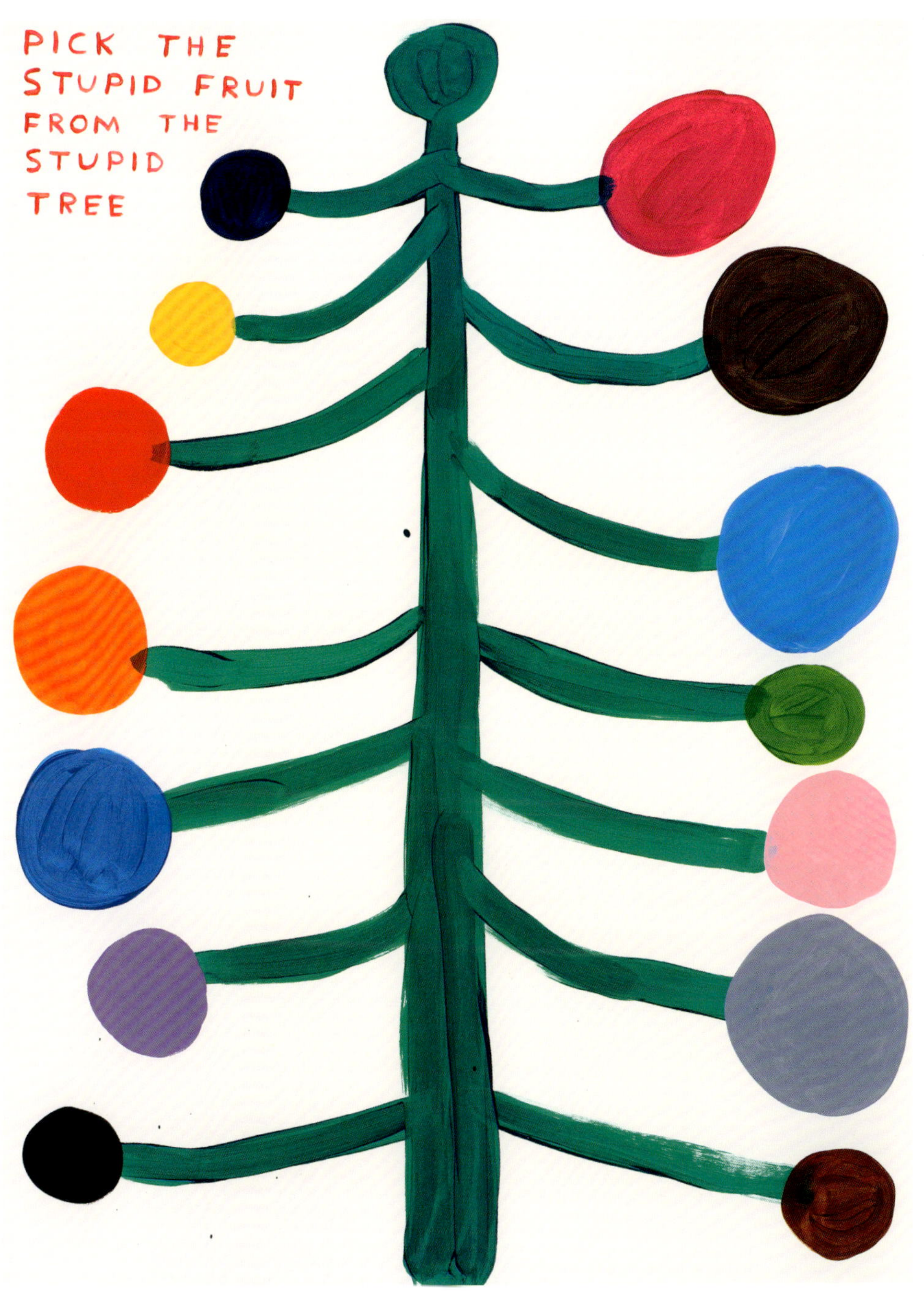
PICK THE
STUPID FRUIT
FROM THE
STUPID
TREE

MY IDEA

I AM GOING TO BREAK INTO
PEOPLE'S HOMES
AND THREATEN THEM
AND TIE THEM UP
THEN I WILL DO PORTRAITS OF
TIED UP THEM
USING OIL PAINT
ON CANVAS

I WILL MAKE A NUMBER OF THESE
AND WILL SHOW THEM WORKS
AT A SMALL COMMERCIAL GALLERY SPACE
IN PICCADILLY
THE EXHIBITION WILL BE CALLED
'PORTRAITS'

ALL YOUR STUPID IDEAS

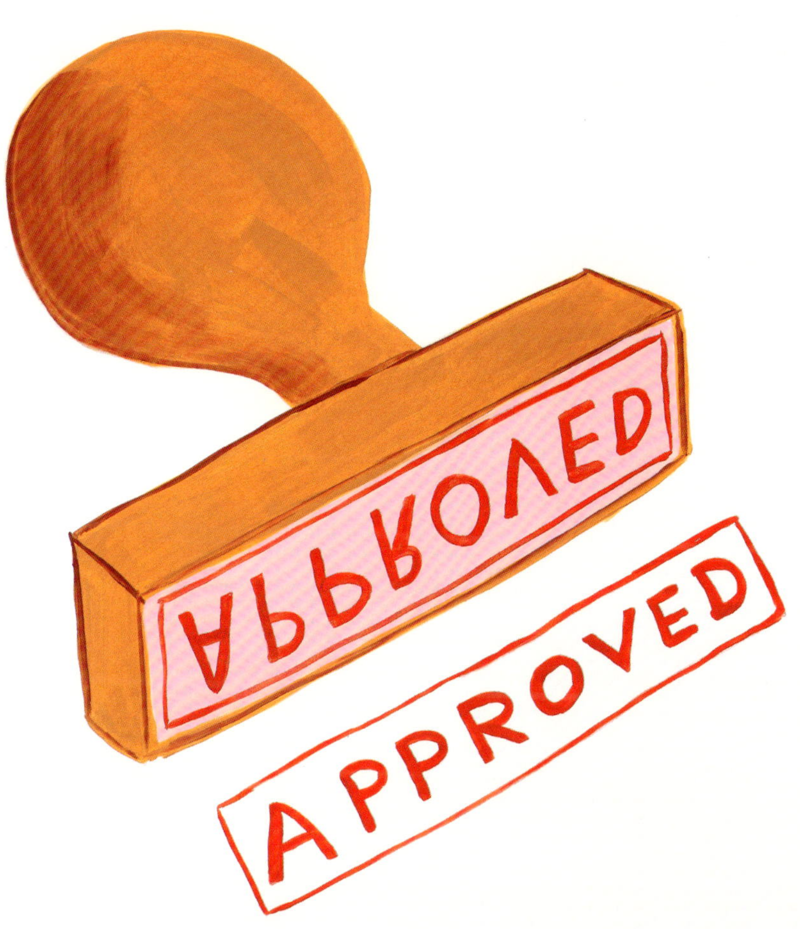

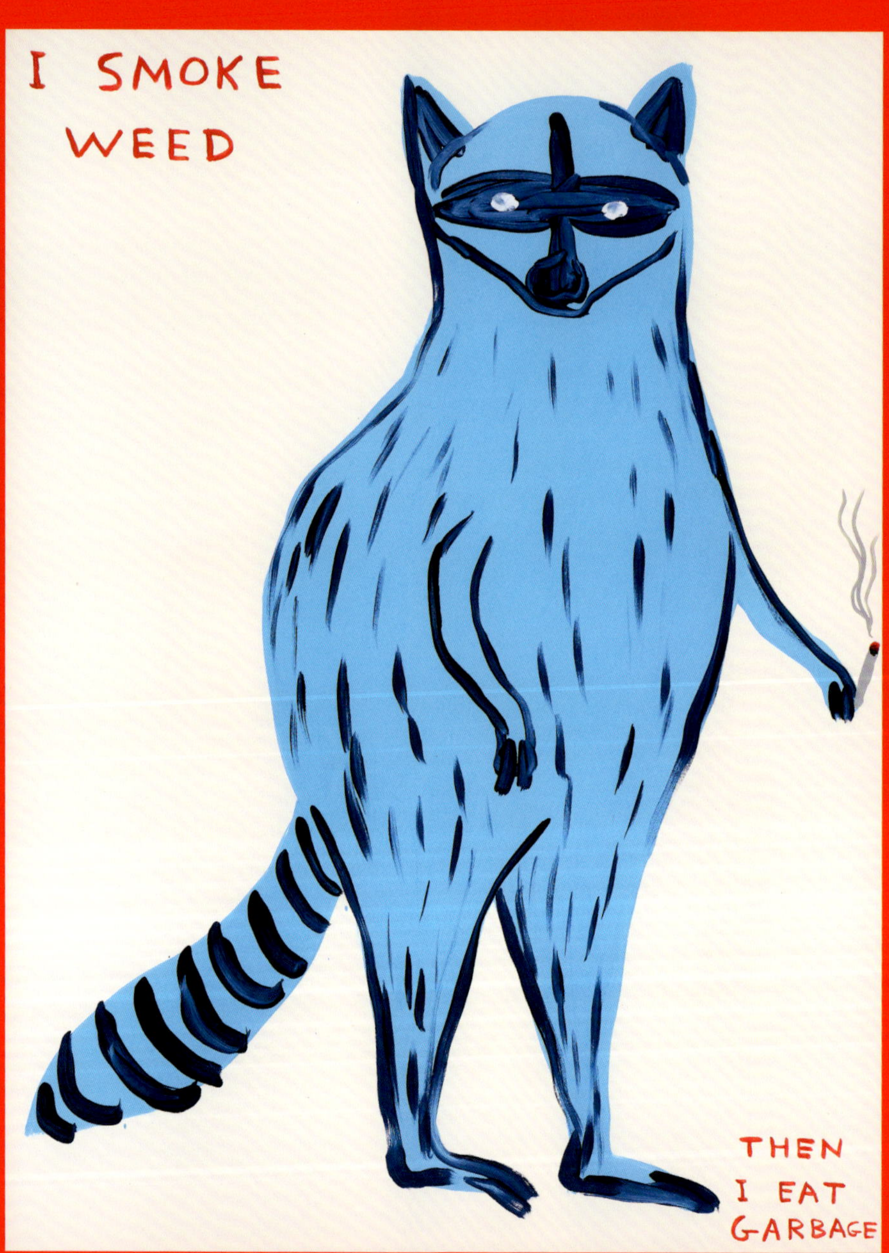
I SMOKE
WEED
THEN
I EAT
GARBAGE

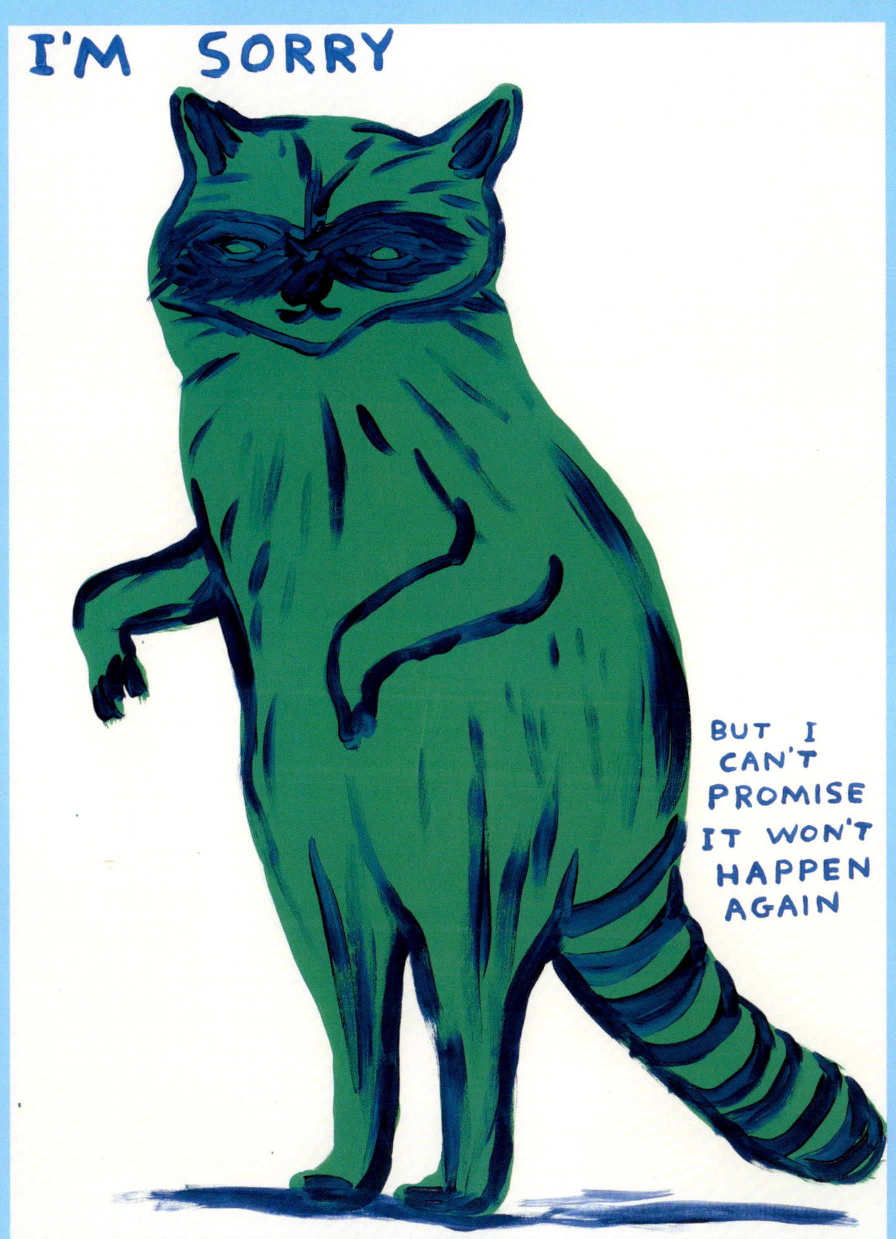
I'M SORRY
BUT I
CAN'T
PROMISE
IT WON'T
HAPPEN
AGAIN

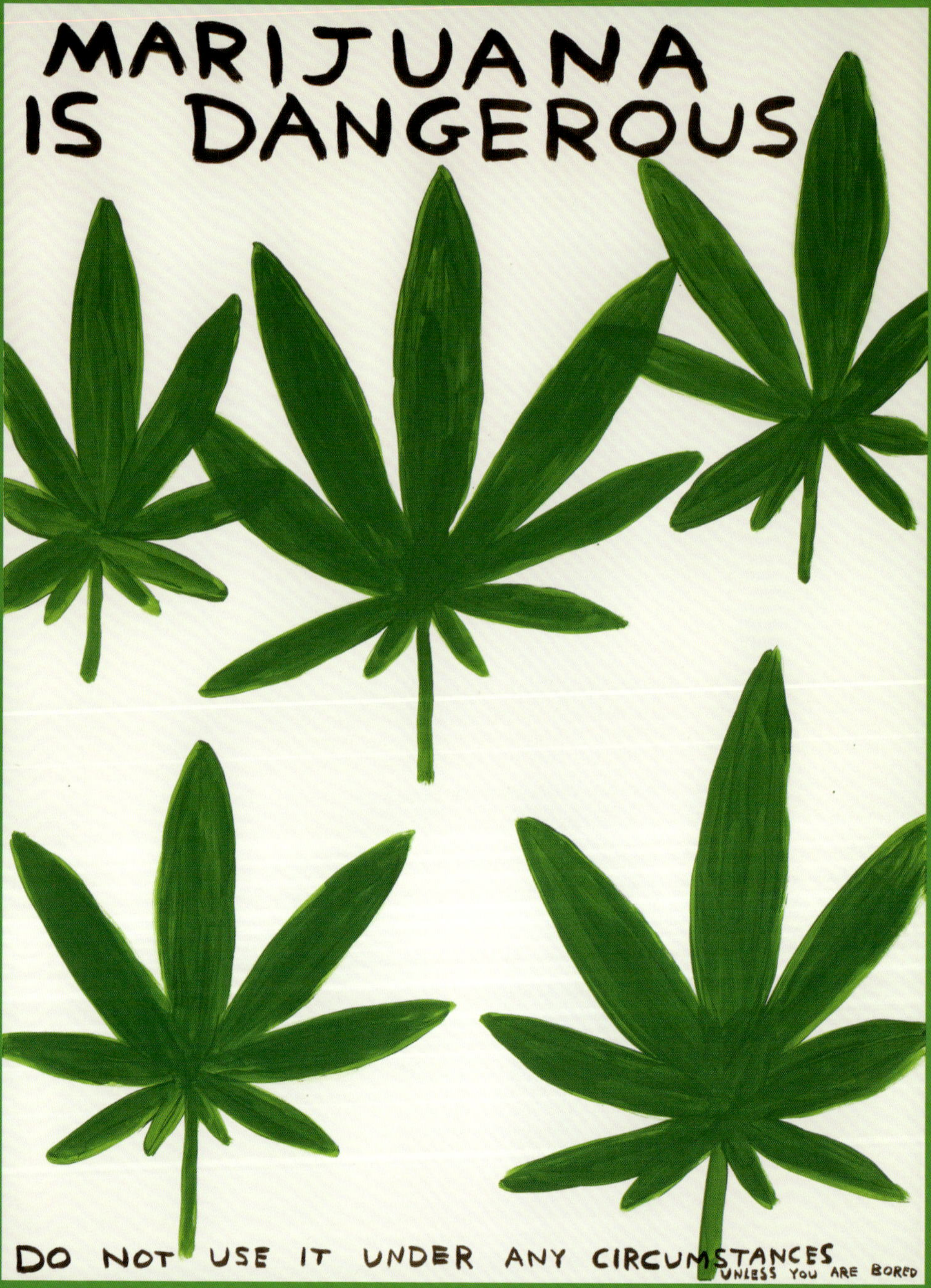

MARIJUANA
IS DANGEROUS

DO NOT USE IT UNDER ANY CIRCUMSTANCES
UNLESS YOU ARE BORED

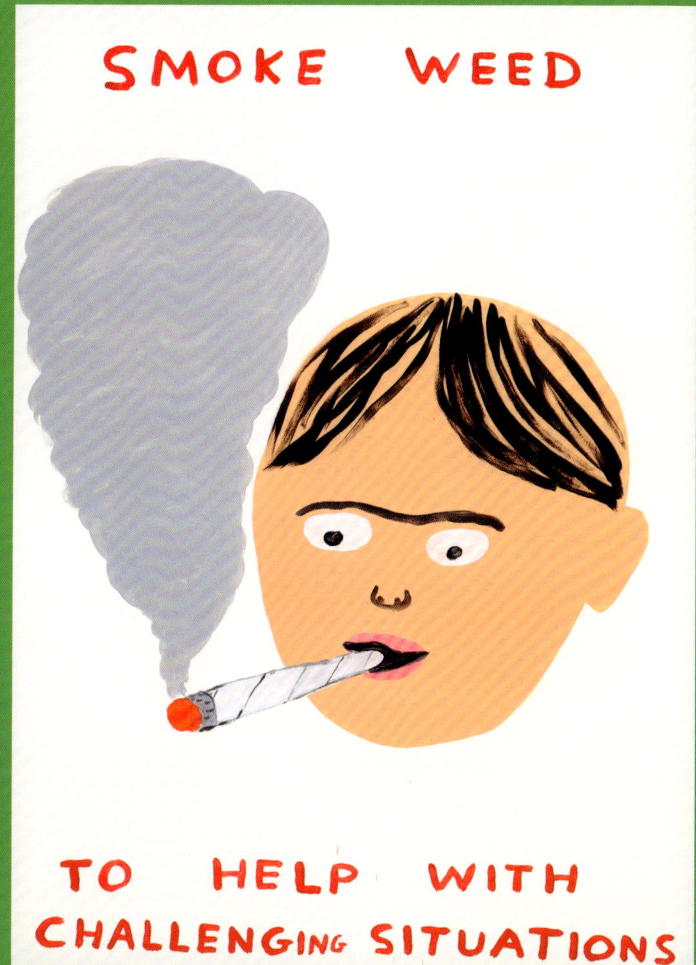
SMOKE WEED
TO HELP WITH
CHALLENGING SITUATIONS

INFORMATION

I AM IN AN AEROPLANE
FLYING HIGH ABOVE YOU
THE PLANE IS FULL OF BOMBS
AND THE HATCH OF THE PLANE IS
AND I AM STANDING OPEN
RIGHT NEXT TO THE BOMBS
AND OVER THE TANNOY
THE CAPTAIN OF THE PLANE IS
SAYING:
"GO ON DAVID; DROP SOME BOMBS"
AND OVER THE TANNOY
THE CO-PILOT OF THE PLANE IS
SAYING;
"GO ON DAVID; DROP SOME BOMBS"
AND THE CHIEF STEWARDESS IS SAYING:
"GO ON DAVID; DROP SOME BOMBS"
AND THE OTHER STEWARDESSES ARE
SAYING:
"GO ON DAVID; DROP SOME BOMBS"
AND SOME OF THE OTHER PASSENGERS
ARE SAYING:
"GO ON DAVID; DROP SOME BOMBS"

SO I'M PROBABLY GOING TO DROP
SOME BOMBS ON YOU
AND I THOUGHT I'D BETTER LET YOU
KNOW

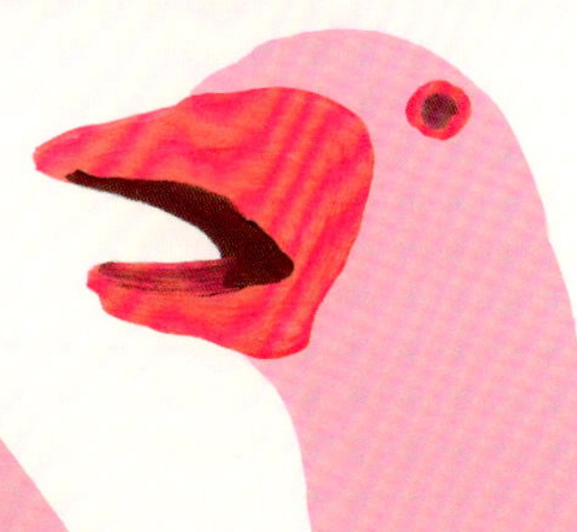
STOP
PANICKING
EVERY
-THING
WILL BE
FINE

INFO

THERE IS TOO MUCH INFO
THERE SHOULD BE LESS
IT WOULD BE BETTER

I WILL NOT DIVULGE ANY NEW INFORMATION – I CAN ONLY TELL YOU THINGS THAT YOU ALREADY KNOW

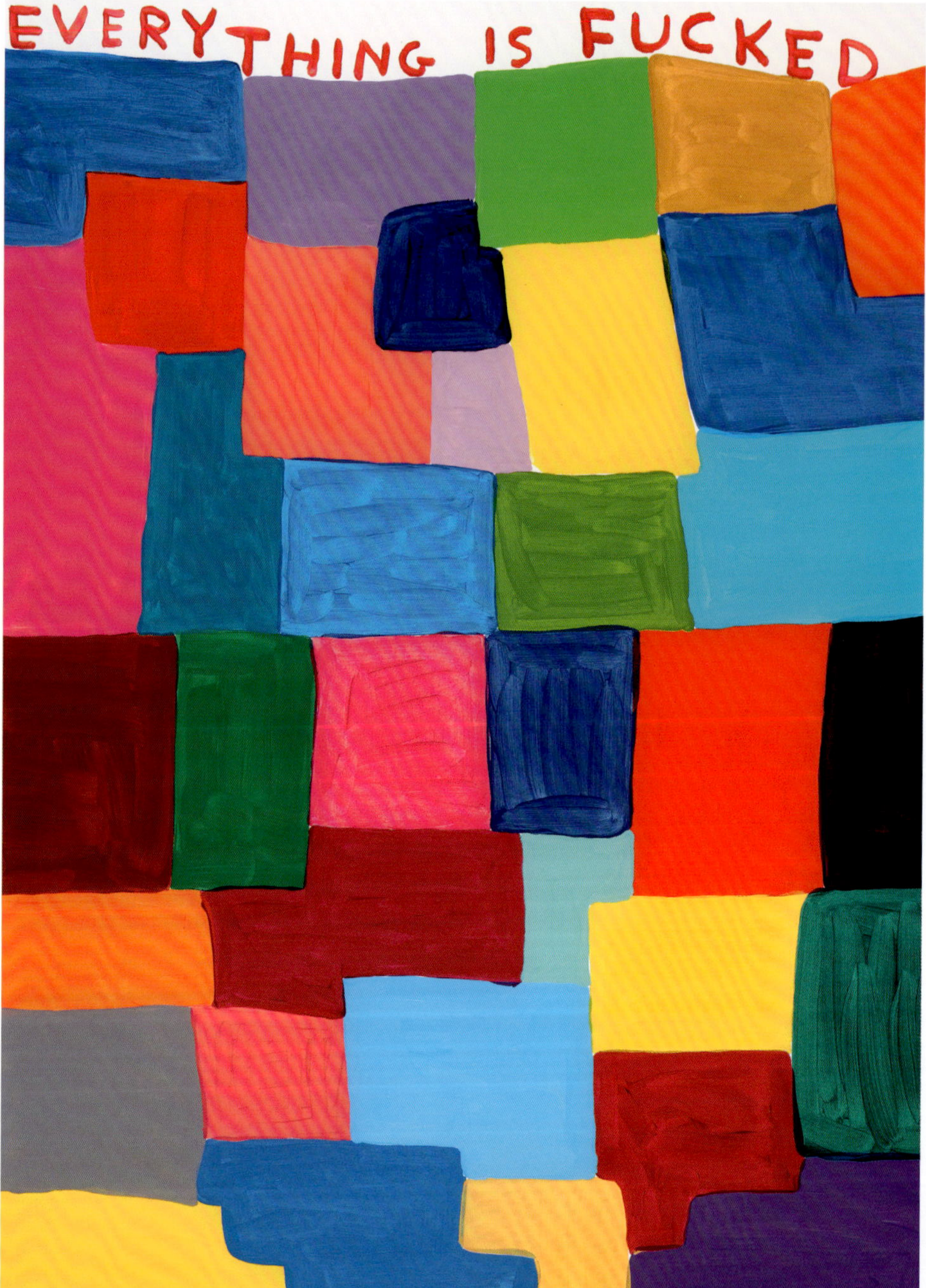
EVERYTHING IS FUCKED

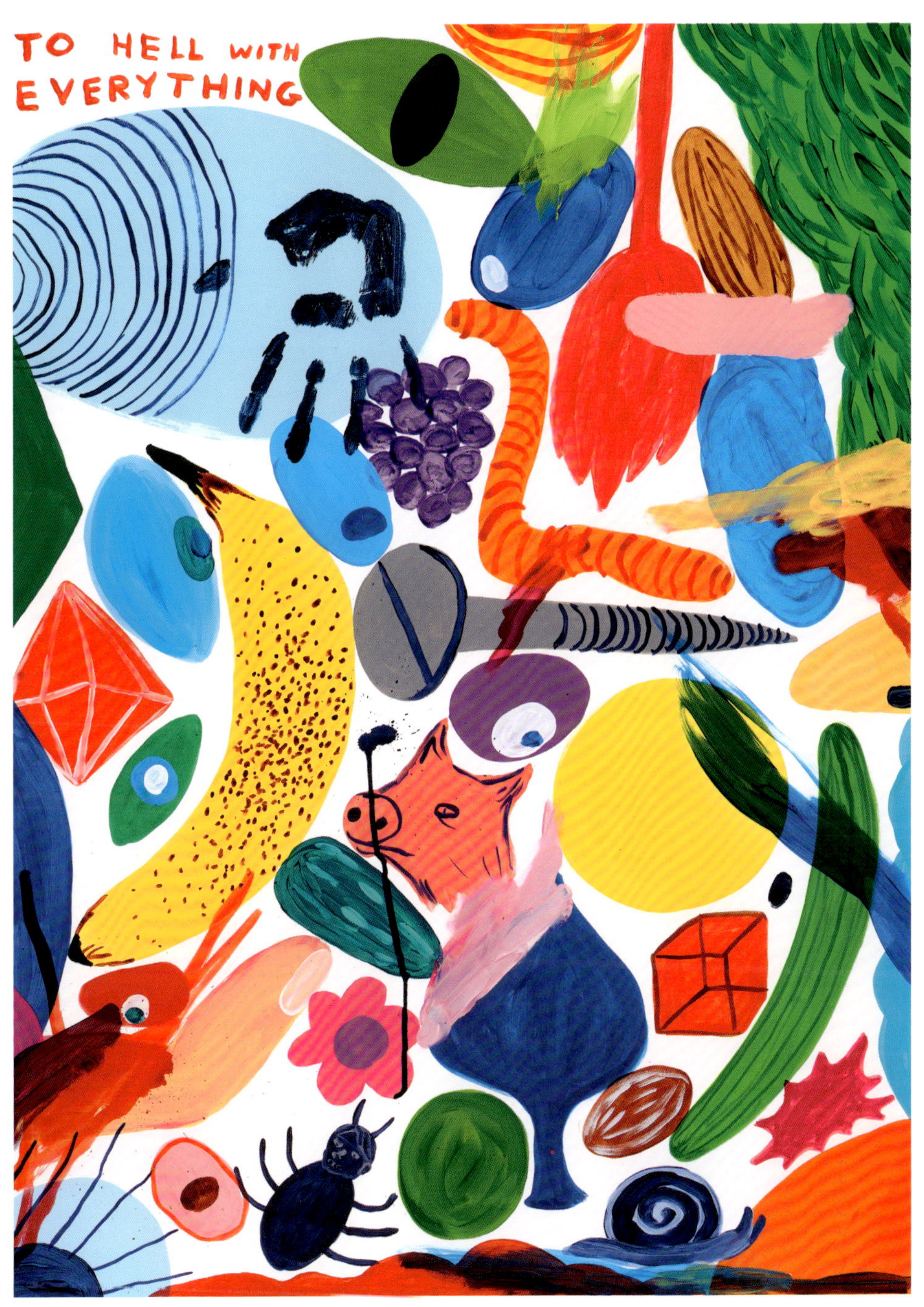
TO HELL WITH
EVERYTHING

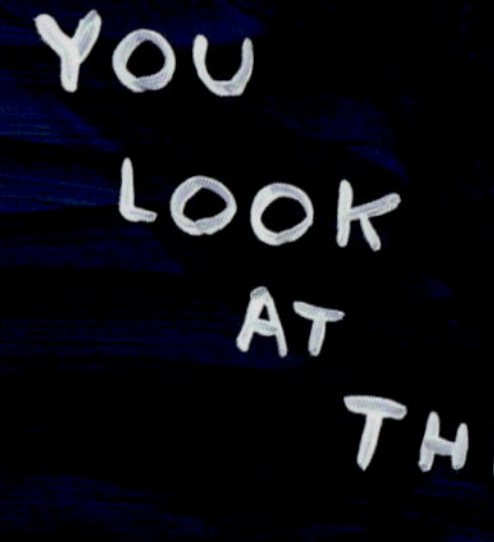
YOU
LOOK
AT
THE
MOON

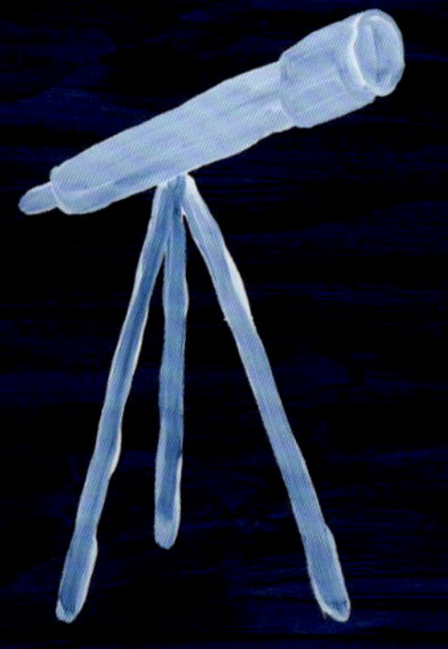
WE
HOWL
AT
THE
MOON

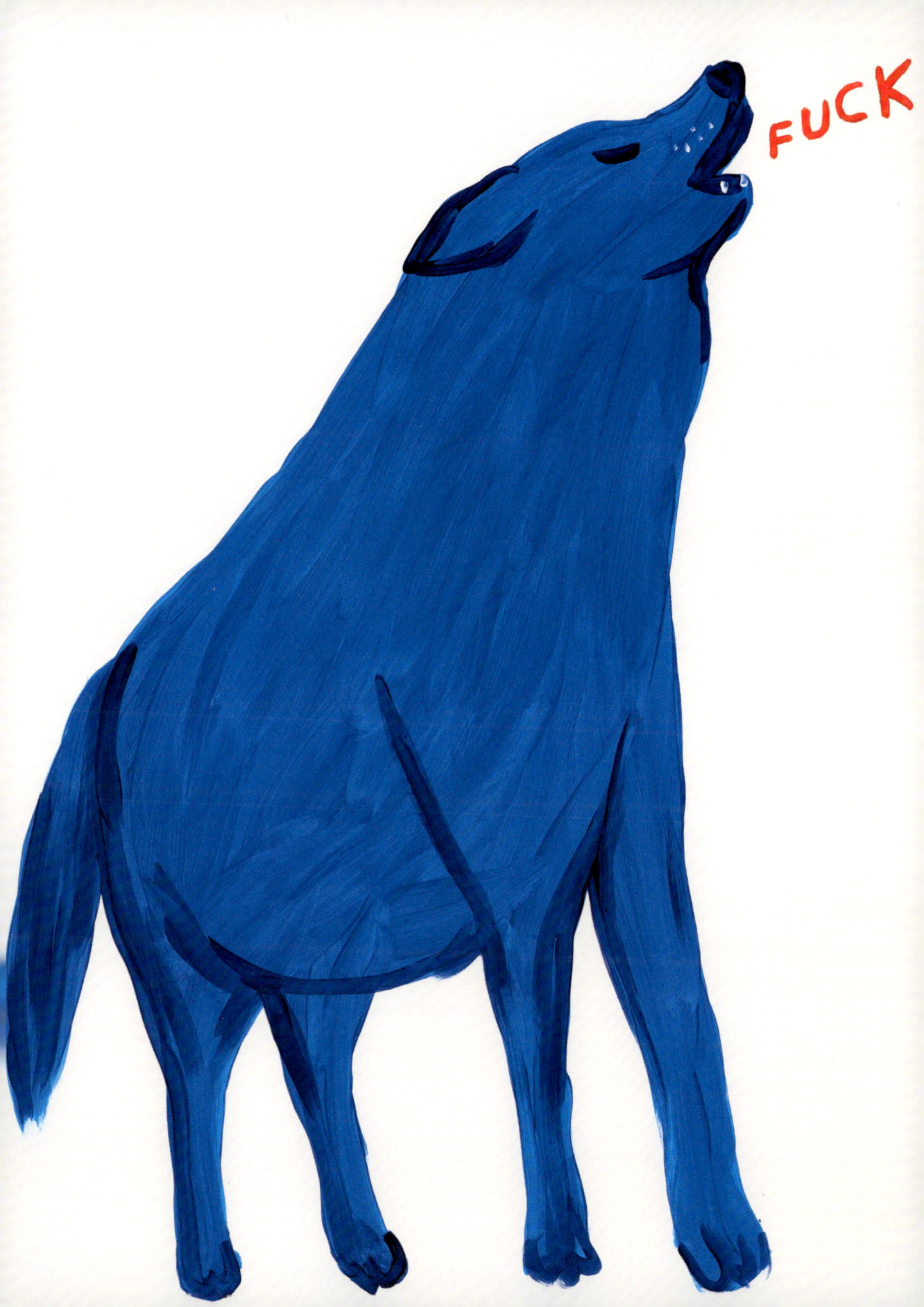
FUCK

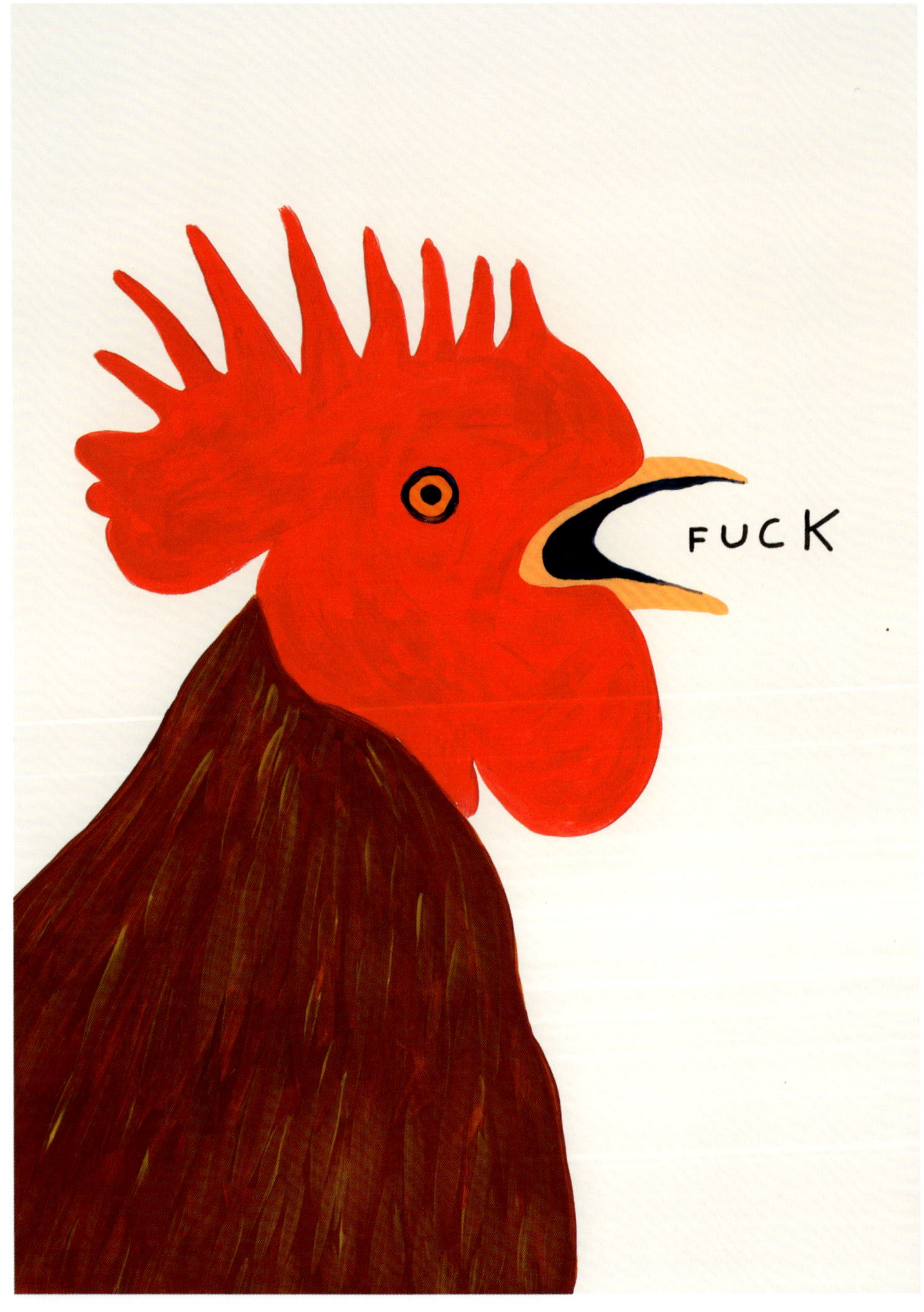
FUCK

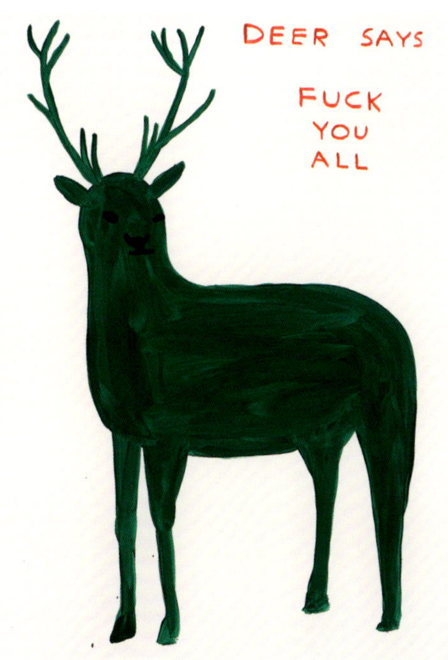
DEER SAYS
FUCK
YOU
ALL
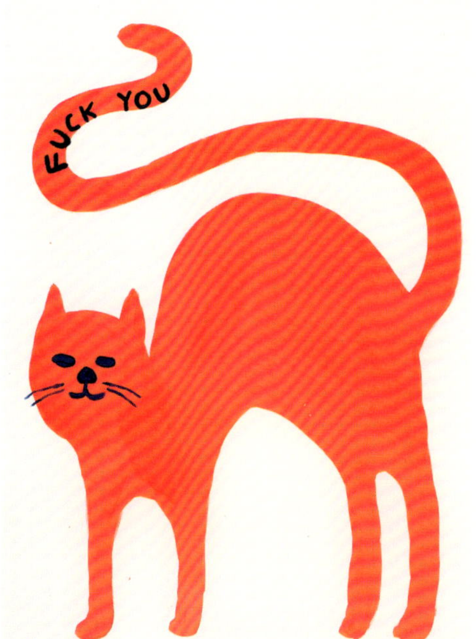
FUCK YOU
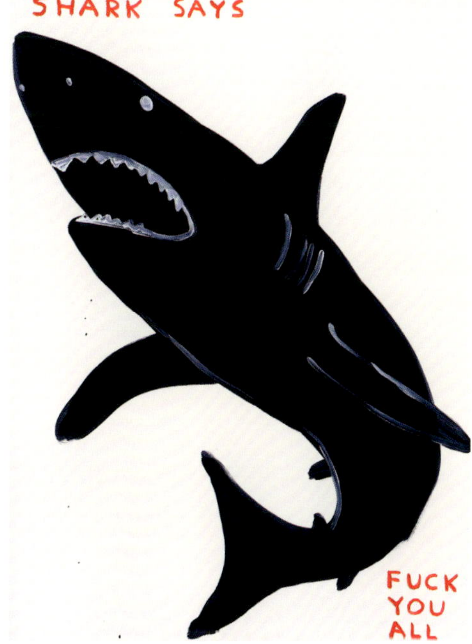
SHARK SAYS
FUCK
YOU
ALL
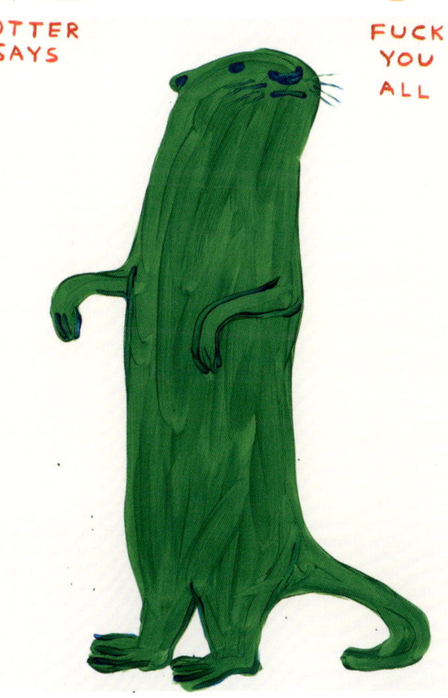
OTTER
SAYS
FUCK
YOU
ALL

BAD

I EAT INSECTS
I DO NOT MEAN TO
THEY FLY INTO MY OPEN MOUTH
I TRY TO SPIT THEM OUT
BUT THEY SEEM TO BREAK APART
AS SOON AS THEY ENTER MY MOUTH
AND I SWALLOW PARTS OF THEM
BY ACCIDENT
IT IS QUITE UNPLEASANT
THEY TASTE BAD
AND ARE OF LITTLE NUTRITIONAL
VALUE

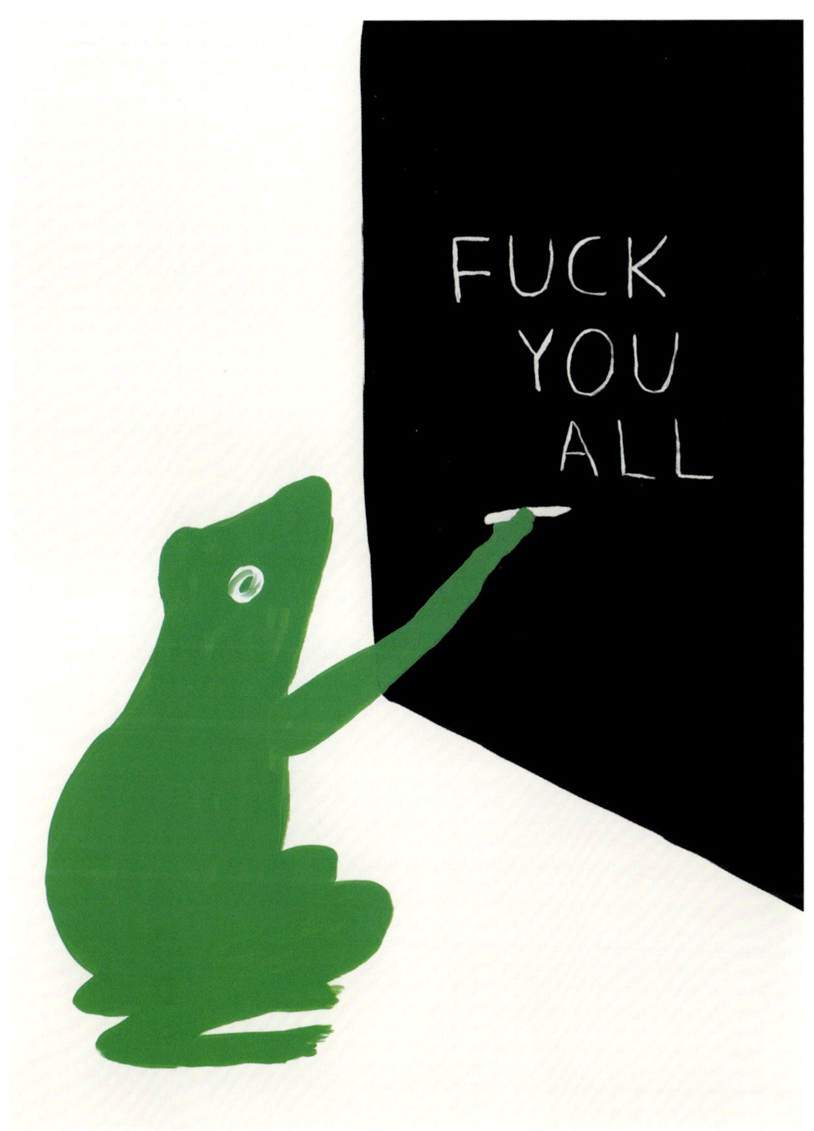
FUCK
YOU
ALL

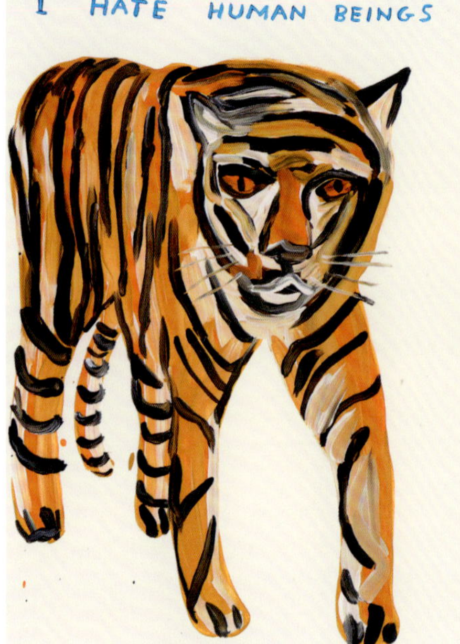
I HATE HUMAN BEINGS

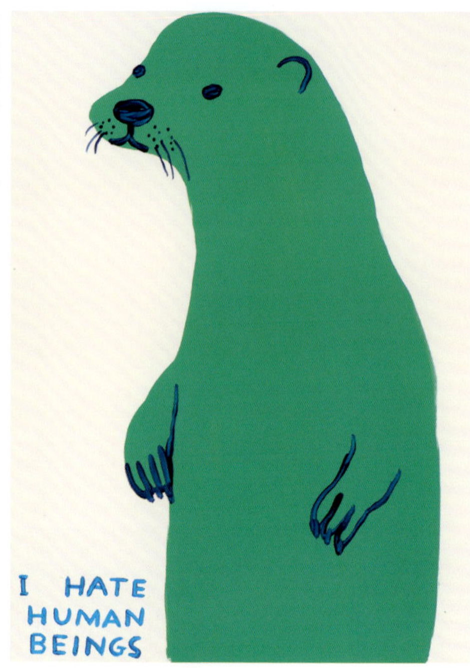
I HATE
HUMAN
BEINGS

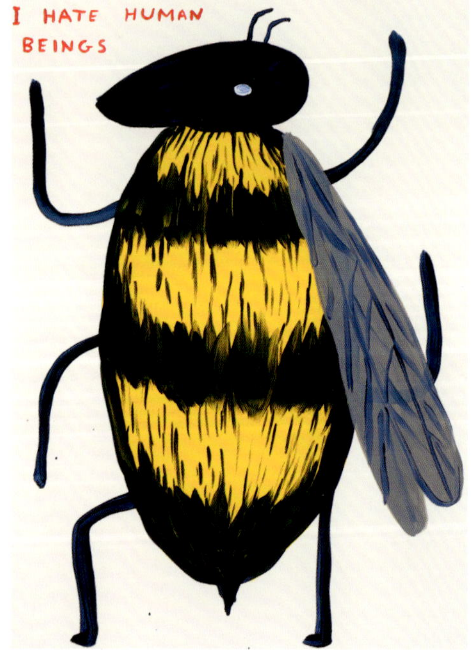
I HATE HUMAN
BEINGS

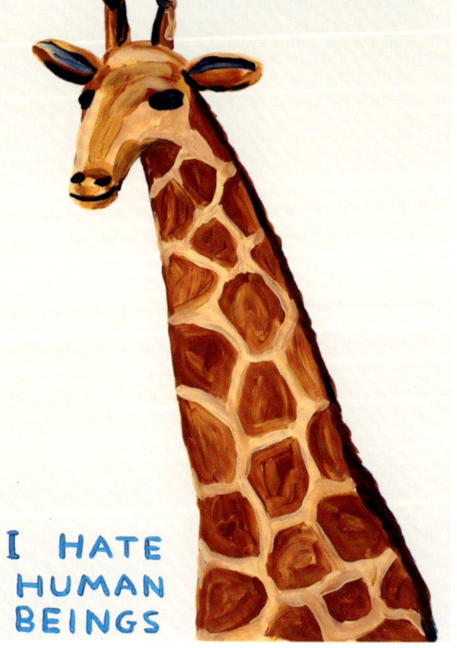
I HATE
HUMAN
BEINGS

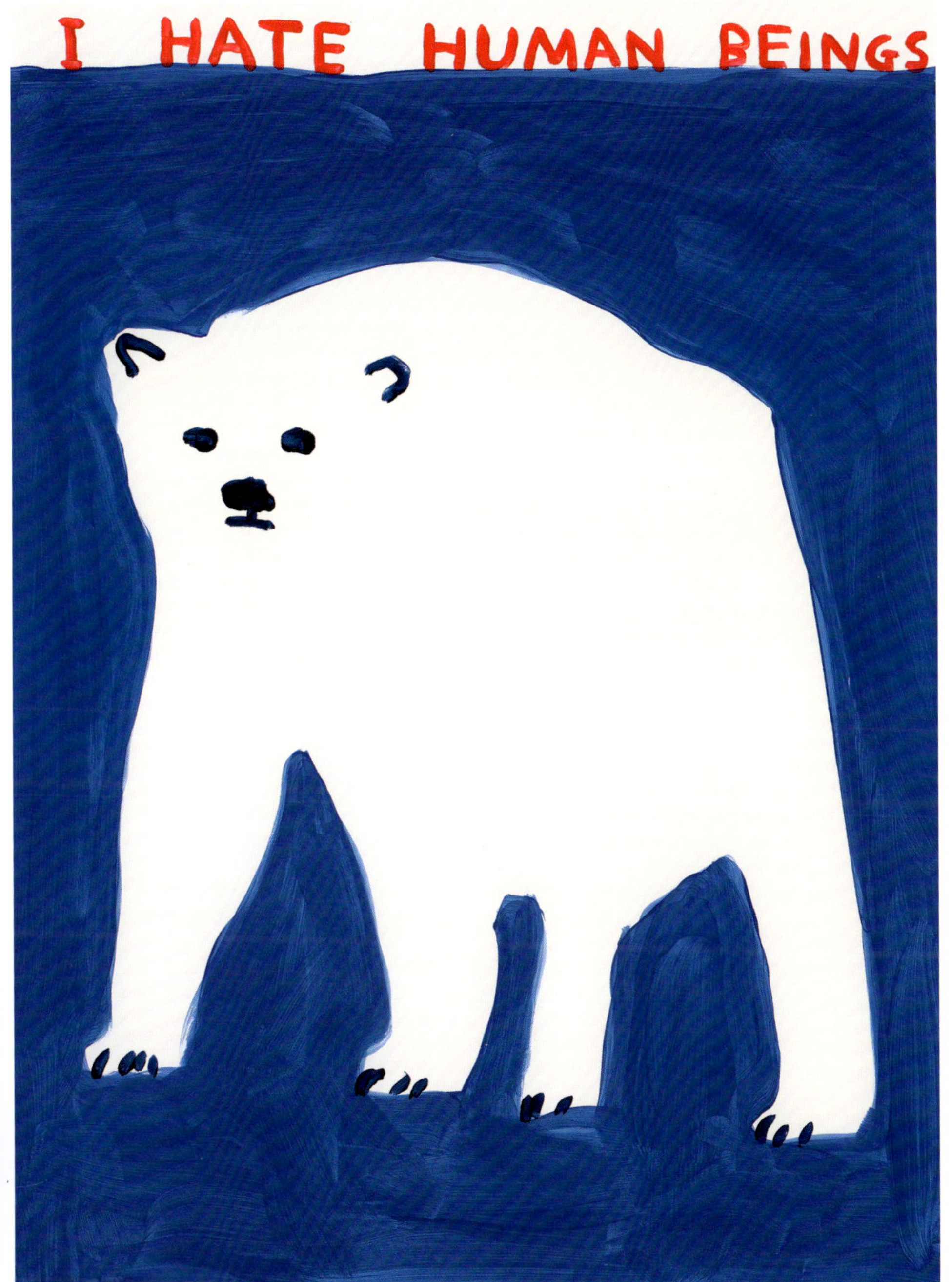
I HATE HUMAN BEINGS

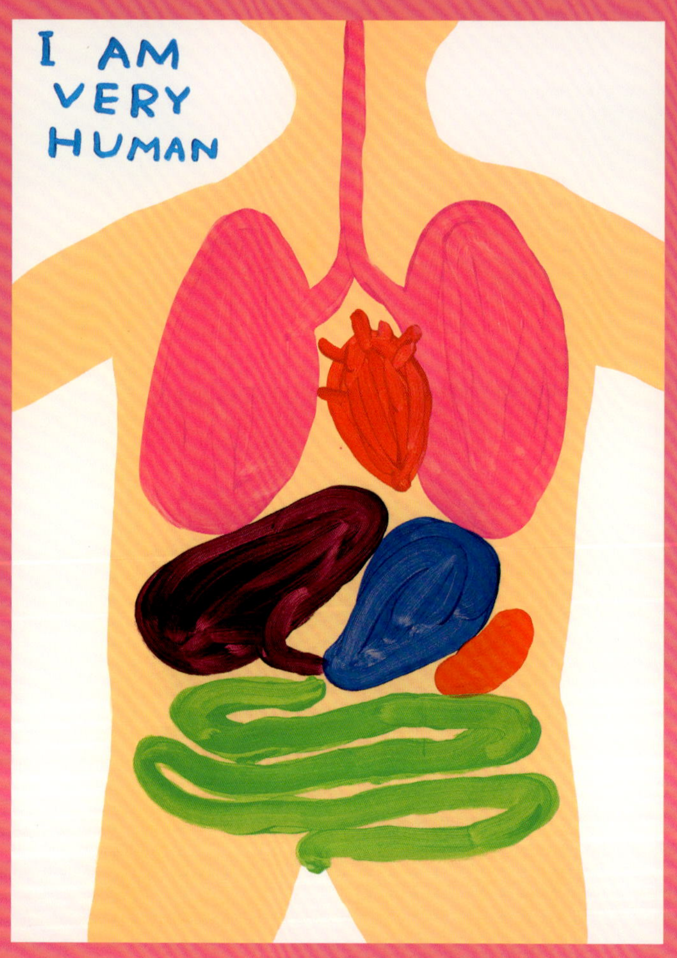
I AM
VERY
HUMAN

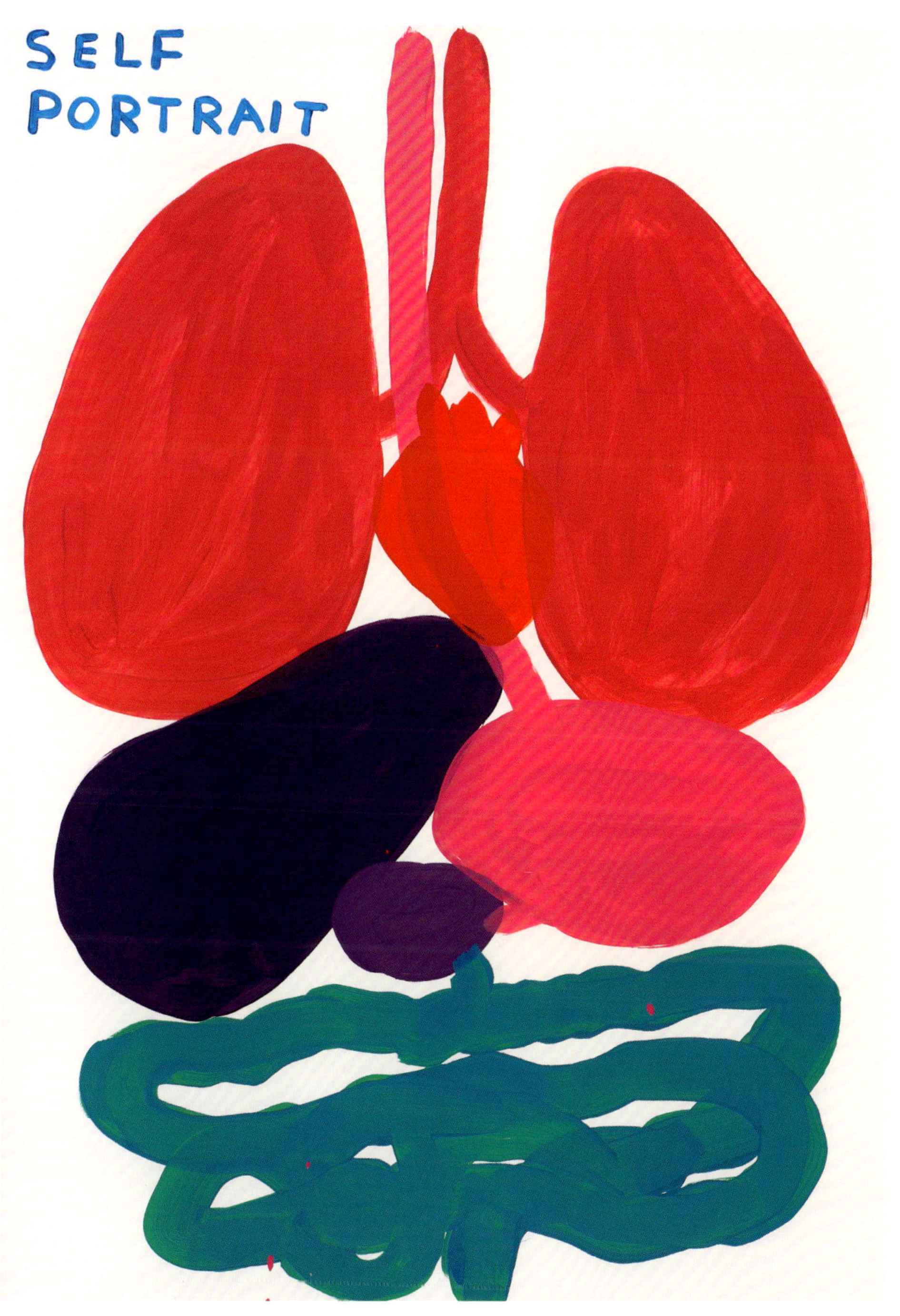
SELF
PORTRAIT

GO TO HELL

GO TO HELL
I'VE BEEN TO HELL
YOU WILL LIKE HELL
I CAN RECOMMEND HELL
TAKE MY ADVICE
AND GO TO HELL

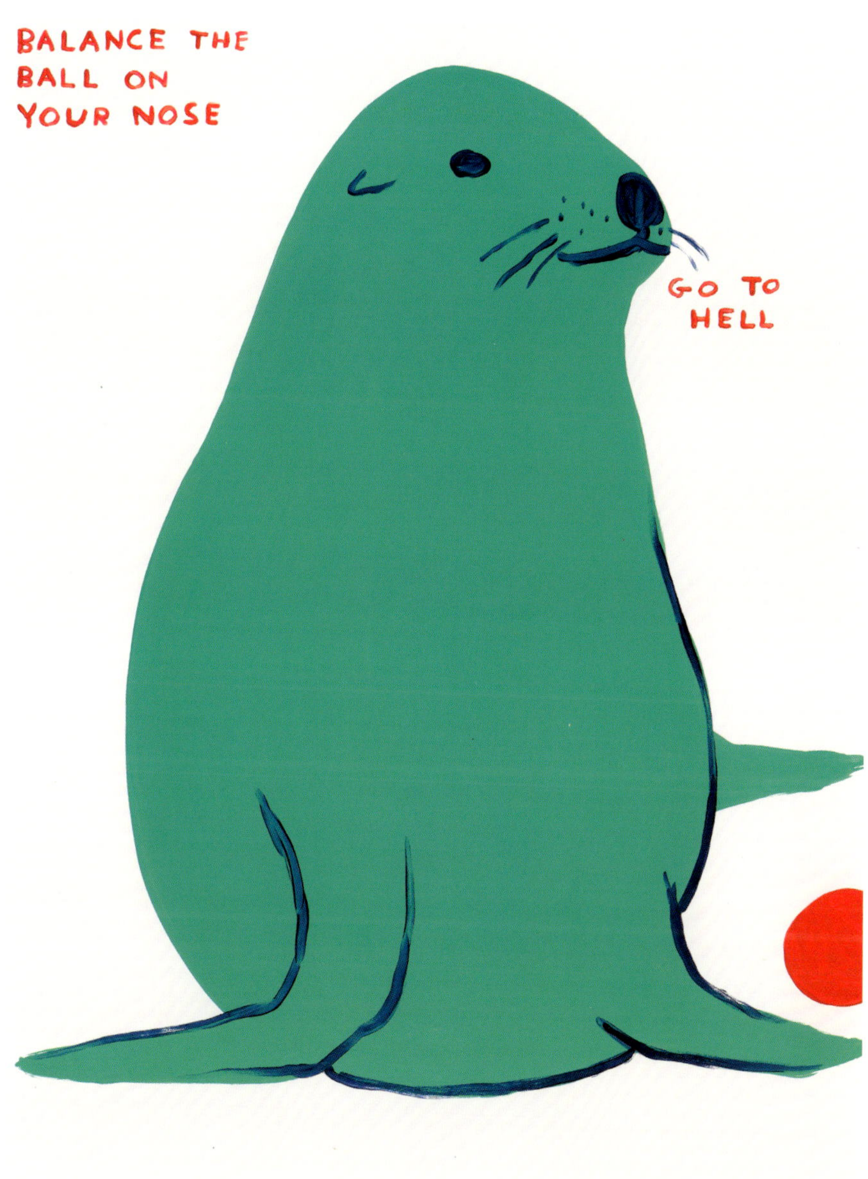
BALANCE THE
BALL ON
YOUR NOSE
GO TO
HELL

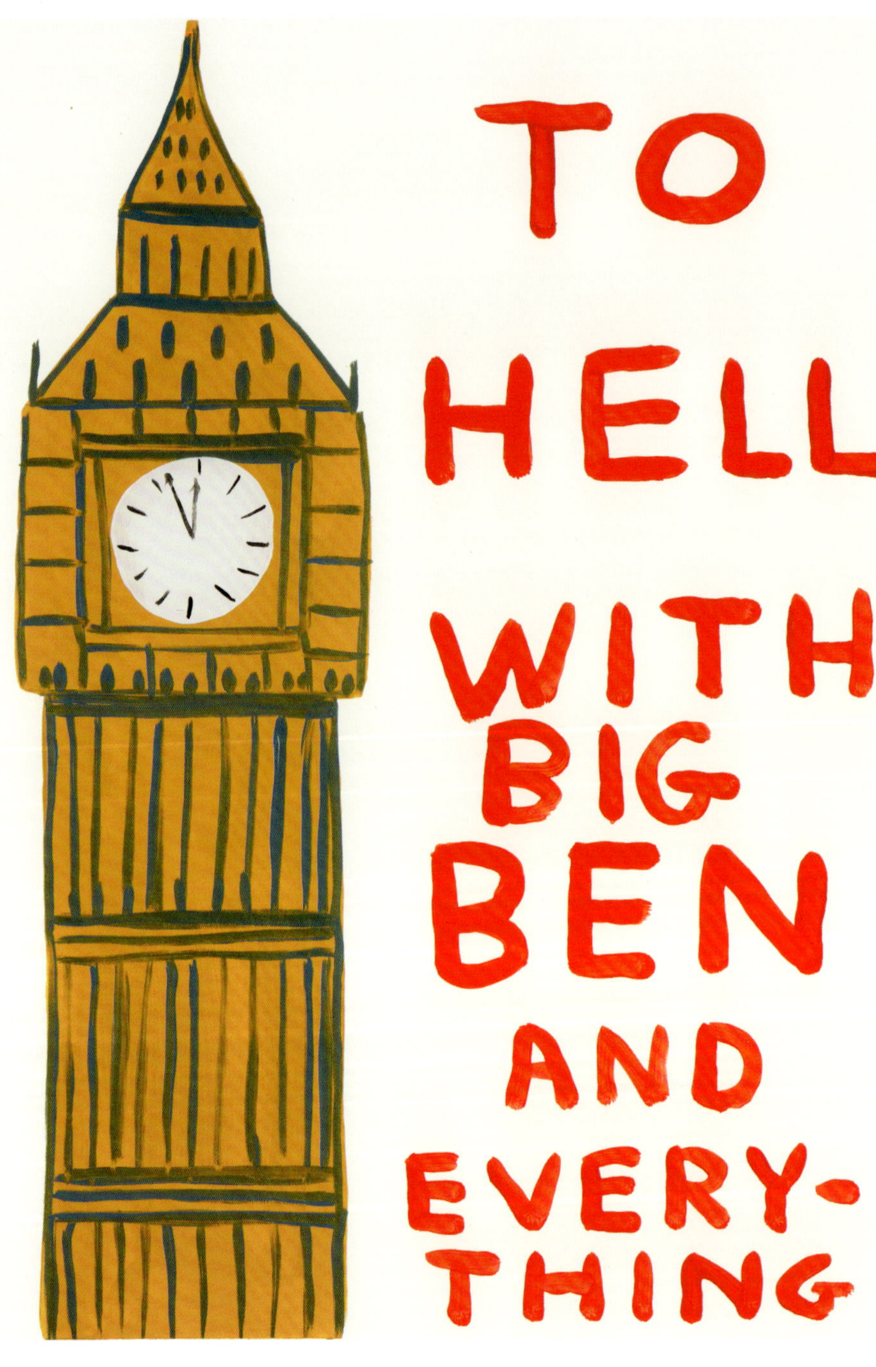
TO
HELL
WITH
BIG
BEN
AND
EVERY-
THING

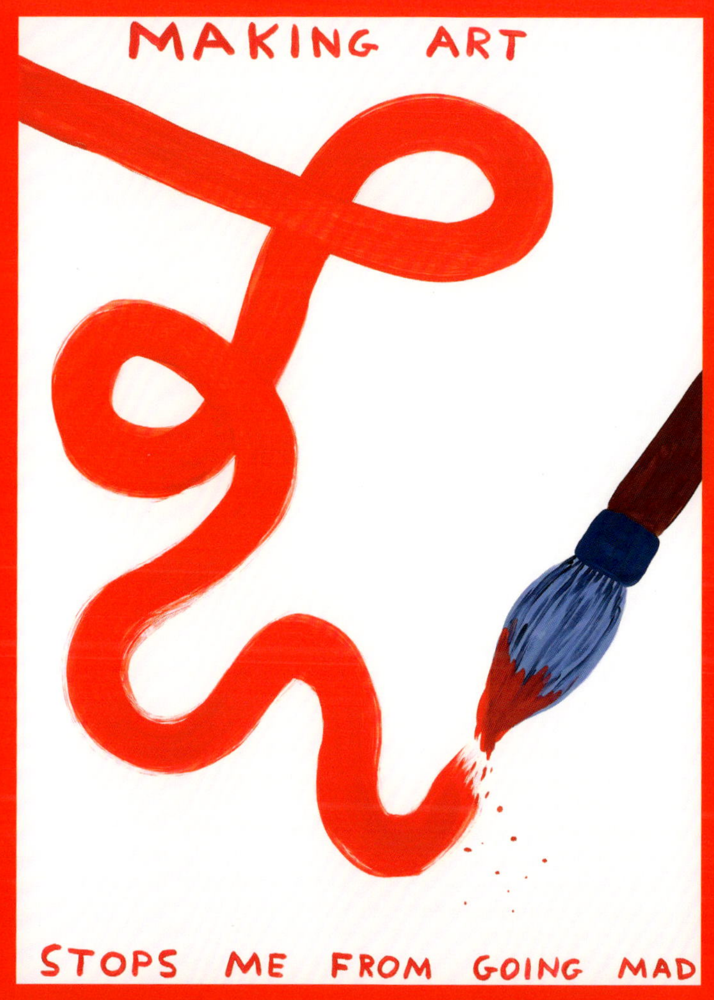
MAKING ART
STOPS ME FROM GOING MAD

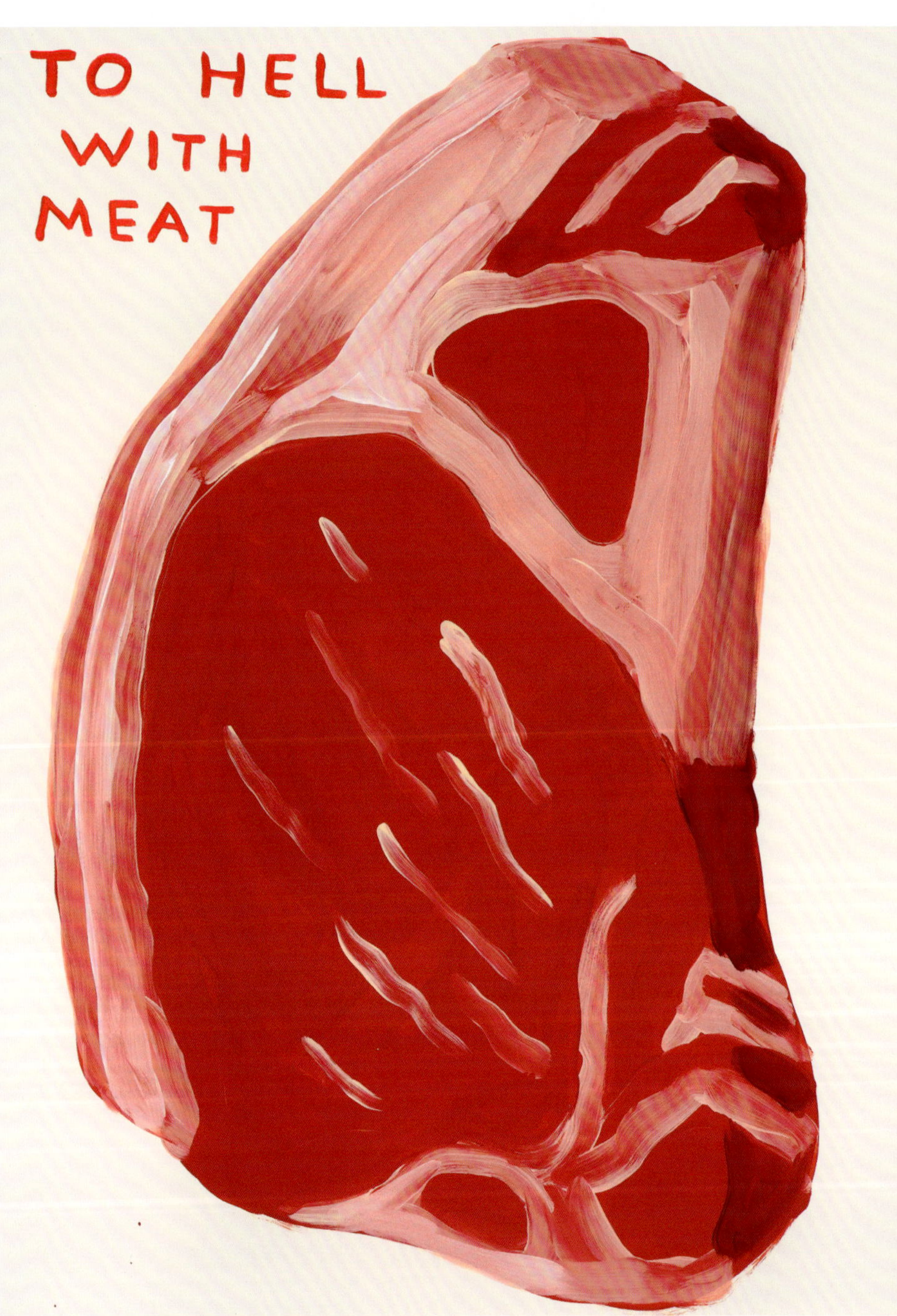
TO HELL
WITH
MEAT

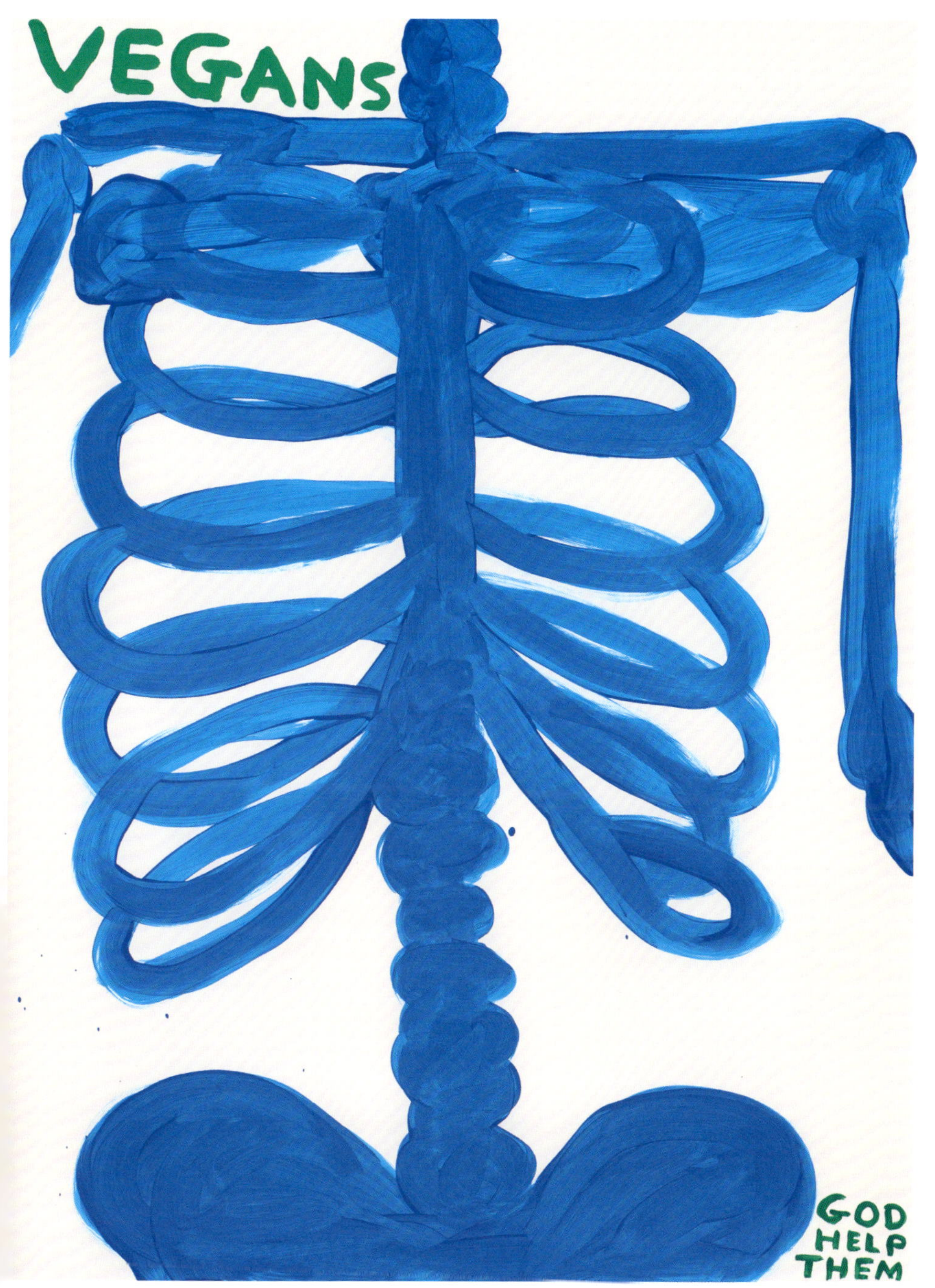
VEGANS
GOD
HELP
THEM

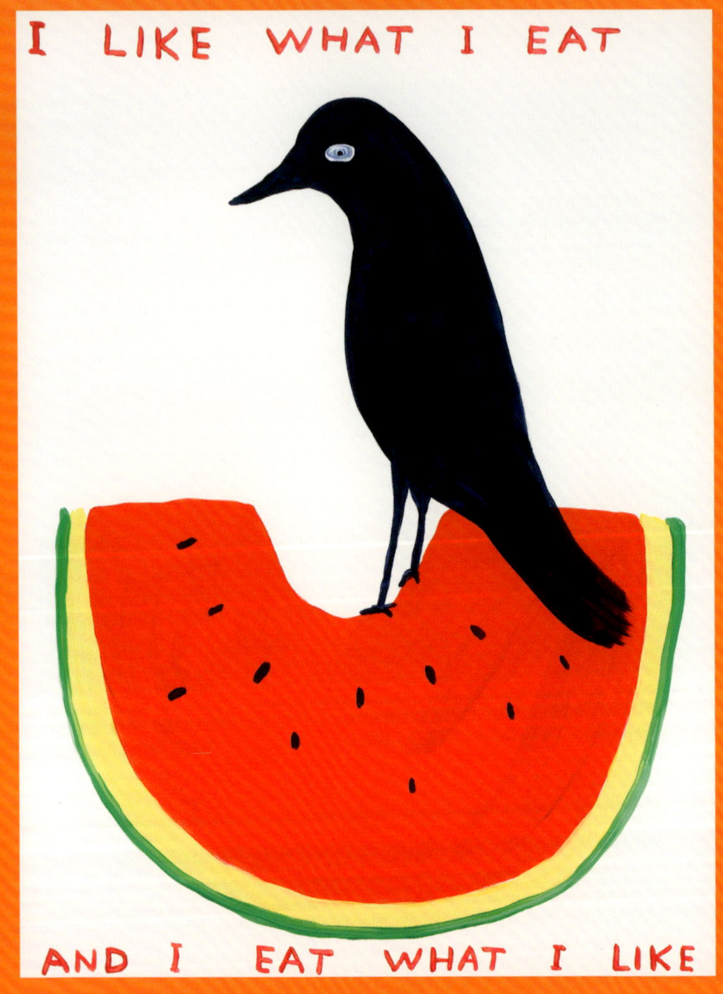
I LIKE WHAT I EAT
AND I EAT WHAT I LIKE

BAD FOOD
IS
GOOD FOOD

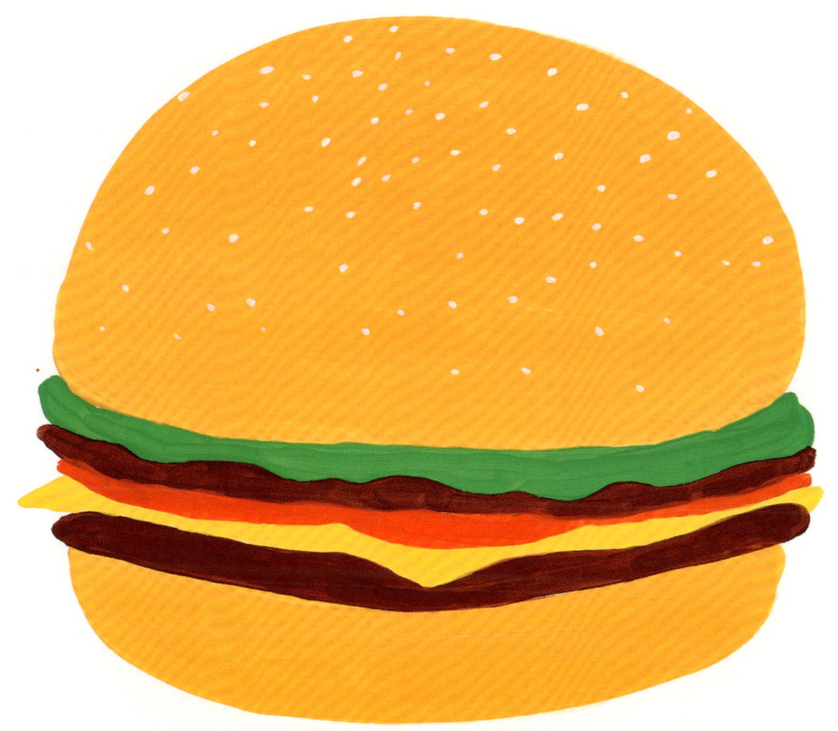

GOOD FOOD
IS
BAD FOOD

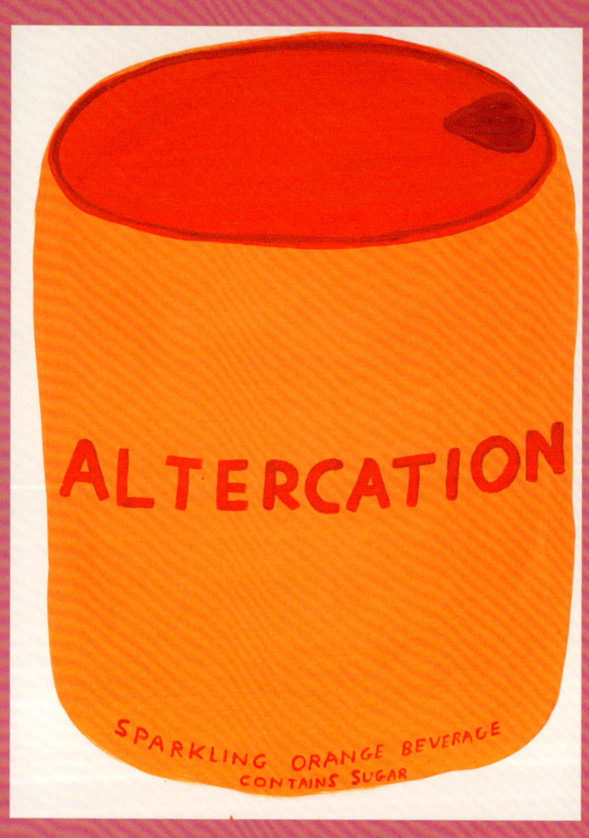
ALTERCATION
SPARKLING ORANGE BEVERAGE
CONTAINS SUGAR

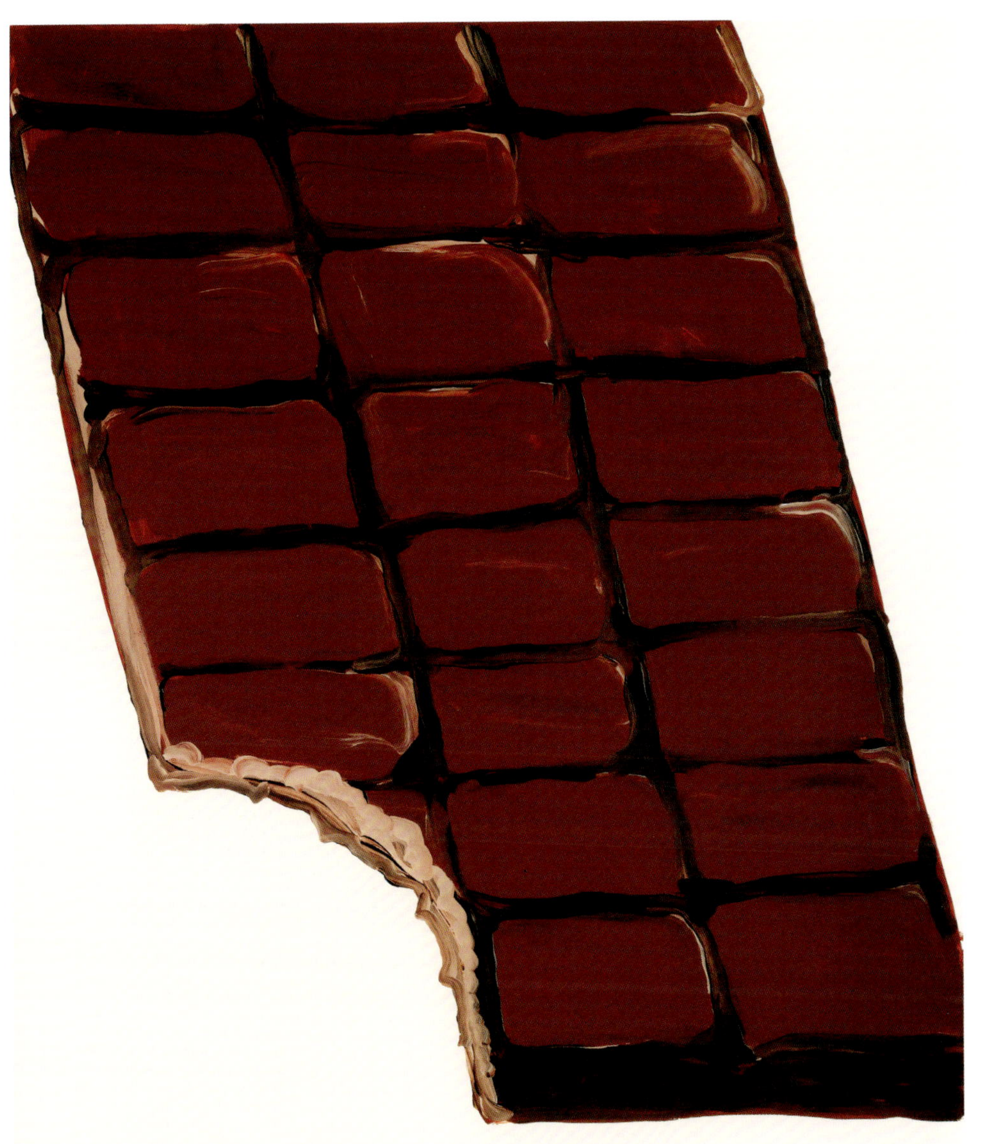

CHOCOLATE IS NOT THE PROBLEM
YOU ARE THE PROBLEM

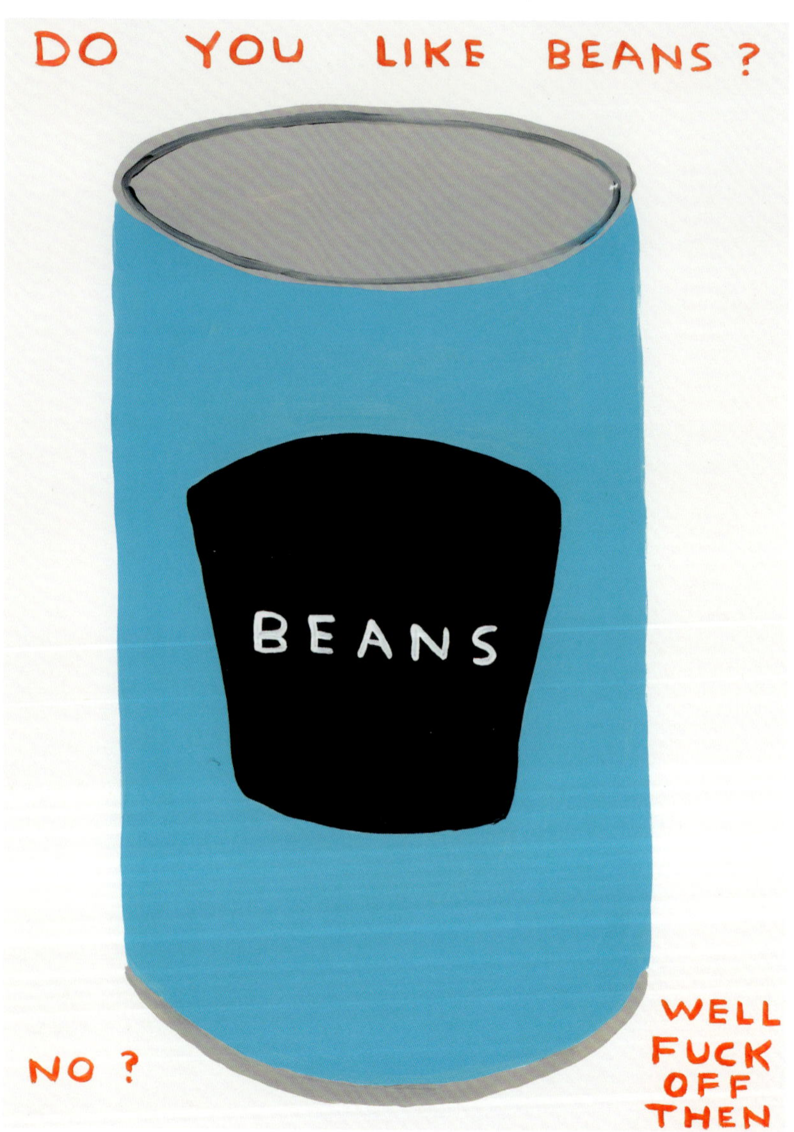
DO YOU LIKE BEANS?
BEANS
NO?
WELL FUCK OFF THEN

GOD SEES YOU

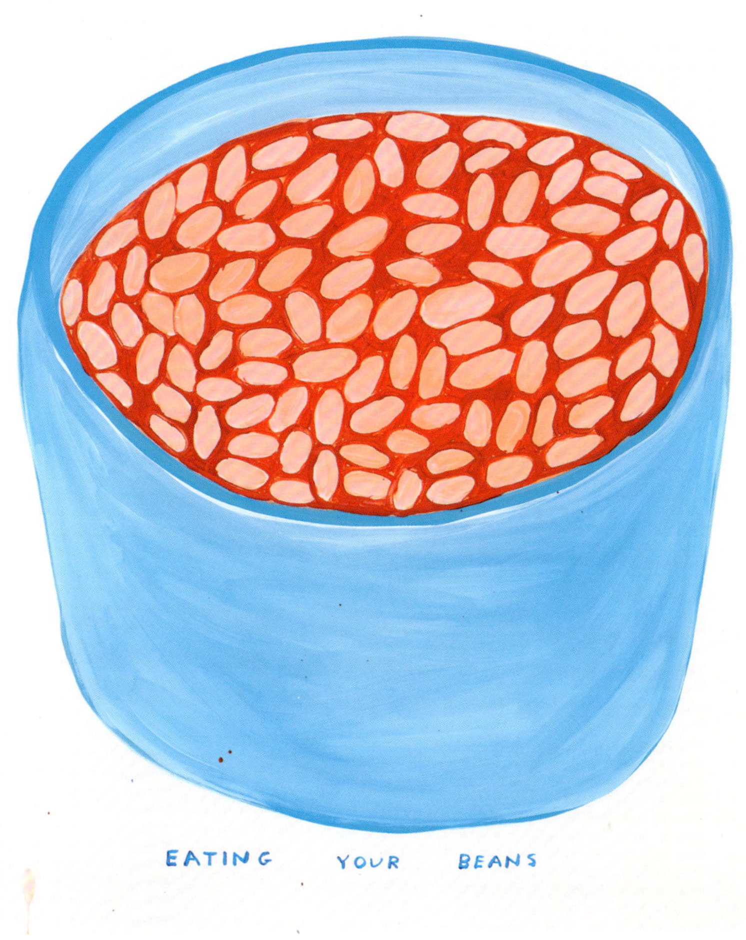

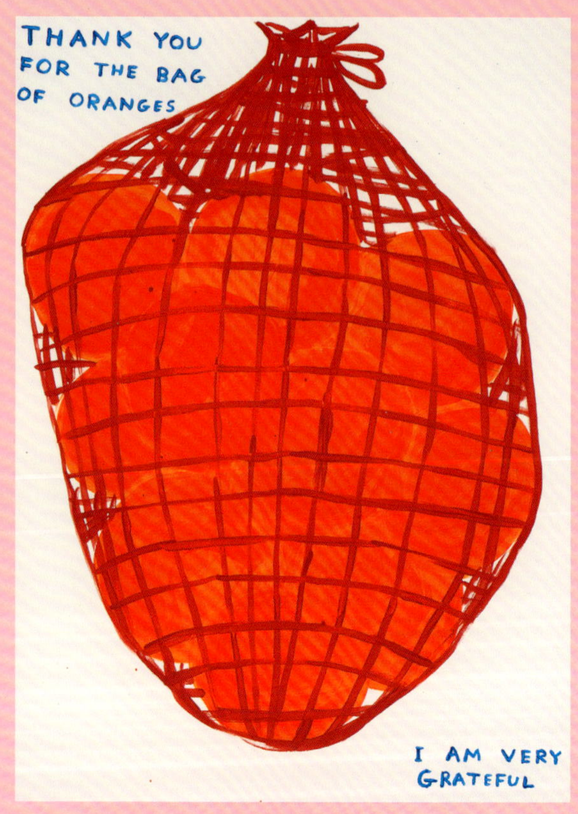
THANK YOU
FOR THE BAG
OF ORANGES
I AM VERY
GRATEFUL

THE JUICE WENT
IN MY EYE

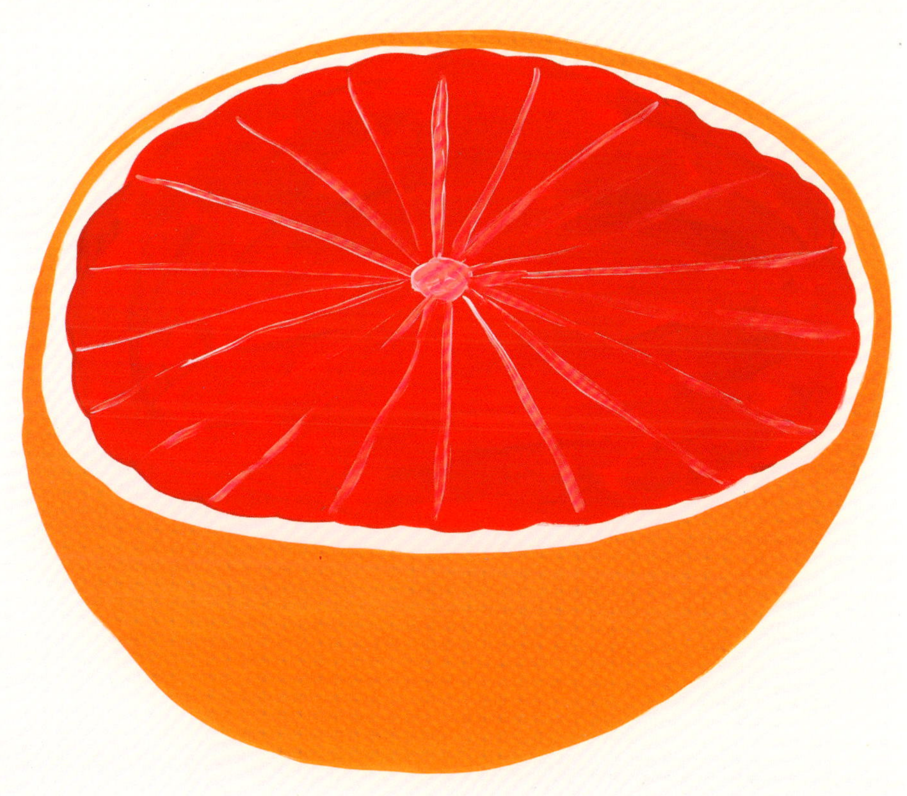

AND NOW I CAN'T SEE

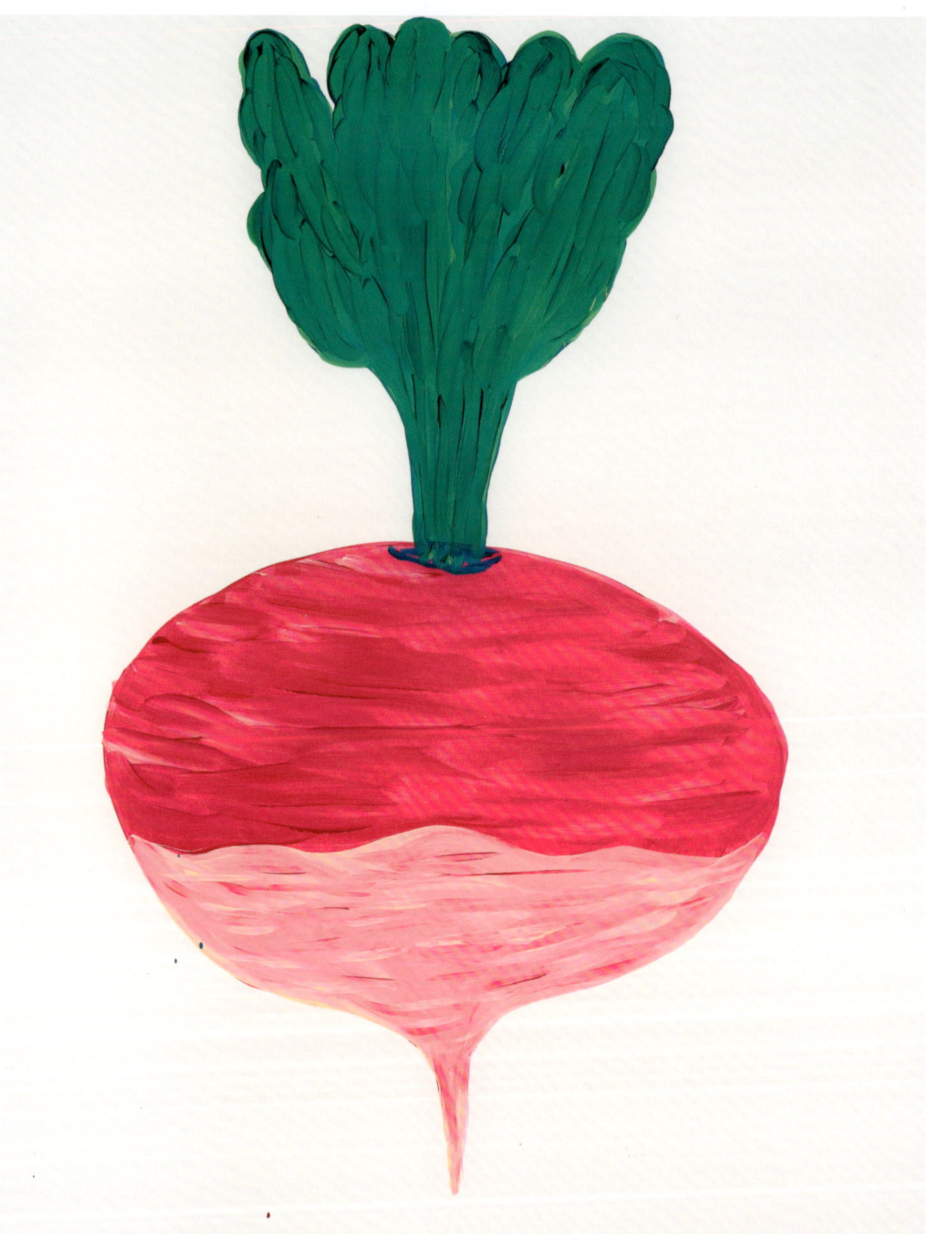

LEGALISE TURNIPS

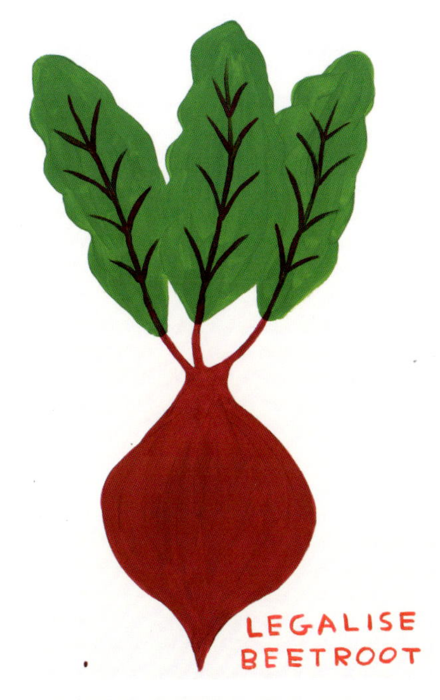
LEGALISE
BEETROOT

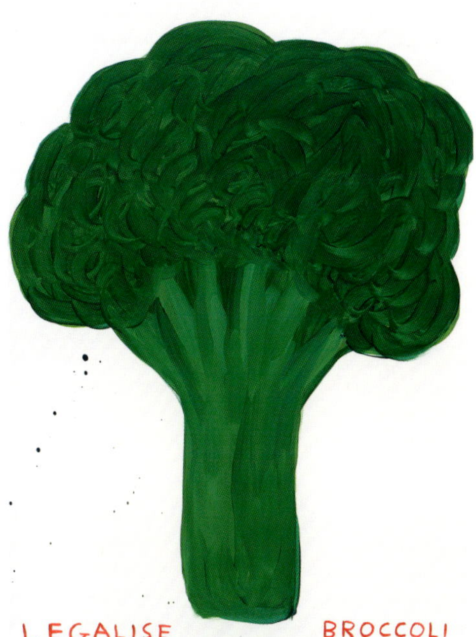
LEGALISE
BROCCOLI

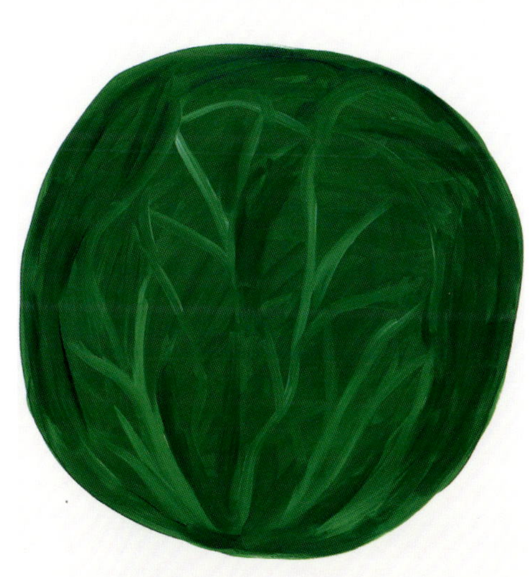

LEGALISE
CABBAGE

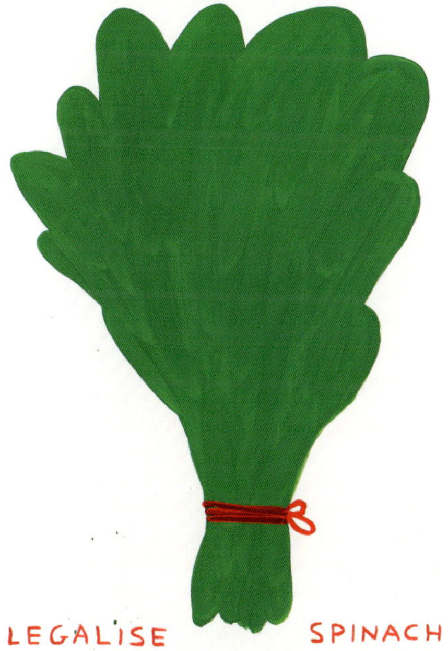
LEGALISE
SPINACH

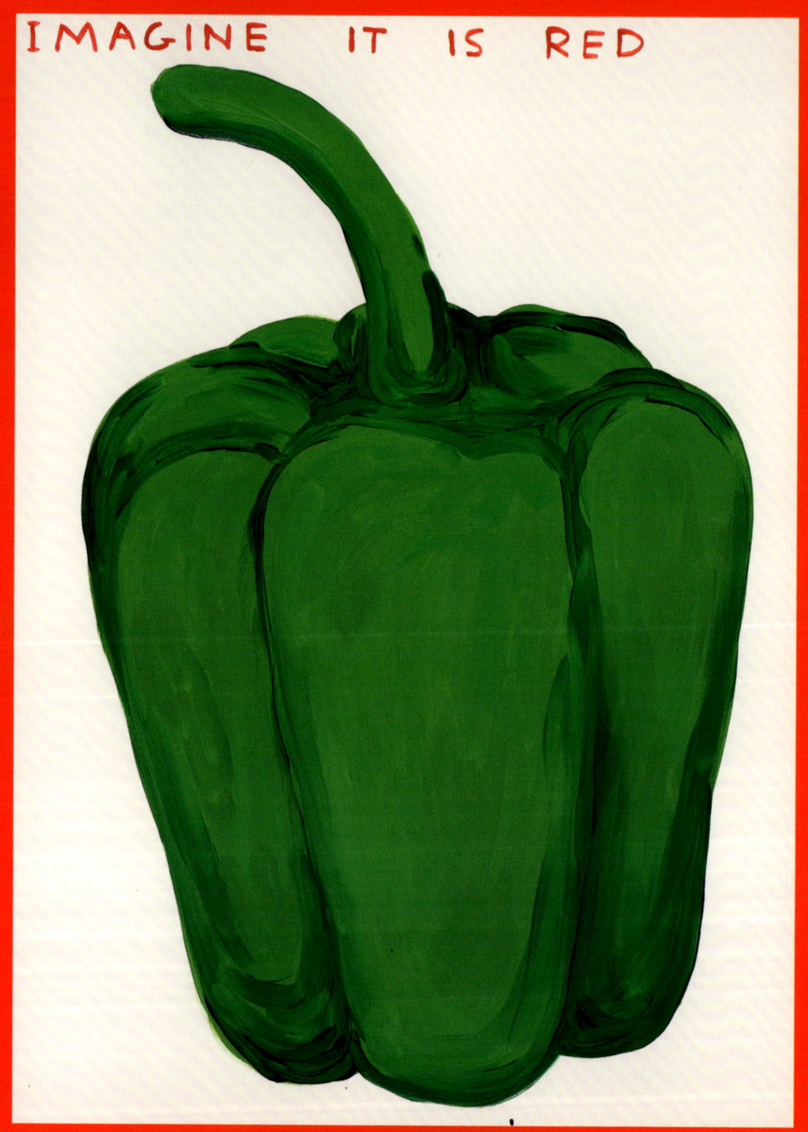
IMAGINE IT IS RED

MAGINE THE GREEN IS RED

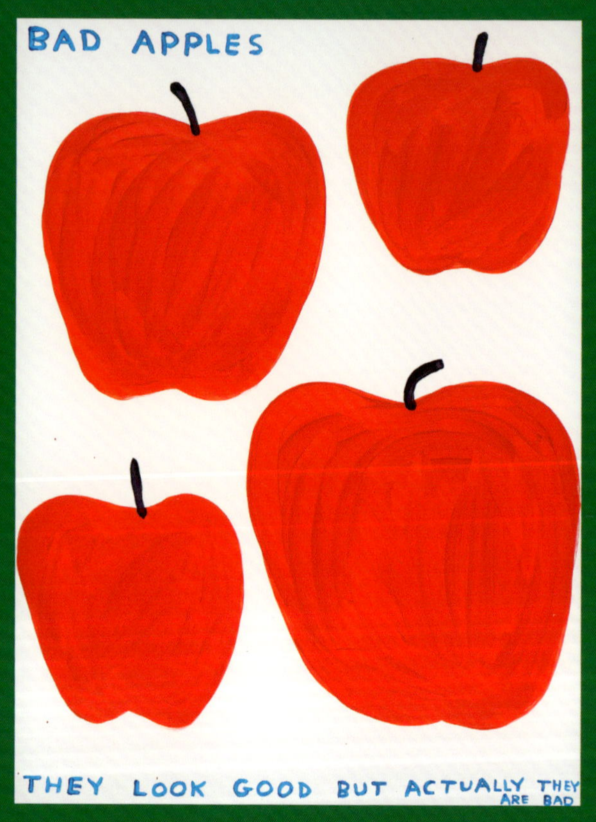
BAD APPLES
THEY LOOK GOOD BUT ACTUALLY THEY ARE BAD

NOT ROTTEN

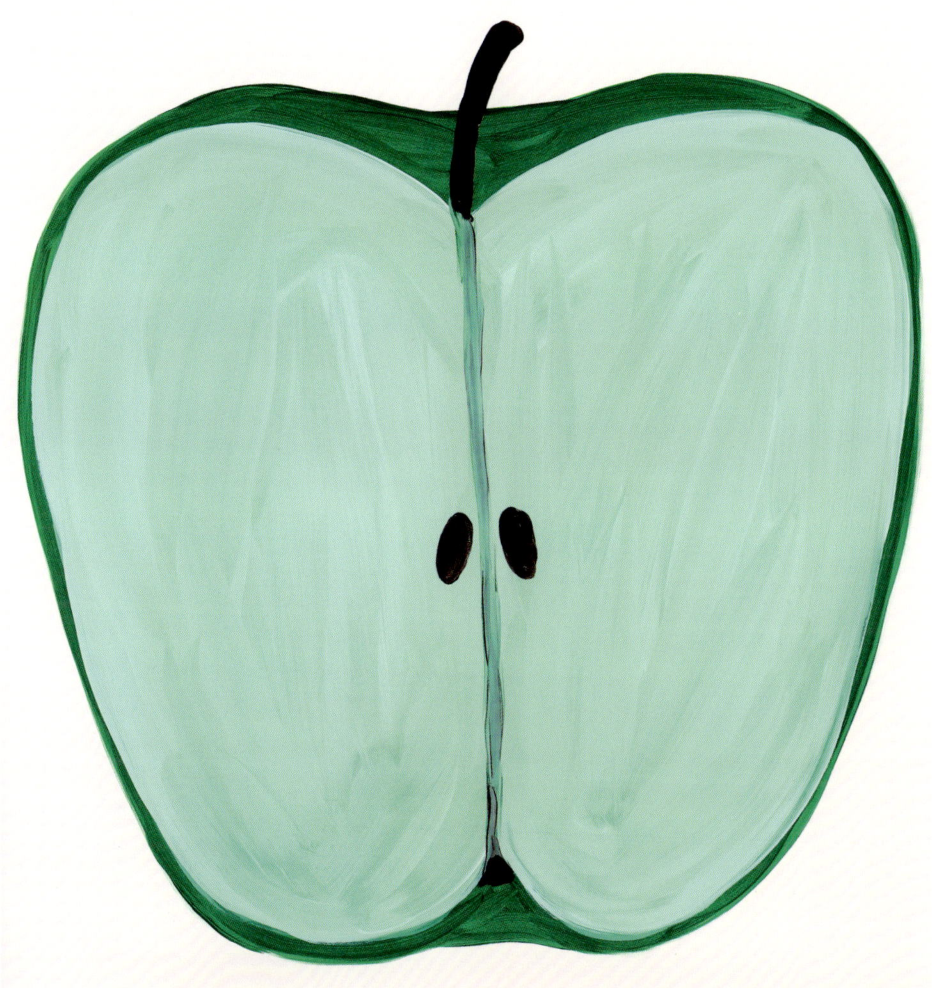

THANK GOODNESS

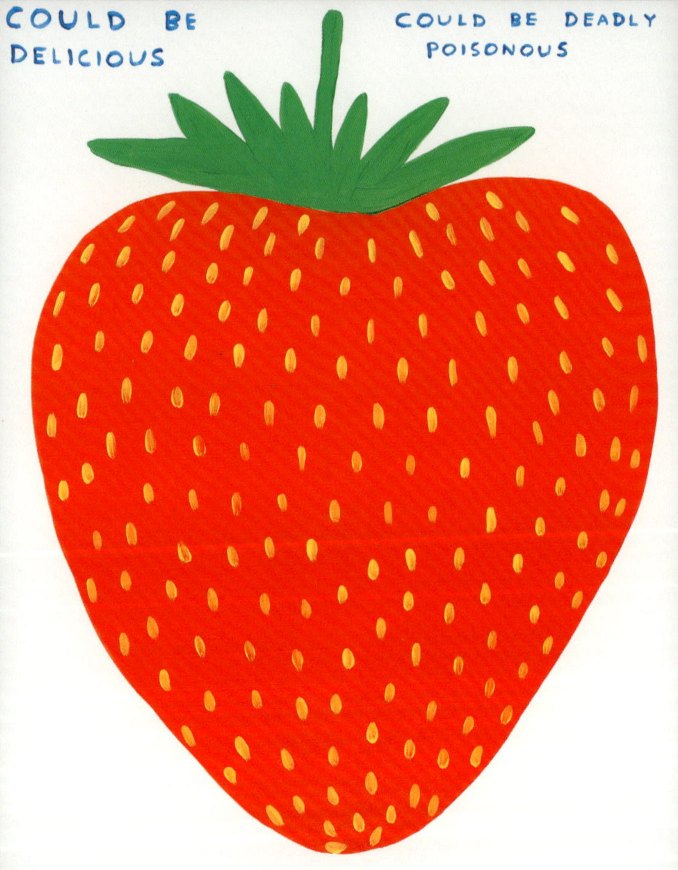
COULD BE
DELICIOUS
COULD BE DEADLY
POISONOUS
COULD BE DEADLY POISONOUS AND DELICIOUS

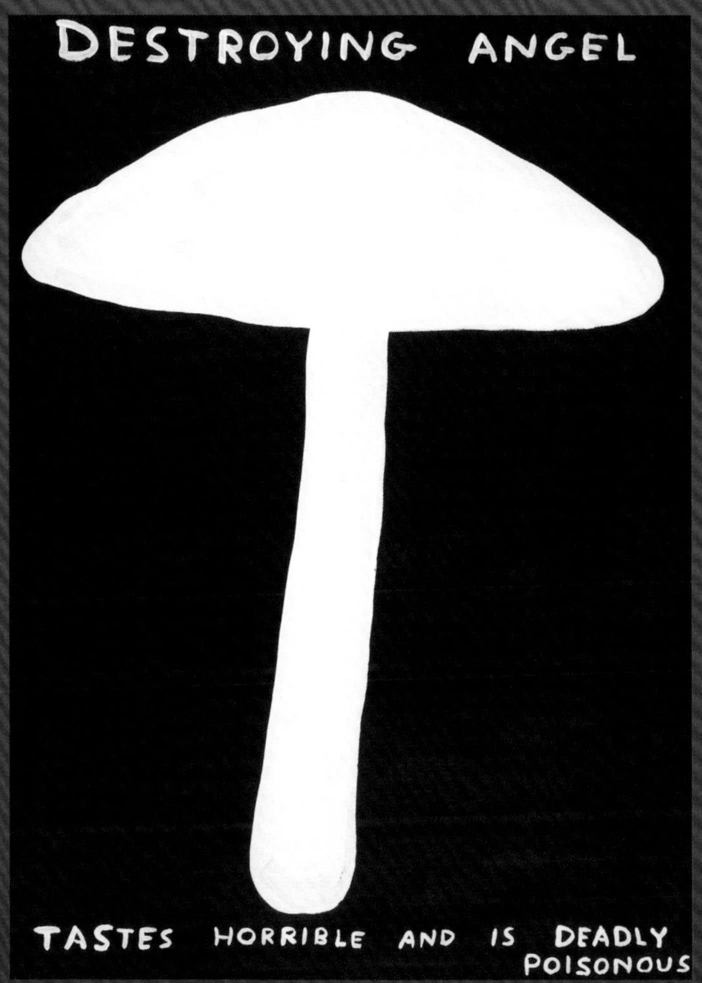
DESTROYING ANGEL
TASTES HORRIBLE AND IS DEADLY
POISONOUS

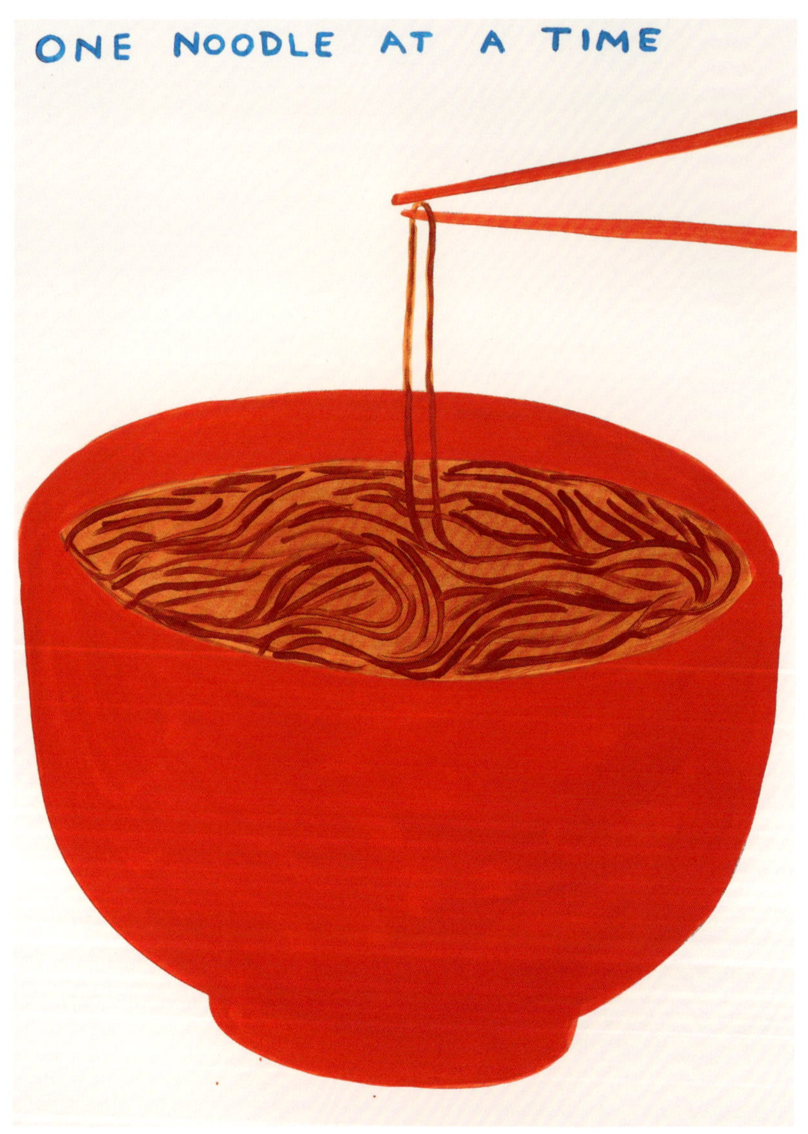
ONE NOODLE AT A TIME

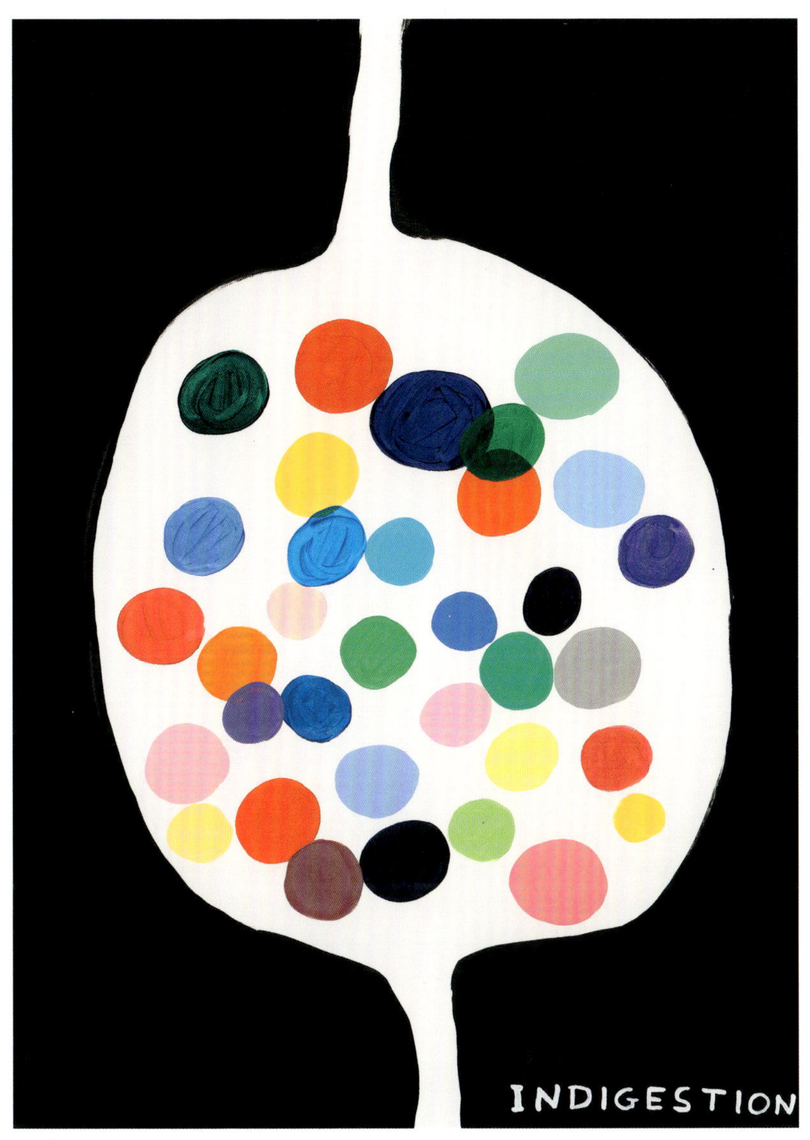
INDIGESTION

AT LAST
SOME GOOD
NEWS

THE BANANAS
ARE RIPE

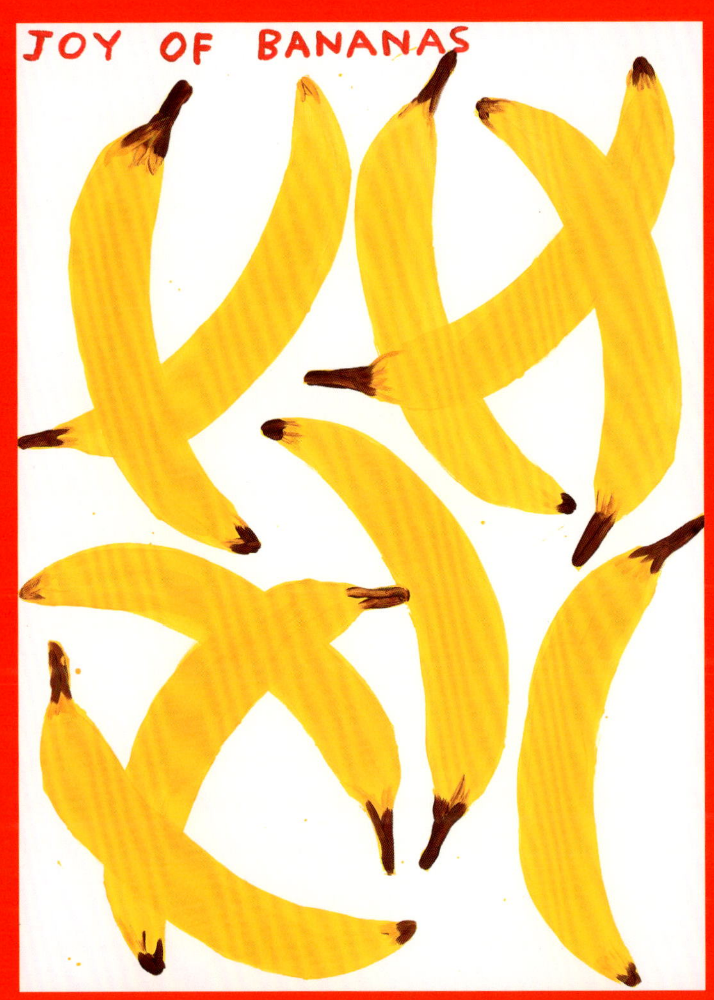
JOY OF BANANAS

INSTRUCTIONS

HOLD THE STICK FIRMLY IN BOTH
HANDS
DO NOT LET IT SLIP FROM YOUR
GRASP
IF IT SLIPS FROM YOUR GRASP
THEN IT IS LOST
AND YOU WILL NOT GET ANOTHER
ONE
THE MIXTURE WILL BE STIFF AT
BUT WILL SOON YIELD TO FIRST
THE STICK
STIR THE MIXTURE
UNTIL IT FROTHS VIOLENTLY
OPEN THE CAGE OF RODENTS
AND POUR THEM INTO THE MIXTURE
CONTINUE TO STIR
CHANT THE INCANTATION
UNTIL THE GHOSTLY FACES START TO
APPEAR
REMOVE THE MIXTURE FROM THE HEAT
AND ALLOW IT TO COOL
POUR IT INTO BOWLS
AND SERVE WITH CRUSTY BREAD

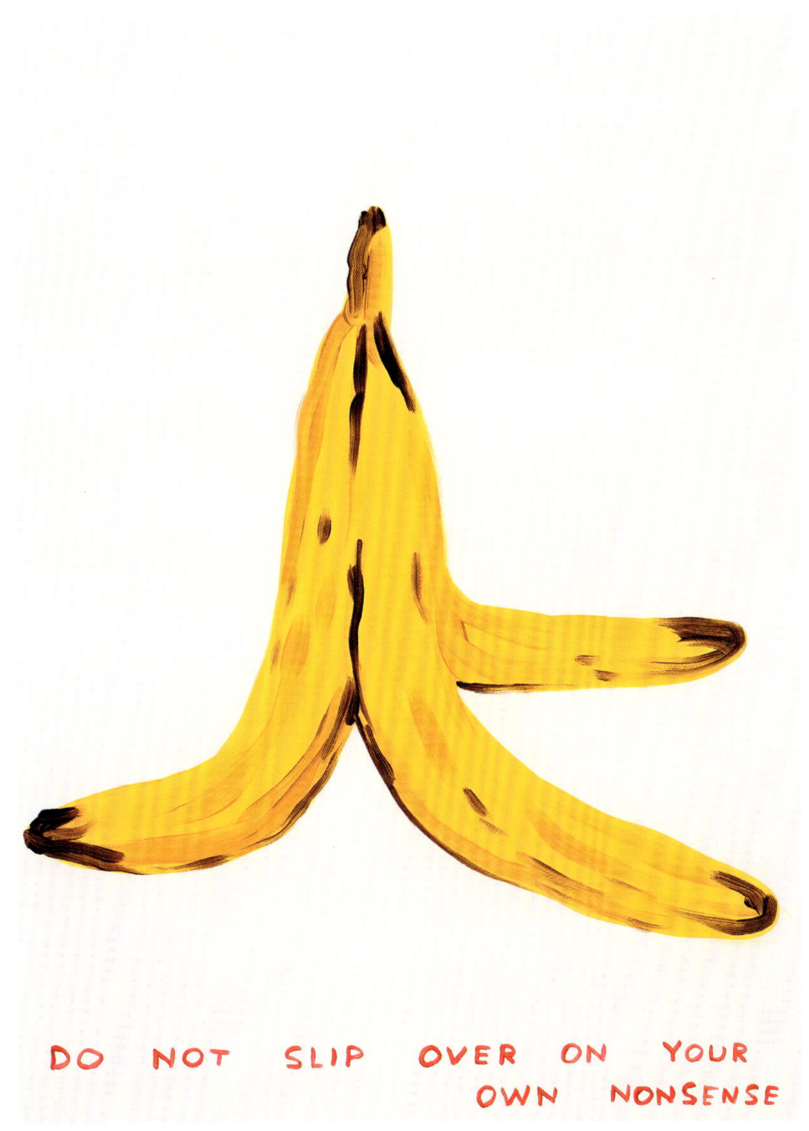
DO NOT SLIP OVER ON YOUR
OWN NONSENSE

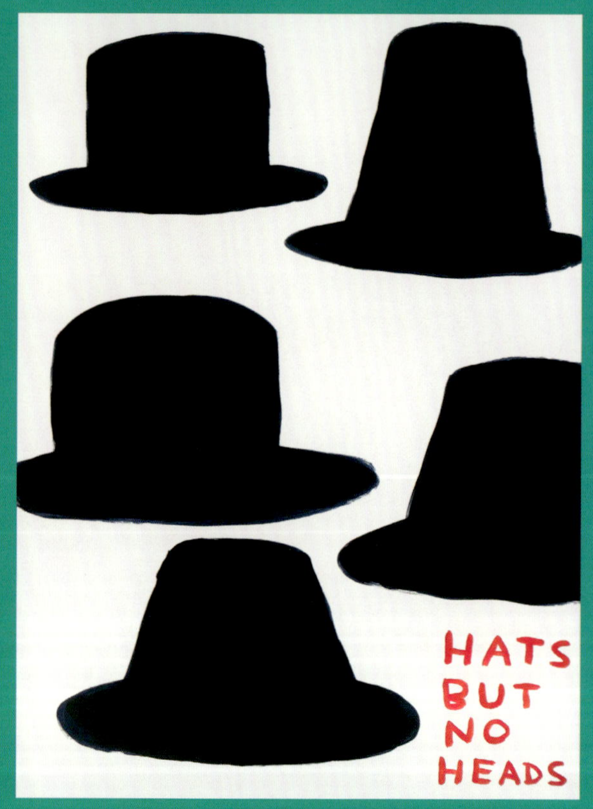
HATS
BUT
NO
HEADS

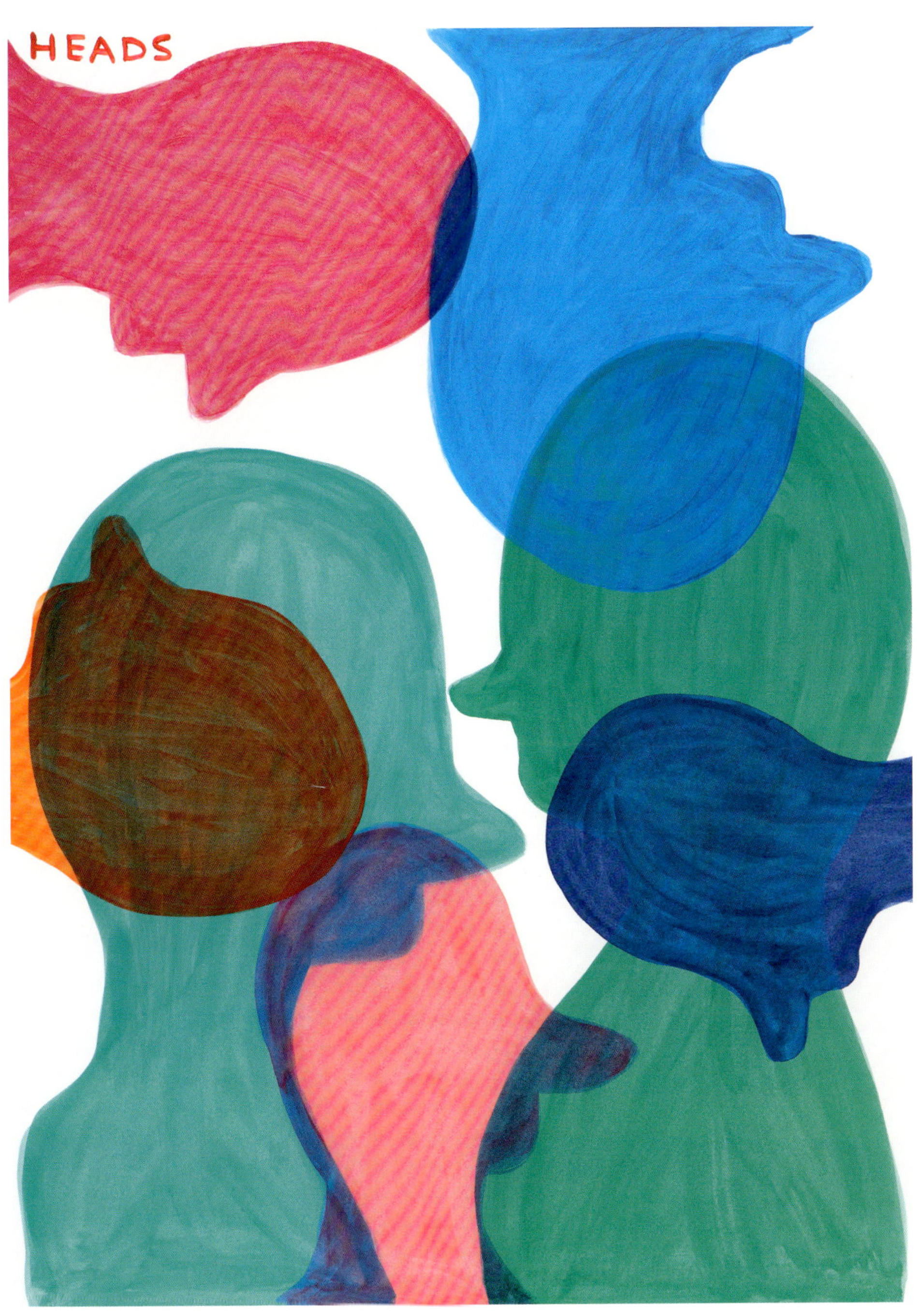
HEADS

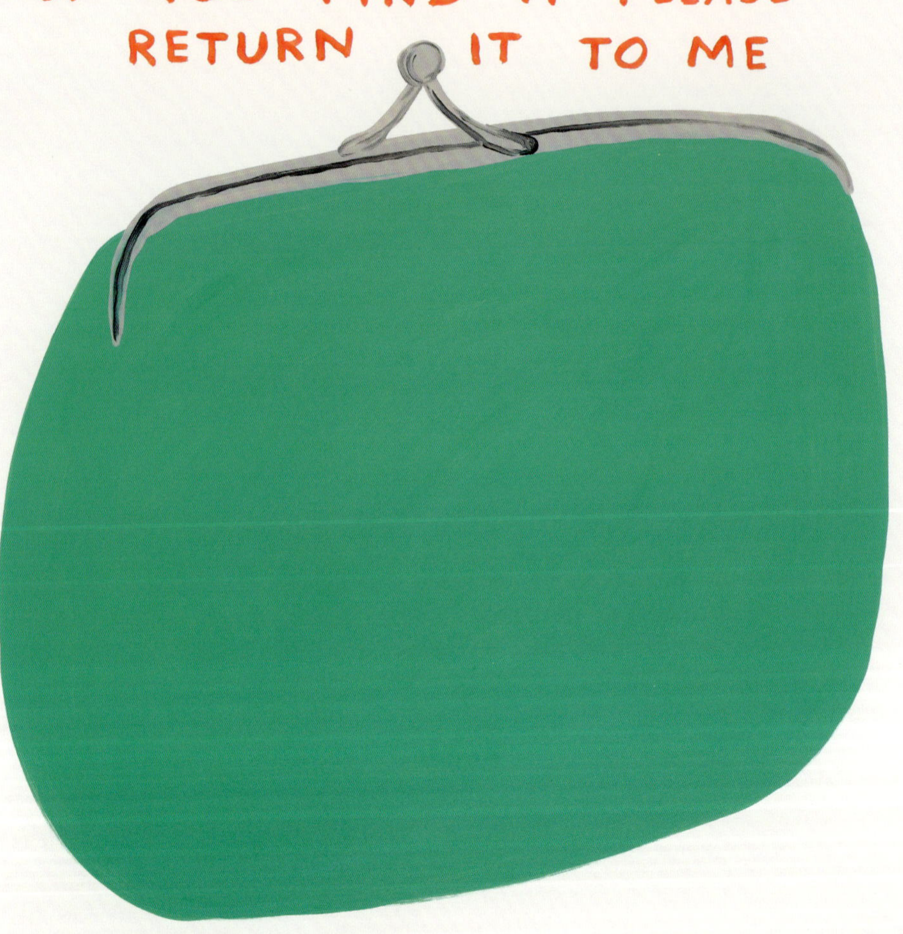
I LEFT MY PURSE ON
THE BUS
IF YOU FIND IT PLEASE
RETURN IT TO ME
IT CONTAINS
ONE MILLION POUNDS

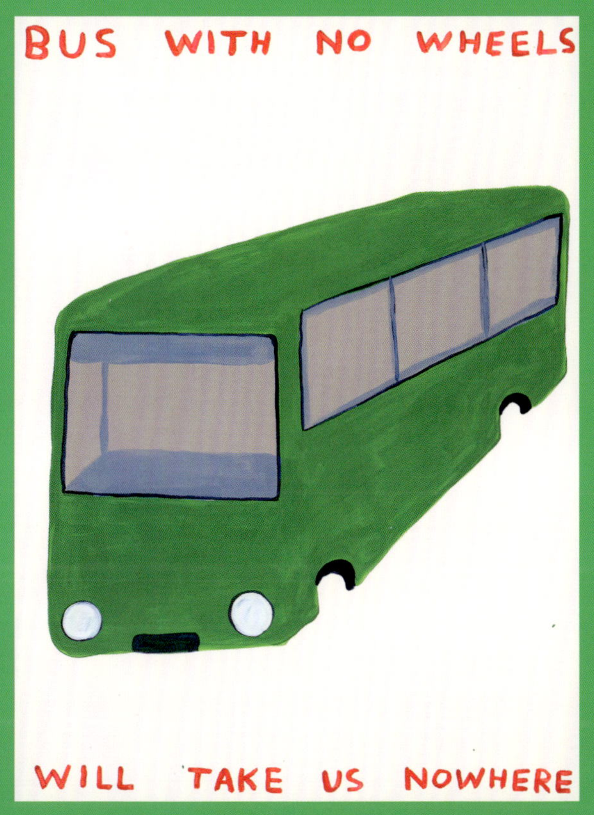
BUS WITH NO WHEELS
WILL TAKE US NOWHERE

CHARGING RHINOCEROS

IGNORE THE WILD RHINOCEROS
THAT IS CHARGING TOWARDS YOU
IF YOU IGNORE HIM
HE WILL FORGET THAT YOU ARE
THERE
AND WILL CHARGE AT SOMEONE
ELSE
TAKE MY ADVICE
I HAVE LIVED IN THE JUNGLE
FOR YEARS
I KNOW WHAT I'M TALKING ABOUT
THIS IS YOUR ONLY CHANCE OF
SURVIVAL

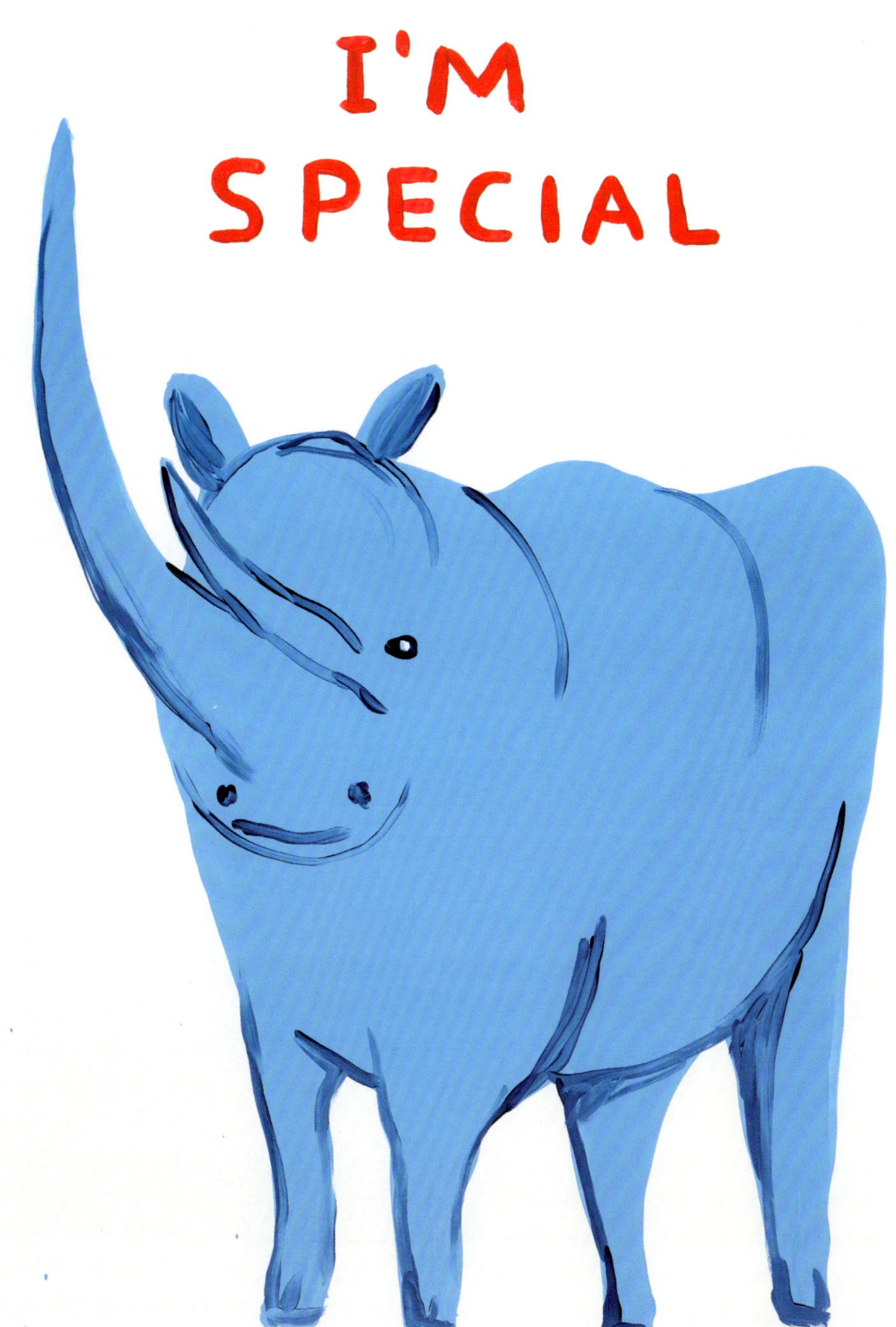
I'M
SPECIAL

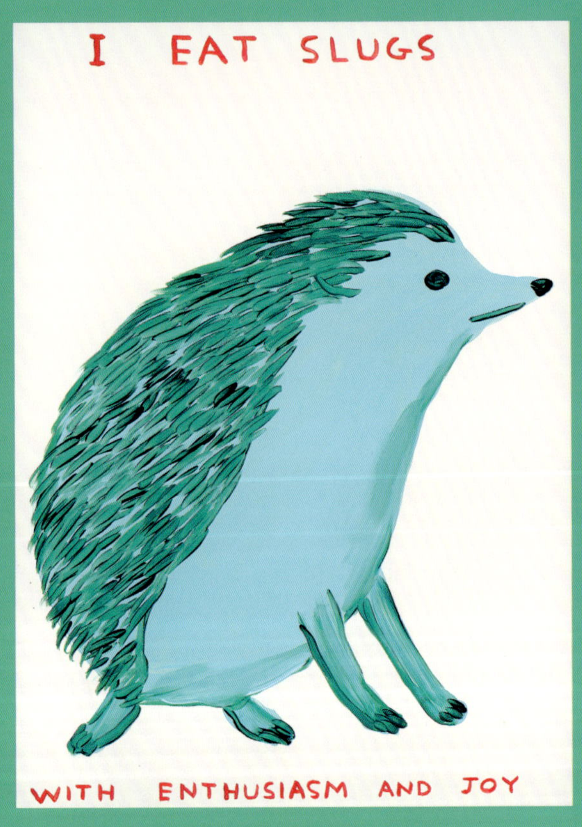
I EAT SLUGS
WITH ENTHUSIASM AND JOY

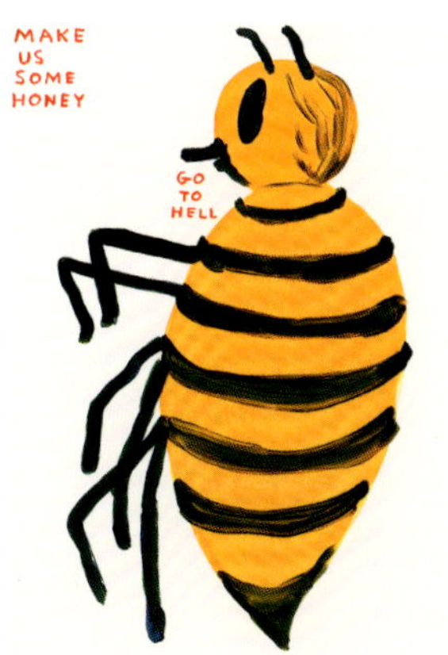
MAKE US SOME HONEY
GO TO HELL

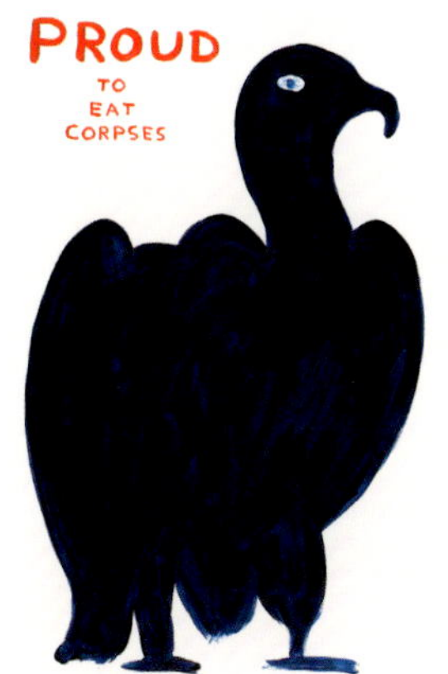
PROUD
TO EAT CORPSES

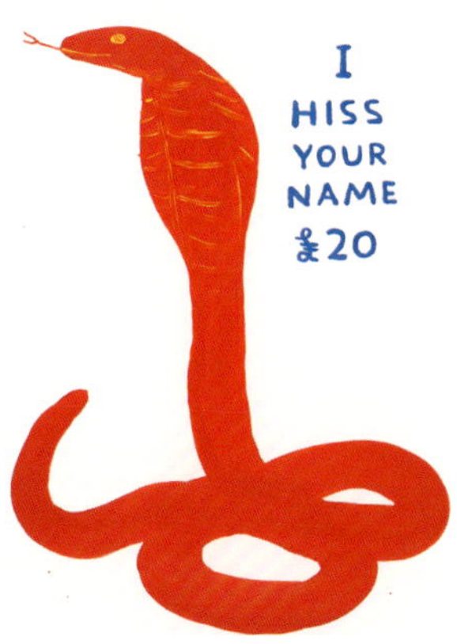
I HISS YOUR NAME
£20

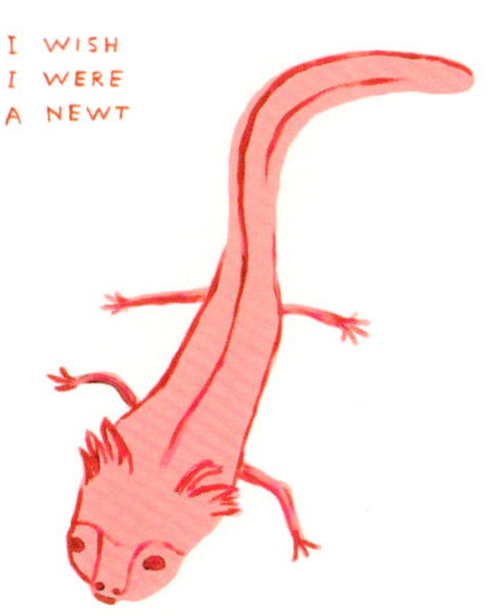
I WISH I WERE A NEWT

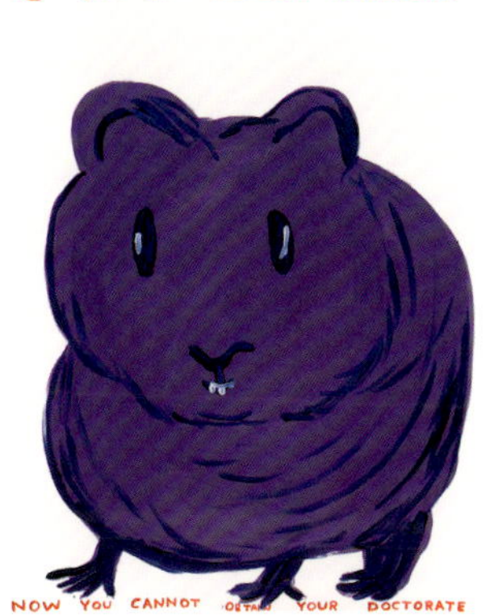
I ATE YOUR THESIS
NOW YOU CANNOT OBTAIN YOUR DOCTORATE

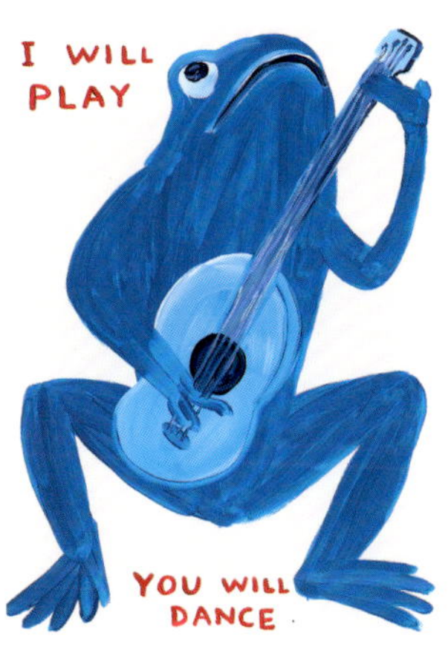
I WILL PLAY
YOU WILL DANCE

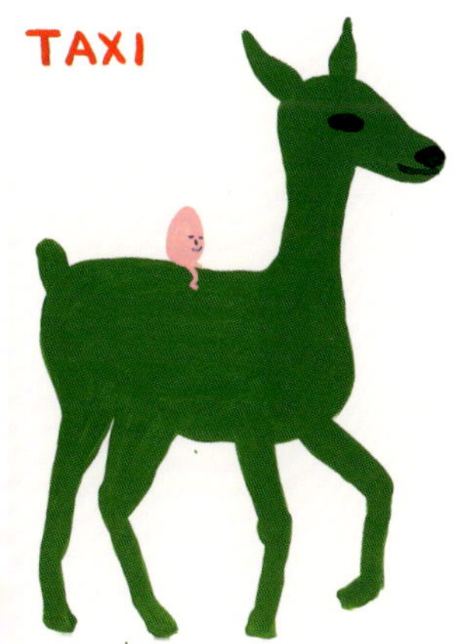
TAXI

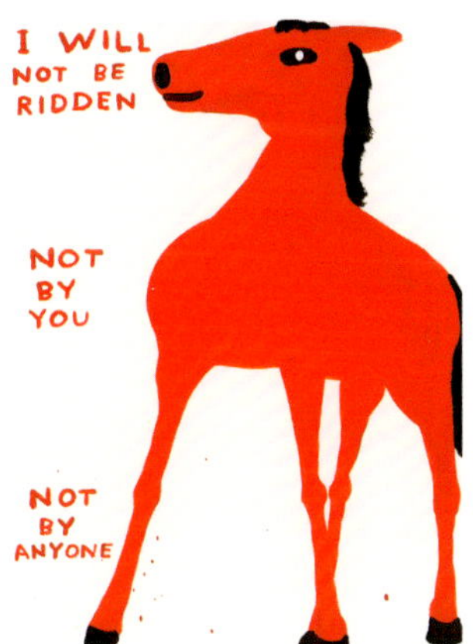
I WILL NOT BE RIDDEN
NOT BY YOU
NOT BY ANYONE

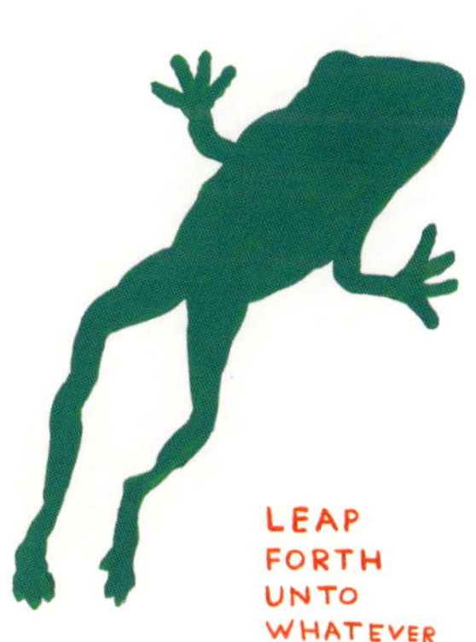
LEAP FORTH UNTO WHATEVER

TYPE OF INSECT

MORAL INSECTS
THEY HAVE A CONSCIENCE:
THEY WON'T DO CERTAIN THINGS
WON'T EAT EACH OTHER
WON'T BITE PEOPLE
ETC.
SOMETIMES ALSO CALLED 'NICE INSECTS'

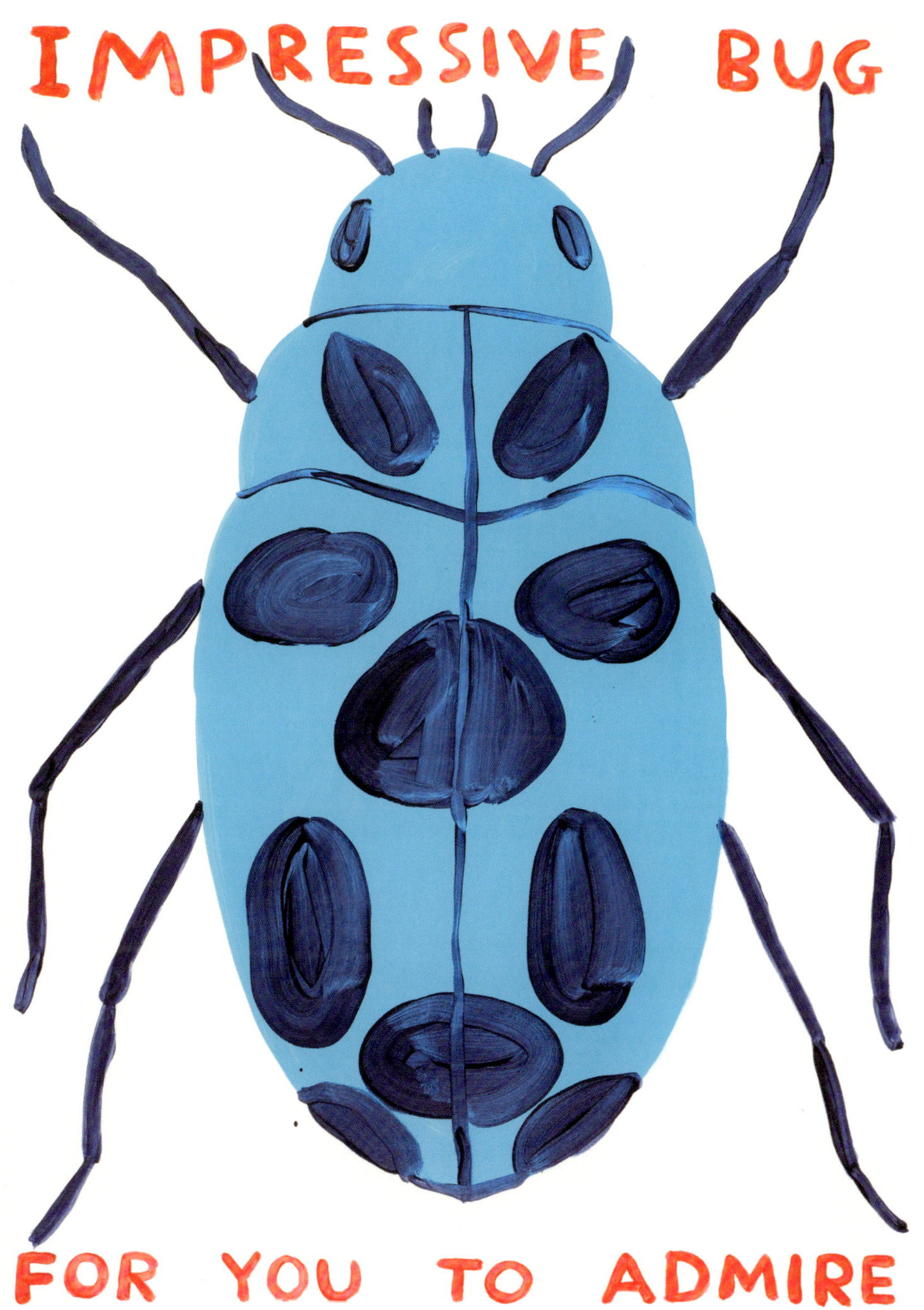
IMPRESSIVE BUG
FOR YOU TO ADMIRE

DIRT

DIRT
WHERE ?
IN THE TEMPLE
SHOULD WE CLEAN IT UP ?
NO
WHY ?
IT IS HOLY DIRT
SO ?
ONLY A PRIEST CAN CLEAR IT UP
IS THERE NOTHING WE CAN DO ?
WE CAN PRAY

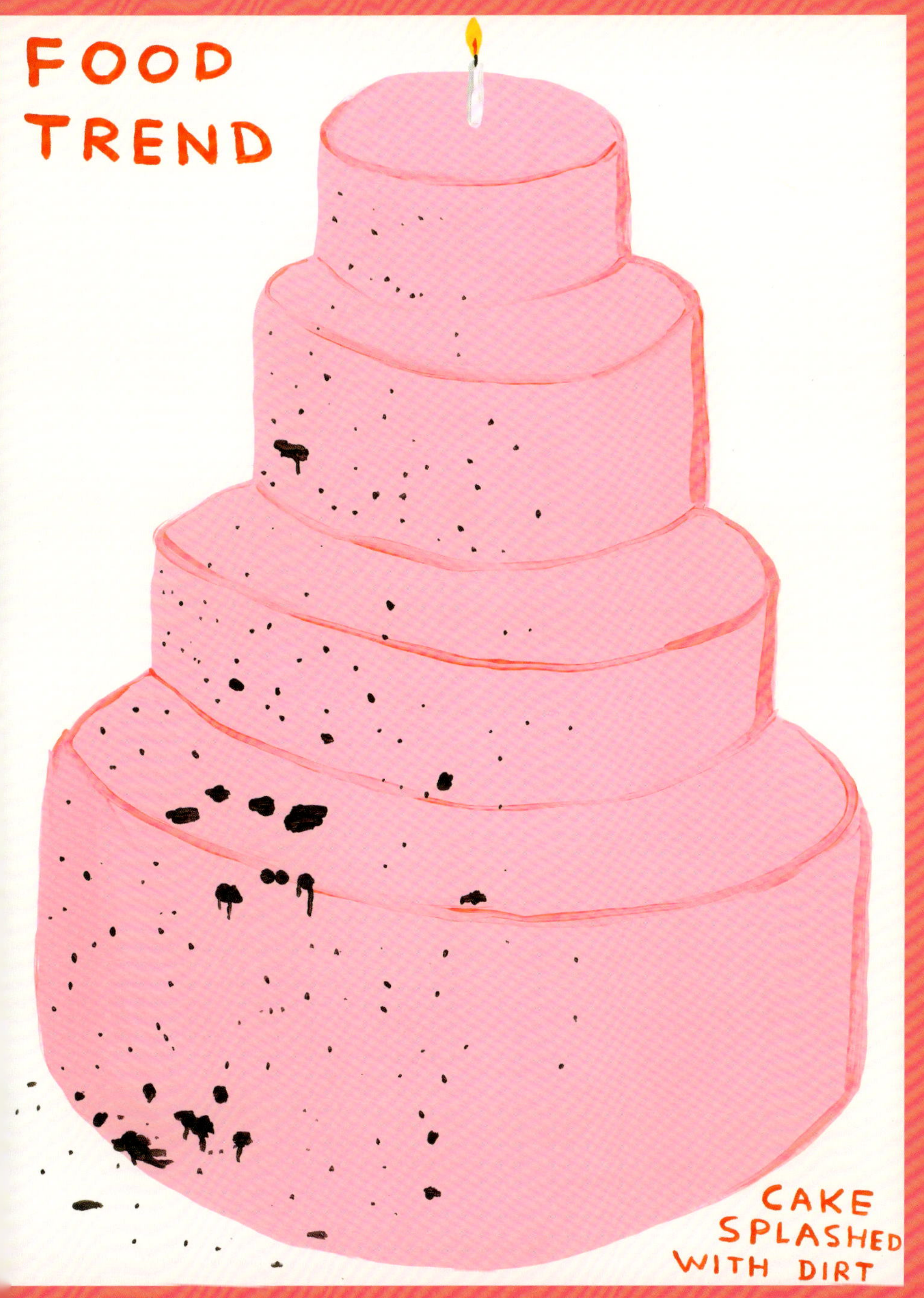
FOOD
TREND
CAKE
SPLASHED
WITH DIRT

TOUCHING DIRT

TOUCH THE DIRT
FEEL IT
DO YOU LIKE IT ?
YOU DO LIKE IT !
ARE YOU SURPRISED THAT YOU LIKE IT?
YOU ARE SURPRISED THAT YOU LIKE IT!
I KNEW YOU WOULD LIKE THE DIRT
I KNOW YOU BETTER THAN YOU KNOW
I AM LIKE AN ADULT YOURSELF
AND YOU ARE LIKE MY BABY
TOUCHING THE DIRT
UNDER MY SUPERVISION

I ATE SOME DIRT
IT TASTED GOOD

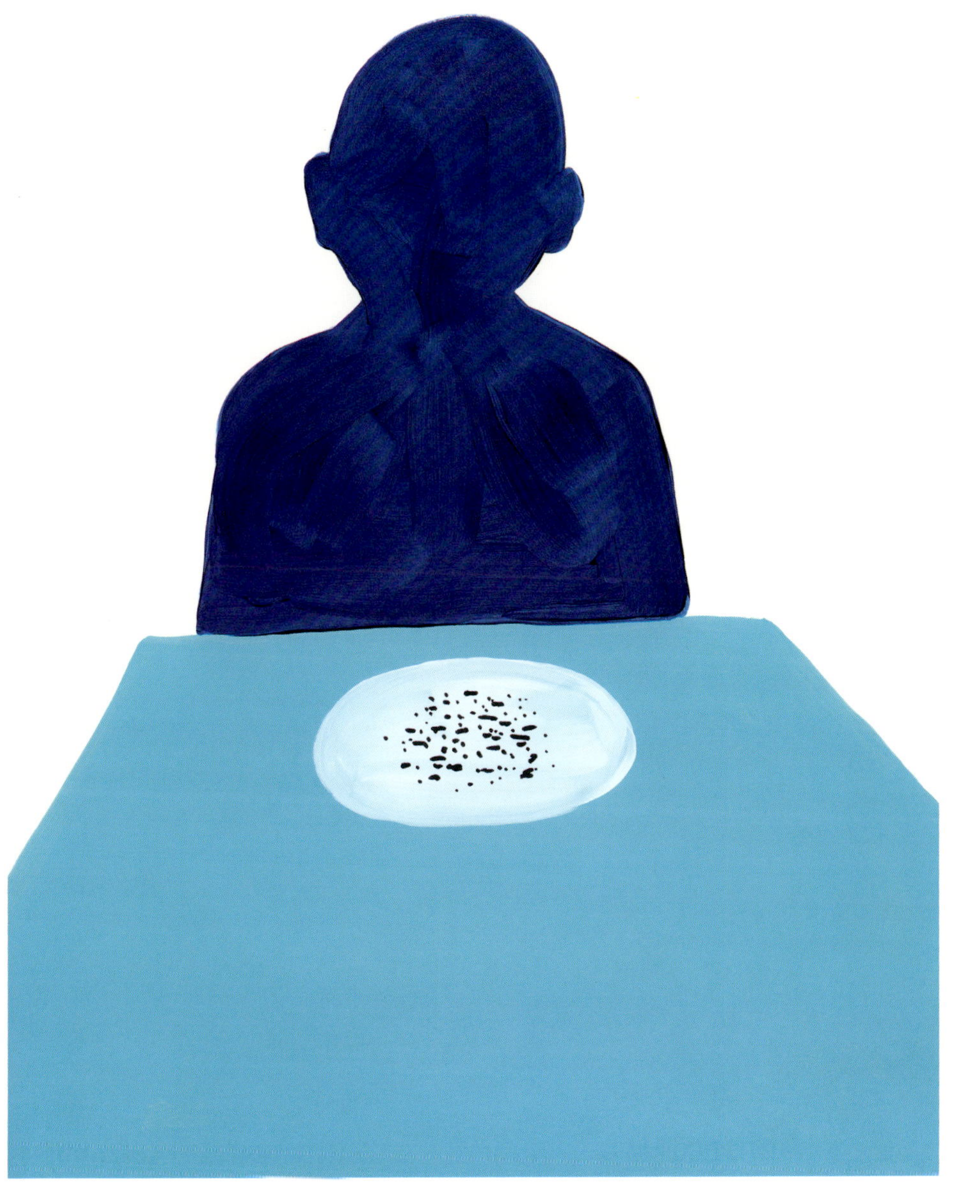

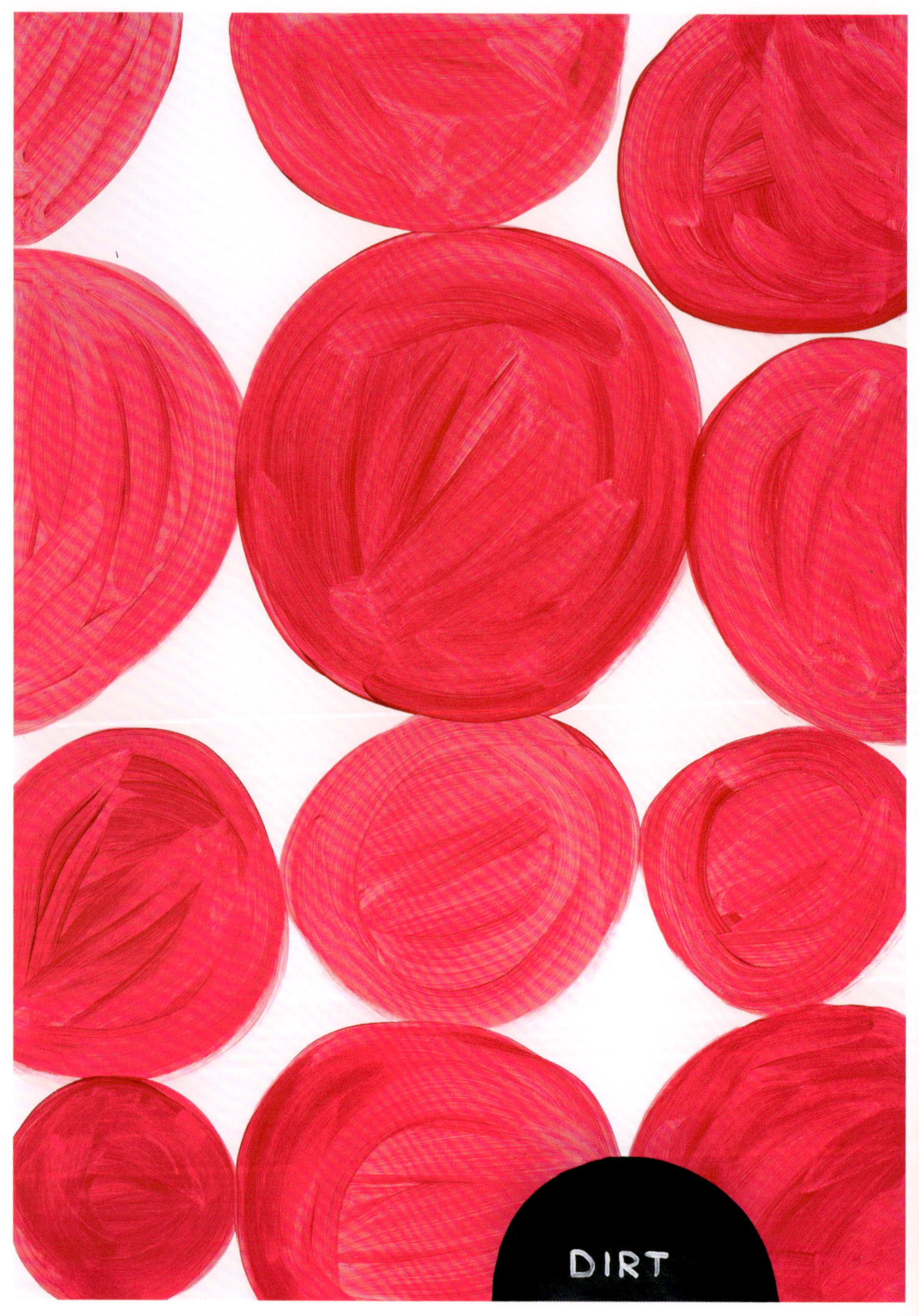
DIRT

DIRTY MARK

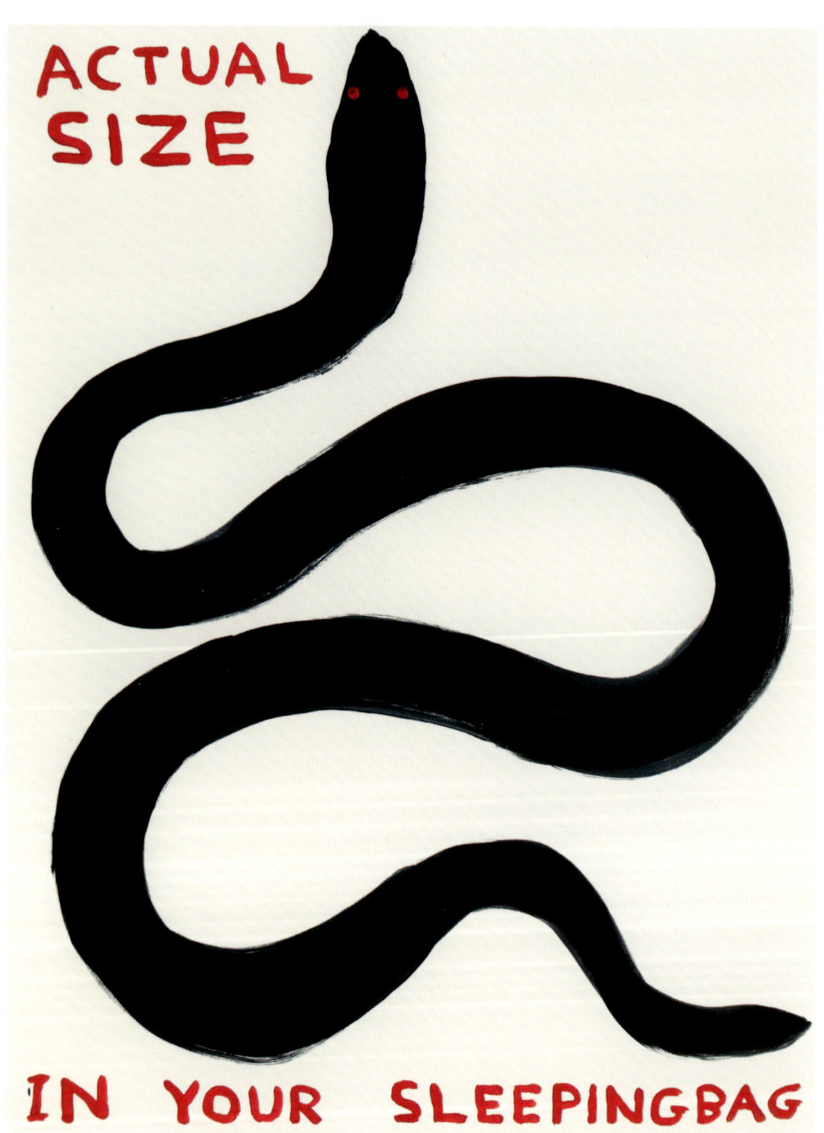
ACTUAL
SIZE
IN YOUR SLEEPINGBAG

STALACTITES
STALAGMITES

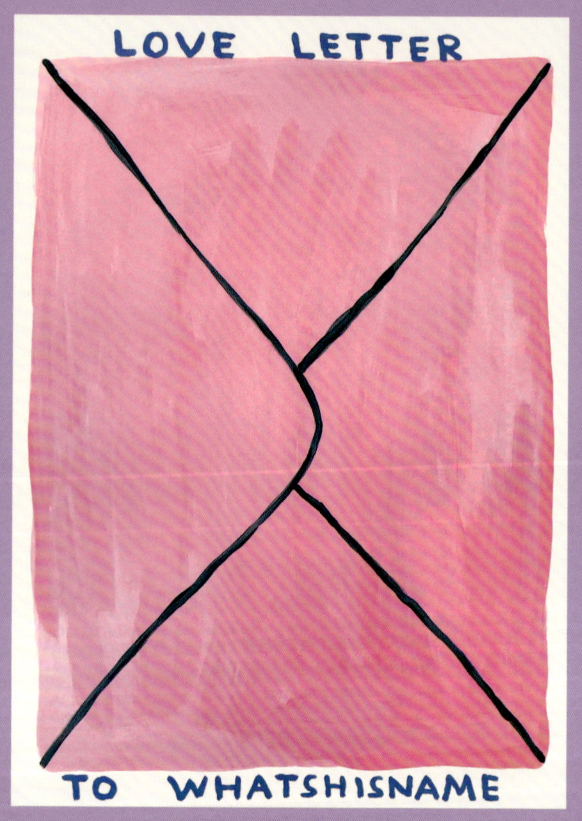
LOVE LETTER
TO WHATSHISNAME

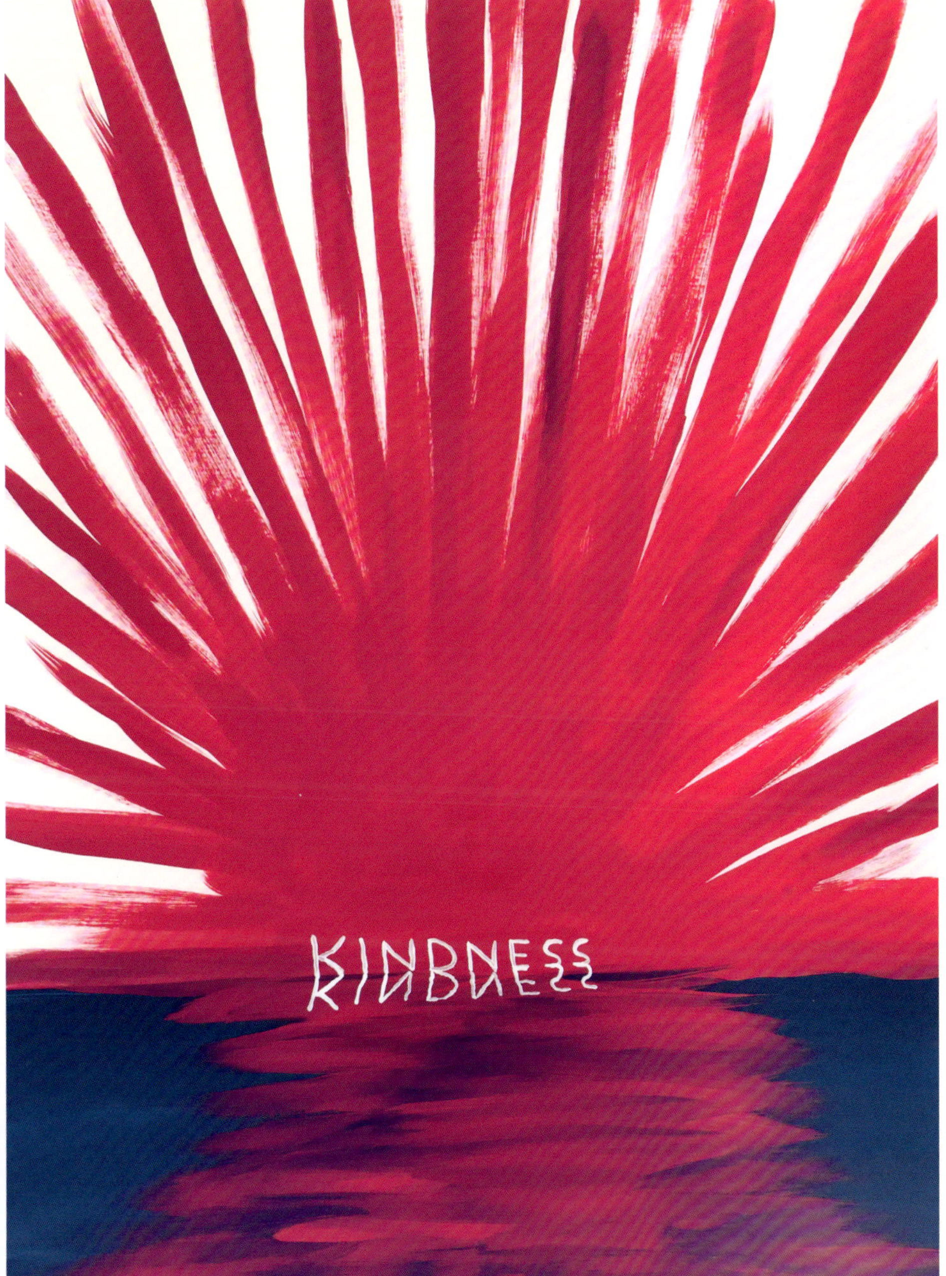
KINDNESS

CAKE

PLEASE MAY I HAVE ANOTHER
SLICE OF CAKE
I ENJOYED THE SLICE OF CAKE
THAT I HAVE JUST EATEN
SO MUCH
THAT I WOULD LIKE TO HAVE
ANOTHER ONE
EVEN THOUGH I AM MORBIDLY
OBESE
AND I HAVE BEEN ADVISED
NOT TO EAT CAKE

CHOCOLATE CAKE
FOR SALE
£1000

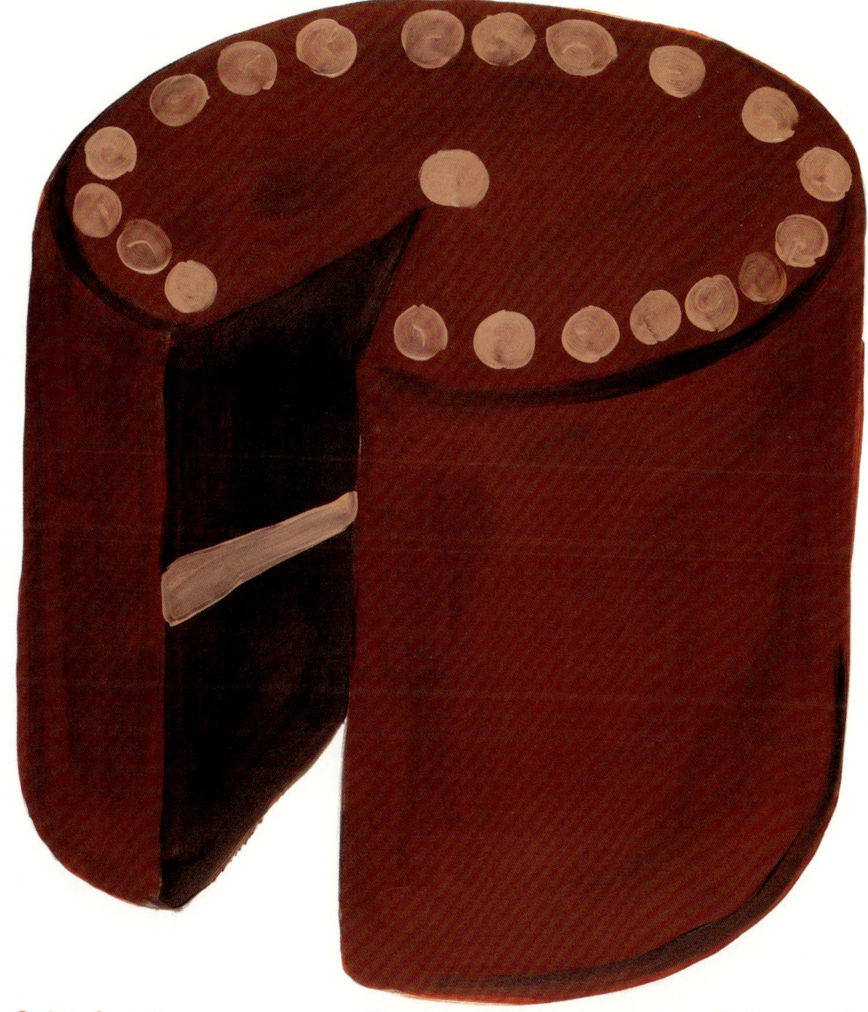

ONLY ONE SLICE MISSING

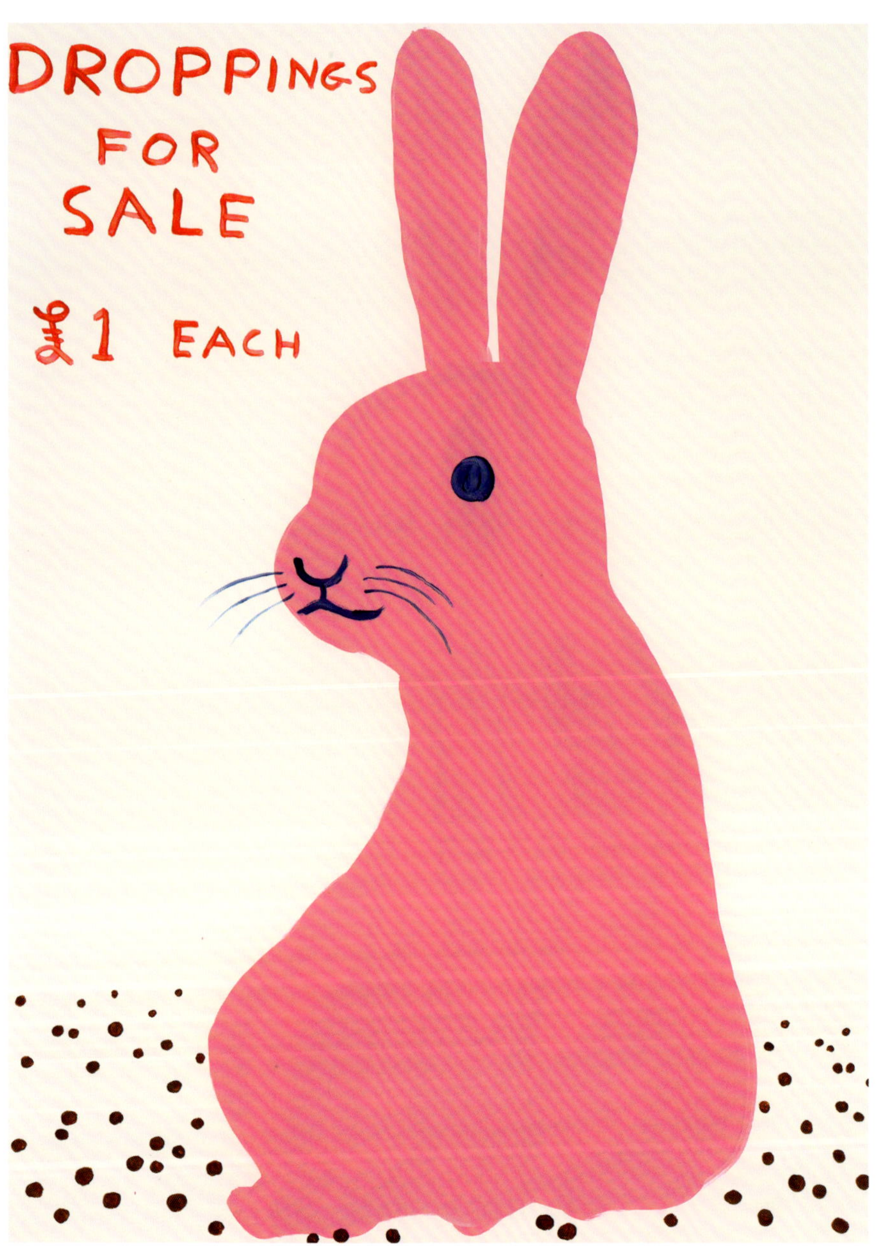
DROPPINGS
FOR
SALE
£1 EACH

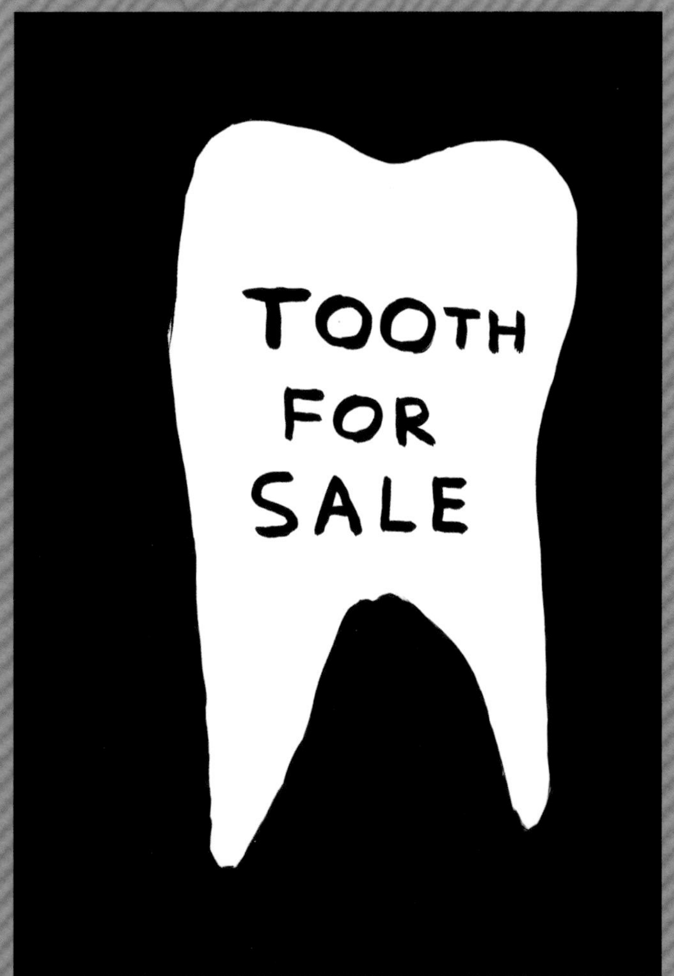
TOOTH
FOR
SALE

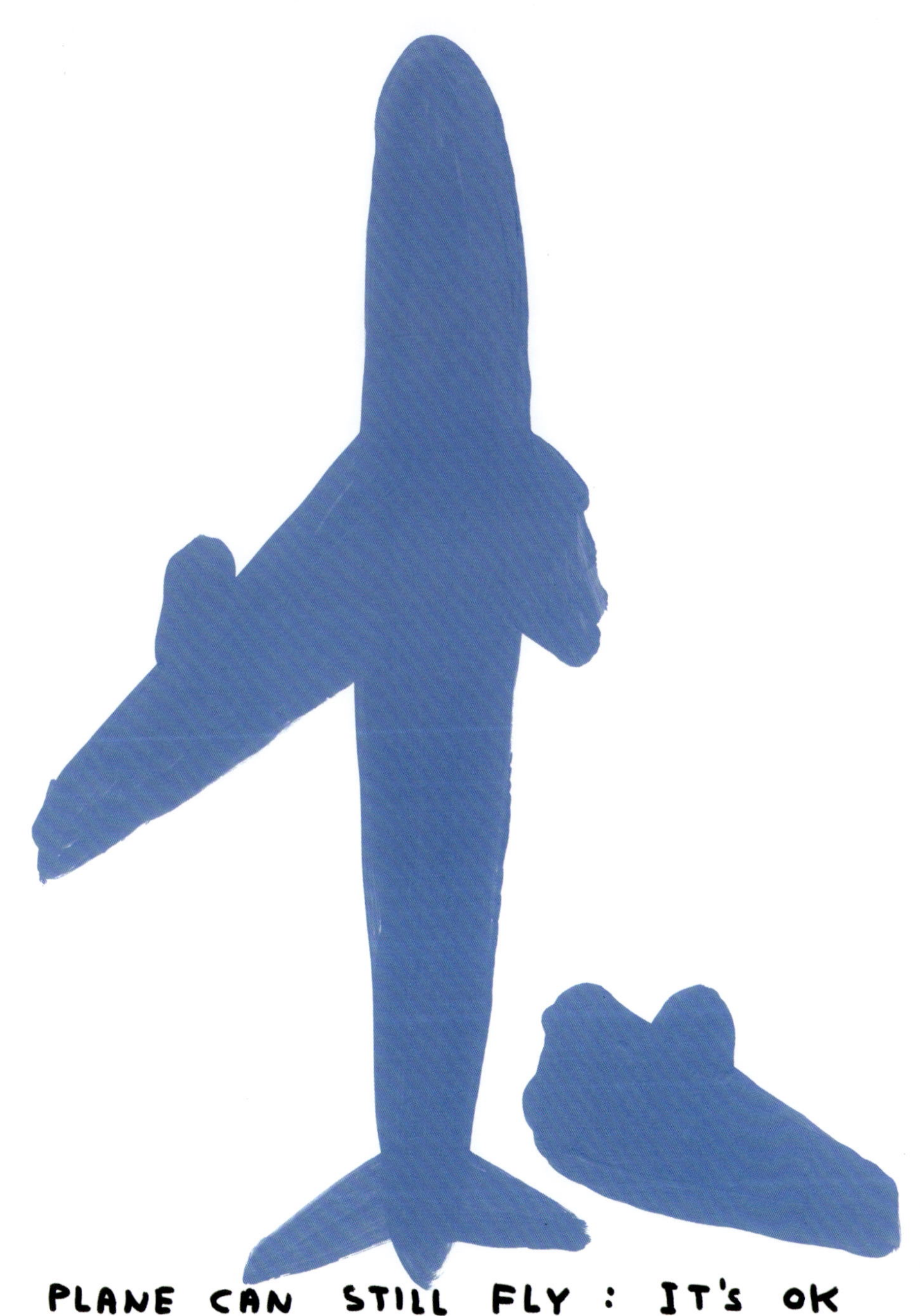

PLANE CAN STILL FLY : IT'S OK

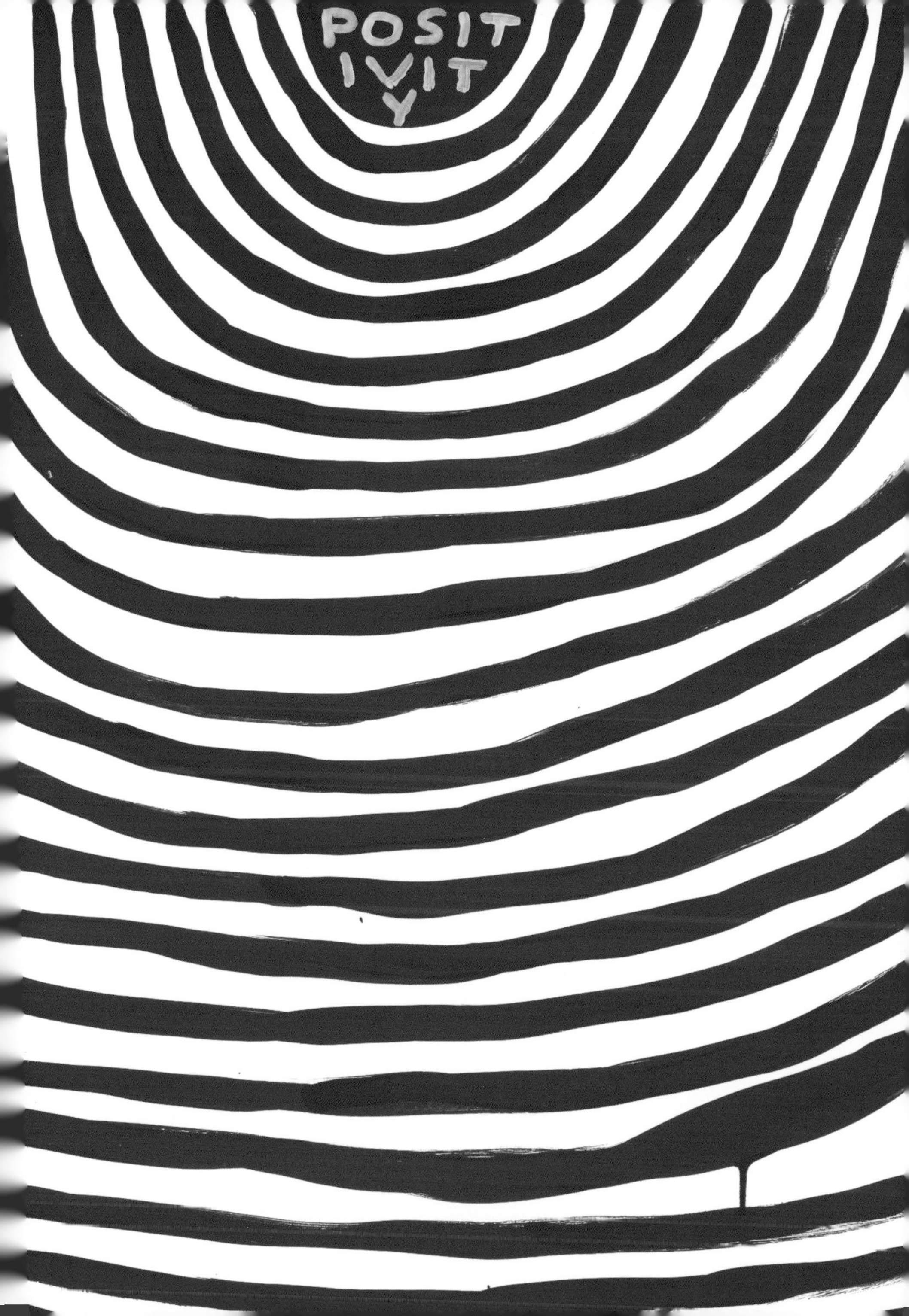
POSIT
IVIT
Y

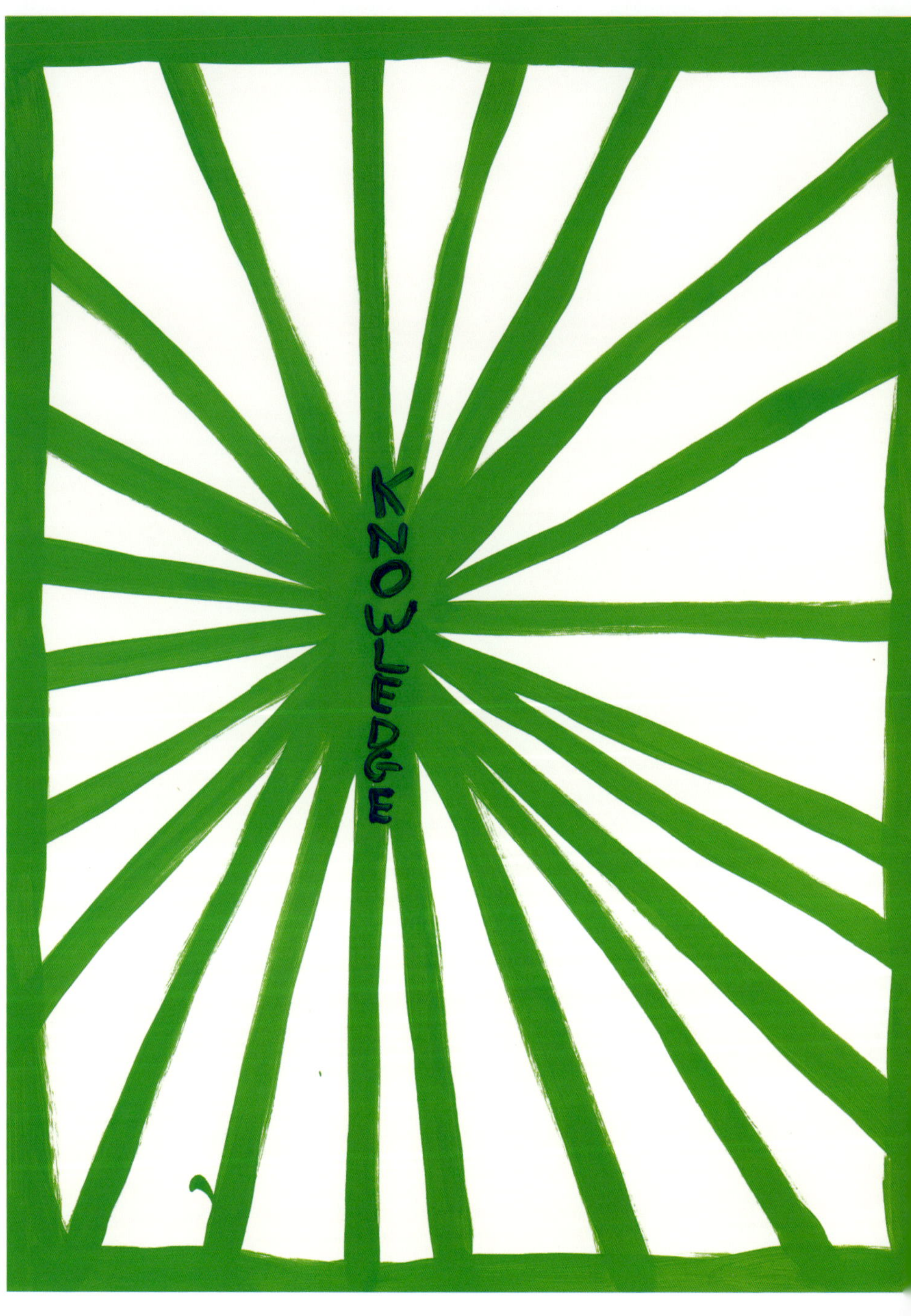
KNOWLEDGE

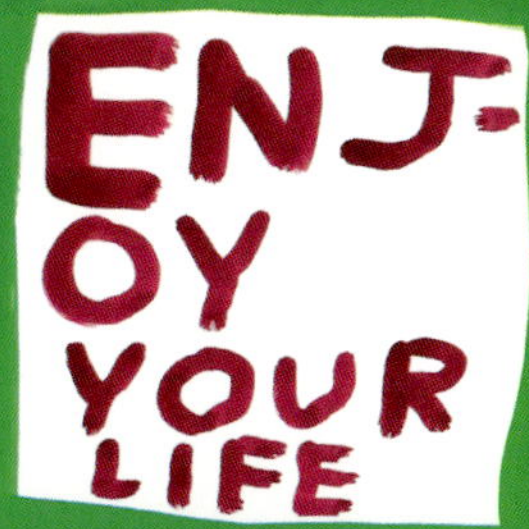
ENJ-
OY
YOUR
LIFE
ENJOY
YOUR
LIFE
ENJOY
YOUR
LIFE

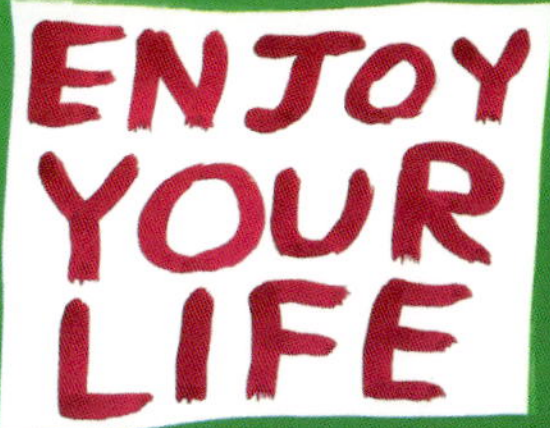
ENJOY
YOUR
LIFE

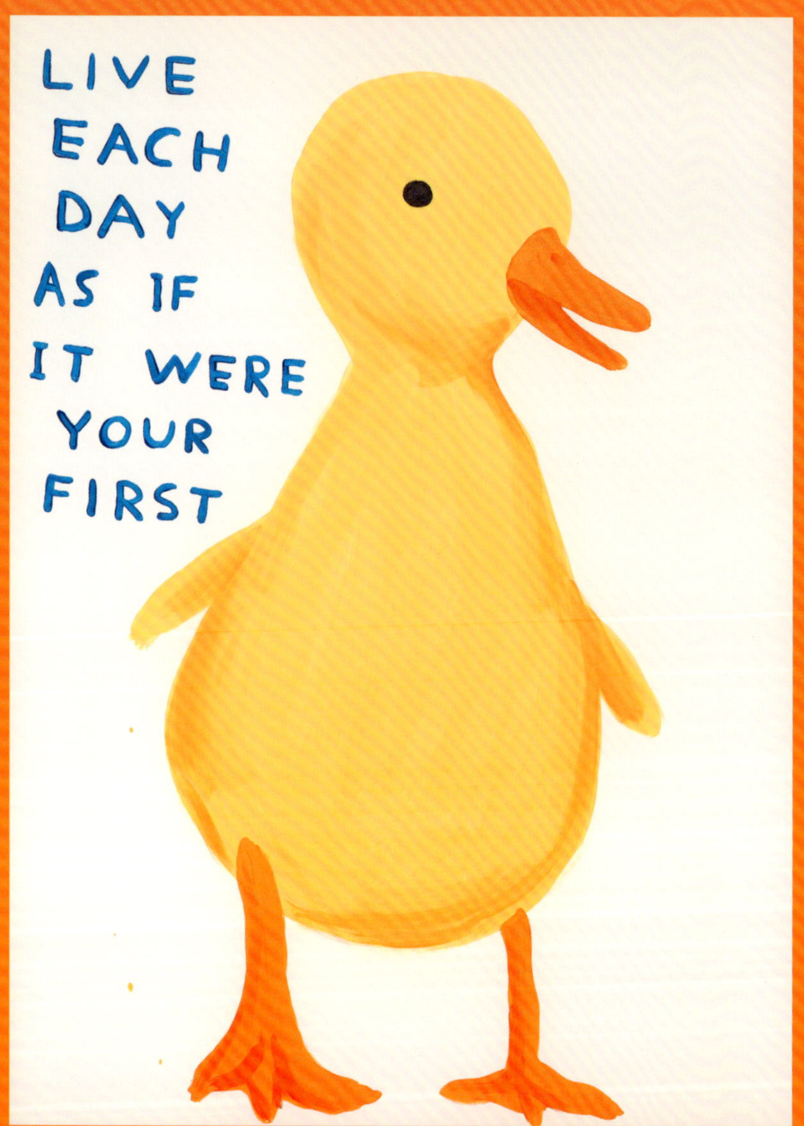
LIVE
EACH
DAY
AS IF
IT WERE
YOUR
FIRST

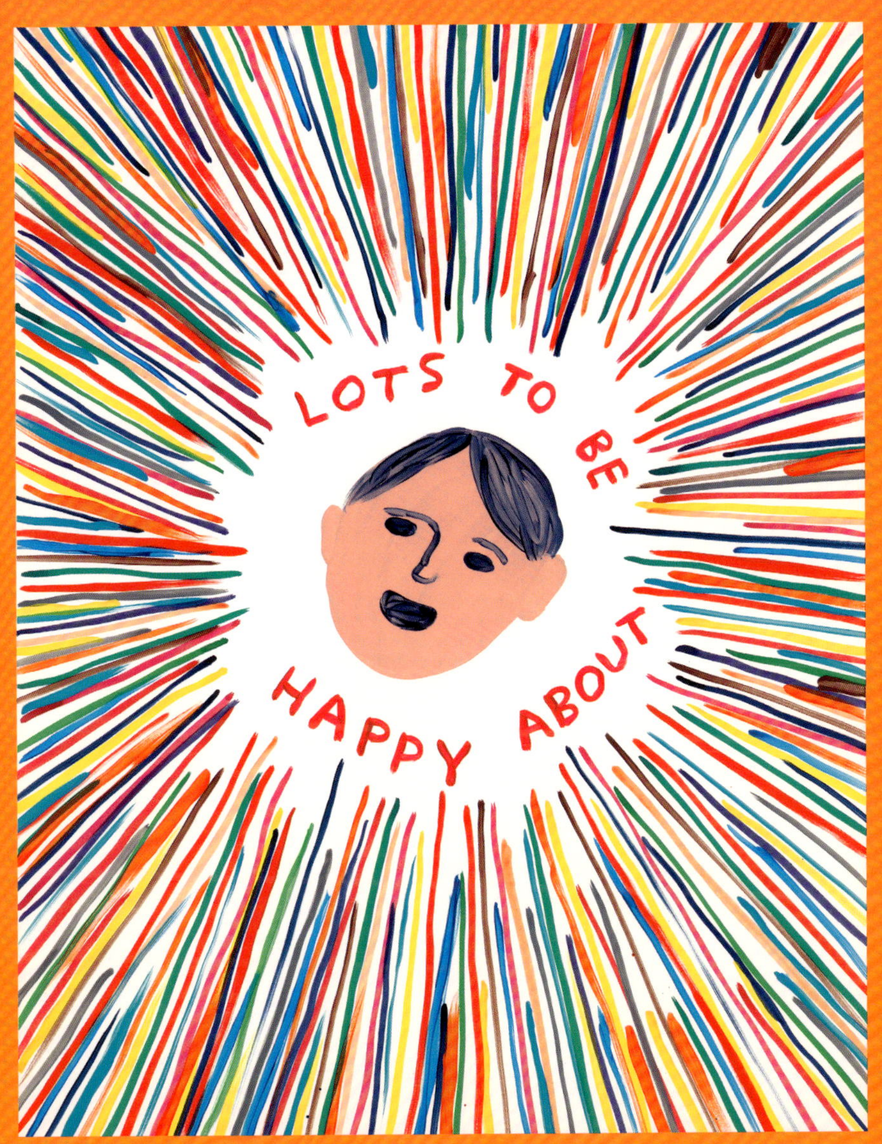
LOTS TO BE
HAPPY ABOUT

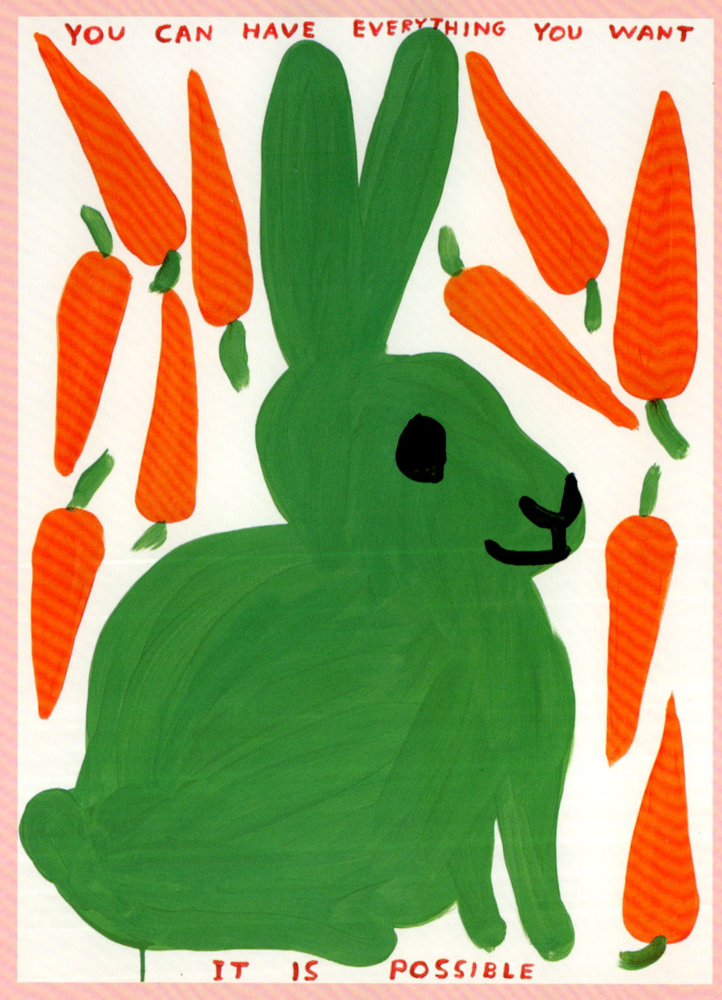
YOU CAN HAVE EVERYTHING YOU WANT
IT IS POSSIBLE

WITNESS MY CONTENTMENT

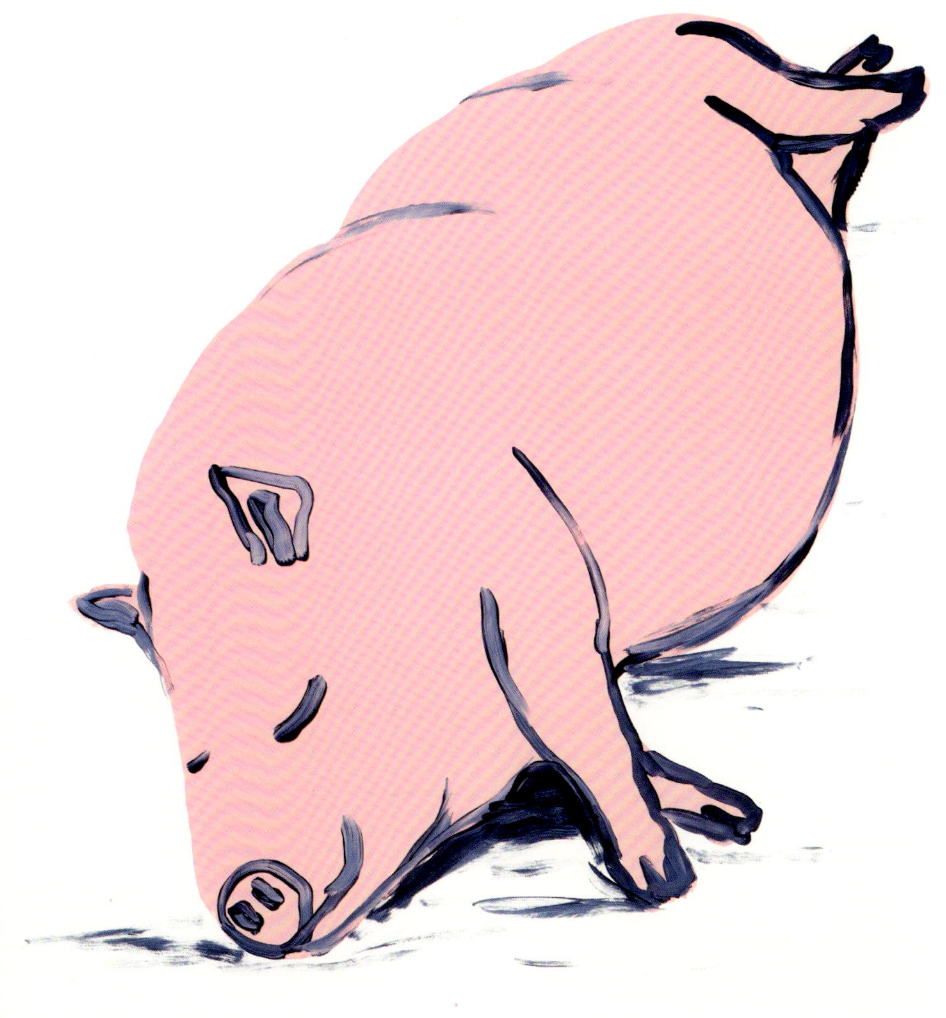

THAT YOU TOO MAY BE CONTENT

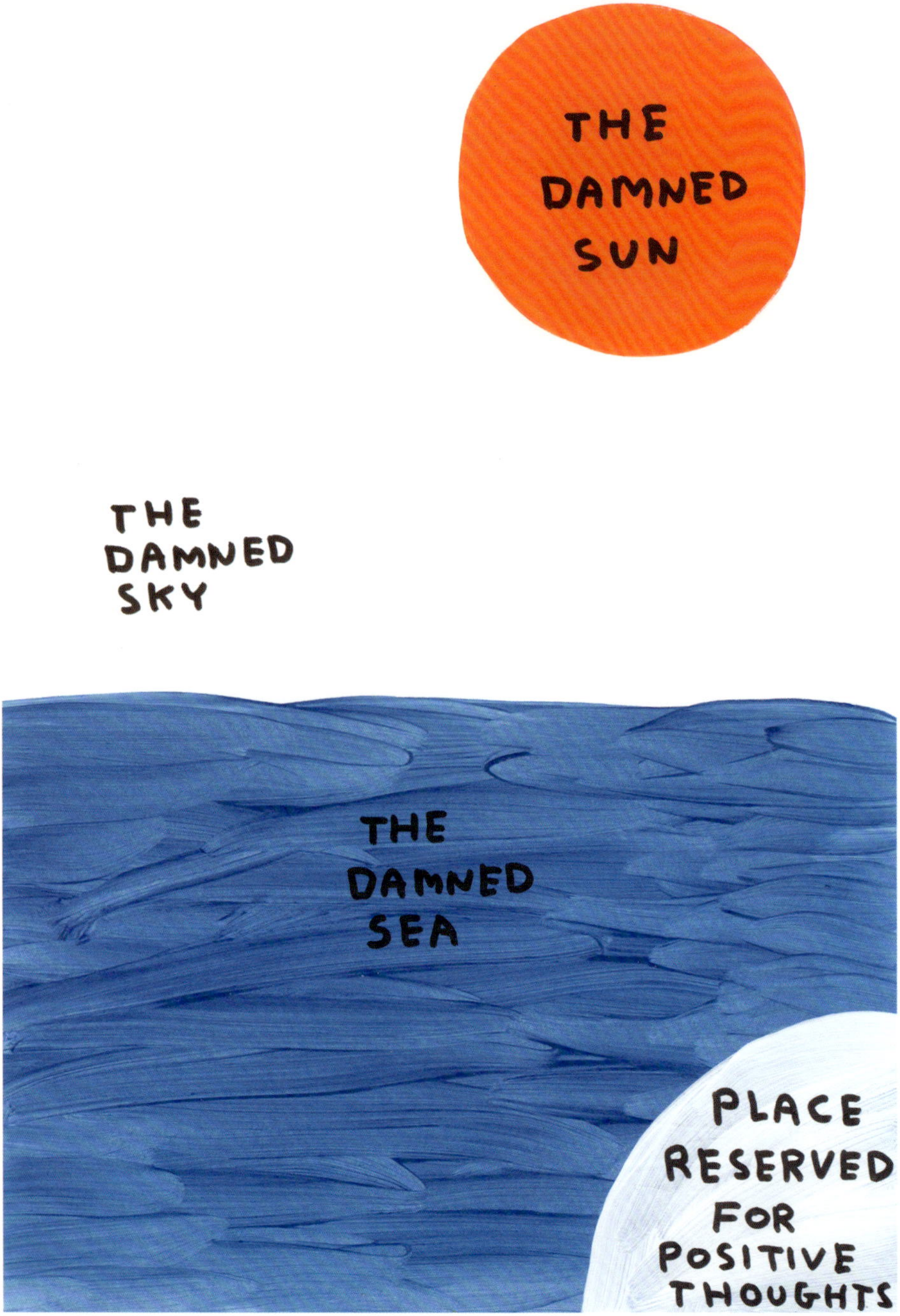

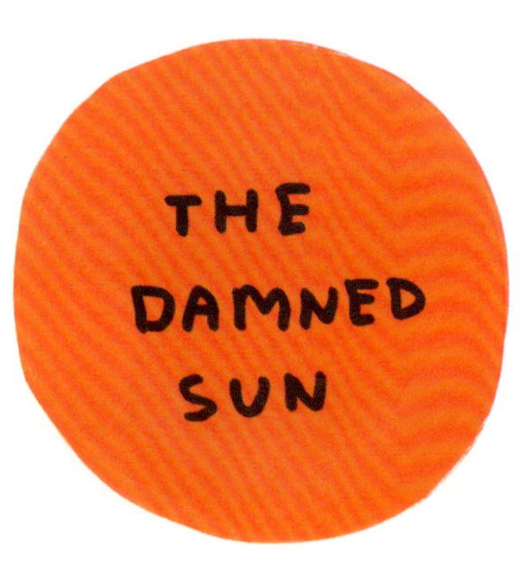

THE
DAMNED
SKY

THE
DAMNED
SEA

PLACE
RESERVED
FOR
POSITIVE
THOUGHTS

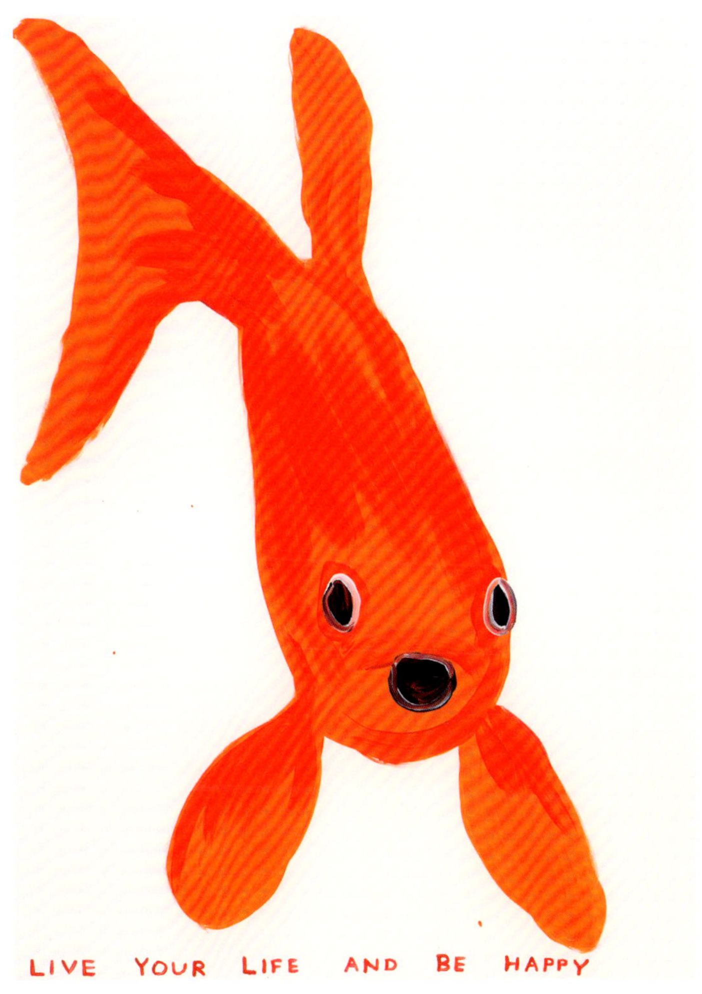
LIVE YOUR LIFE AND BE HAPPY

EVERYBODY

WHERE IS EVERYBODY?
WHERE HAVE THEY ALL GONE?
HAVE THEY GONE ON HOLIDAY?
OR HAVE THEY ALL DIED?
AND TO WHOM AM I ASKING
THESE QUESTIONS?
(I AM ALONE, YOU SEE)

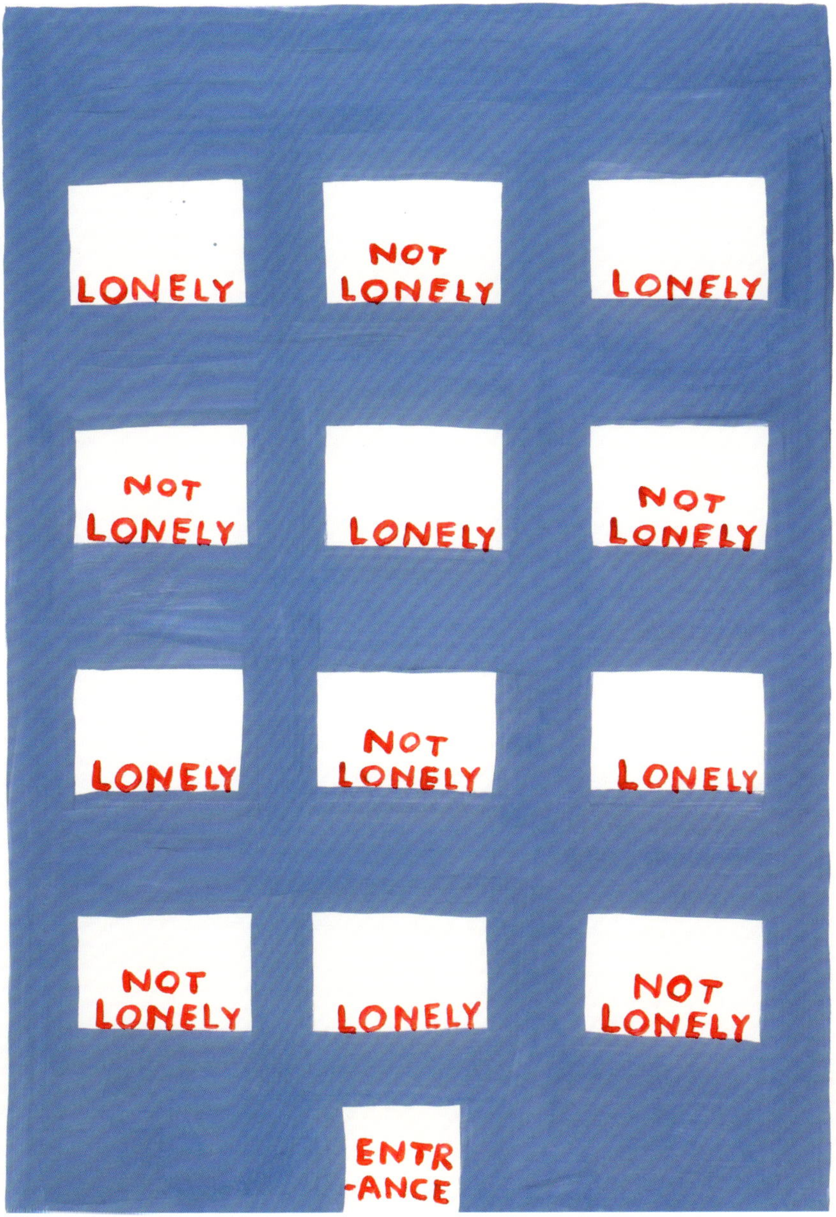

LONELY

NOT
LONELY

LONELY

NOT
LONELY

LONELY

NOT
LONELY

LONELY

NOT
LONELY

LONELY

NOT
LONELY

LONELY

NOT
LONELY

ENTR
-ANCE

HAIR

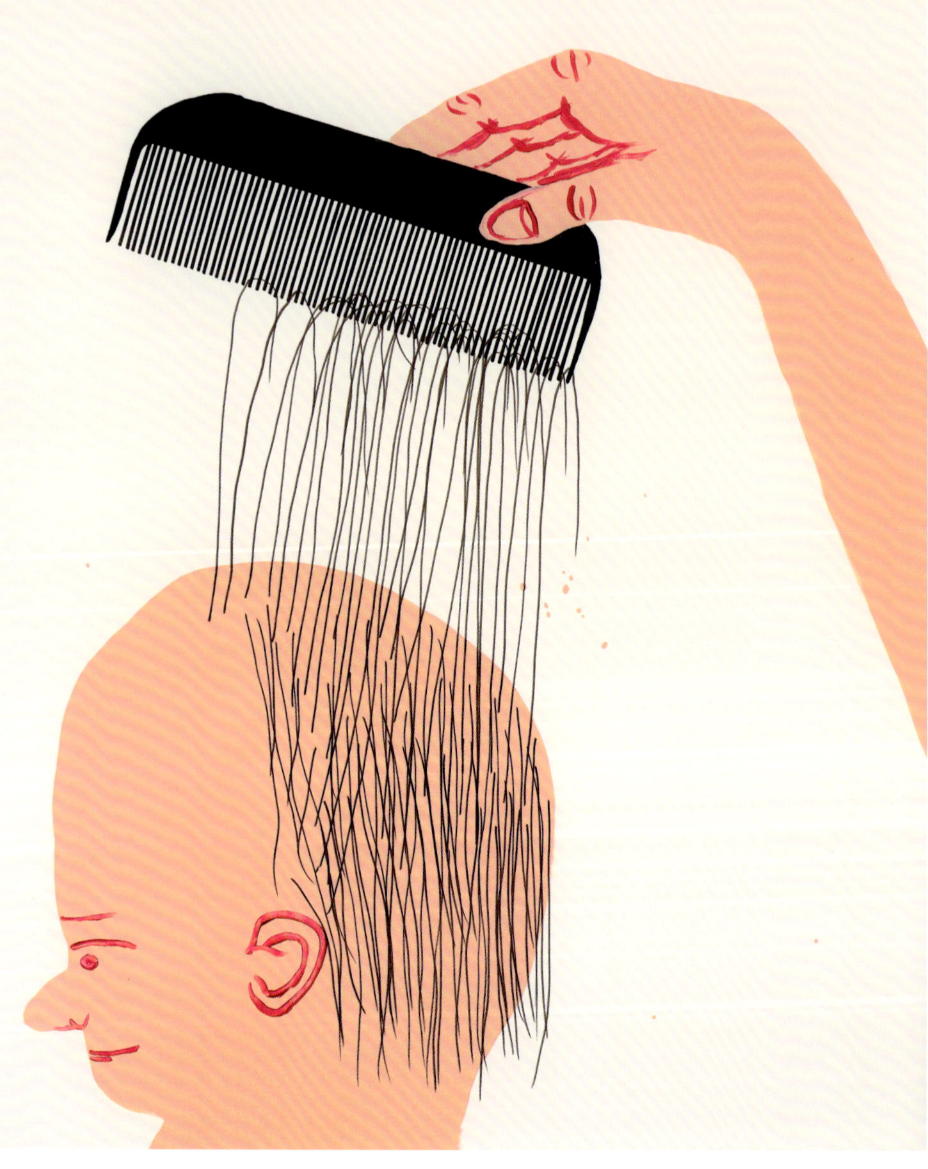

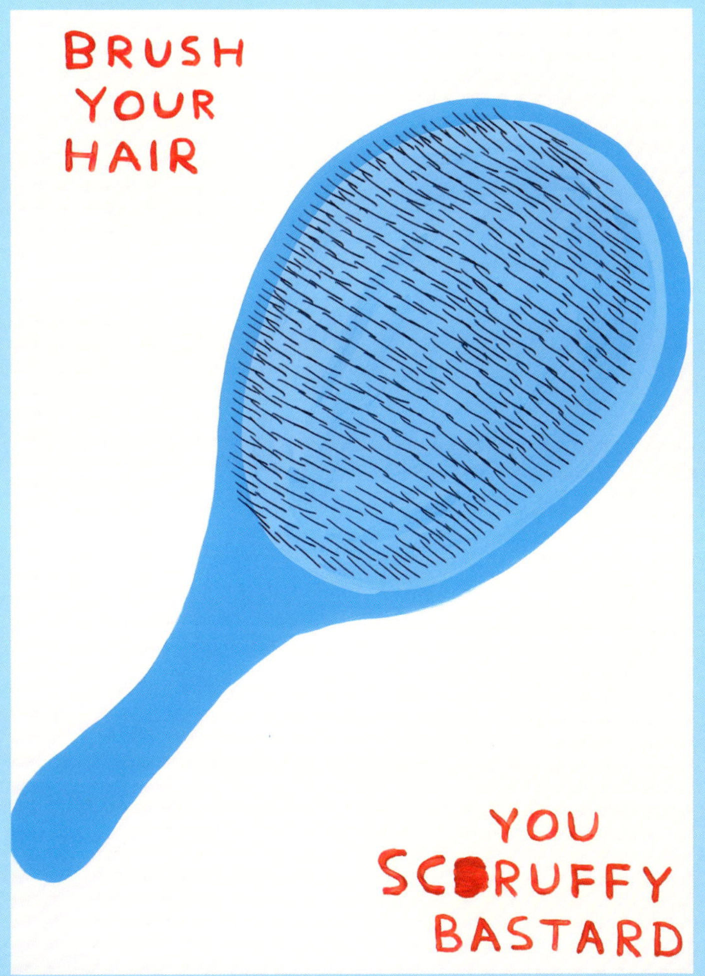
BRUSH
YOUR
HAIR
YOU
SCRUFFY
BASTARD

POLITICIAN

STOP ALL THE INJUSTICE
STOP ALL THE TERRIBLE THINGS
THAT ARE HAPPENING
REPLACE ALL THE BAD THINGS
WITH GOOD THINGS
SO THAT EVERYONE IS HAPPY
I CAN MAKE THIS HAPPEN
VOTE FOR ME
AS PRESIDENT OF THE WORLD

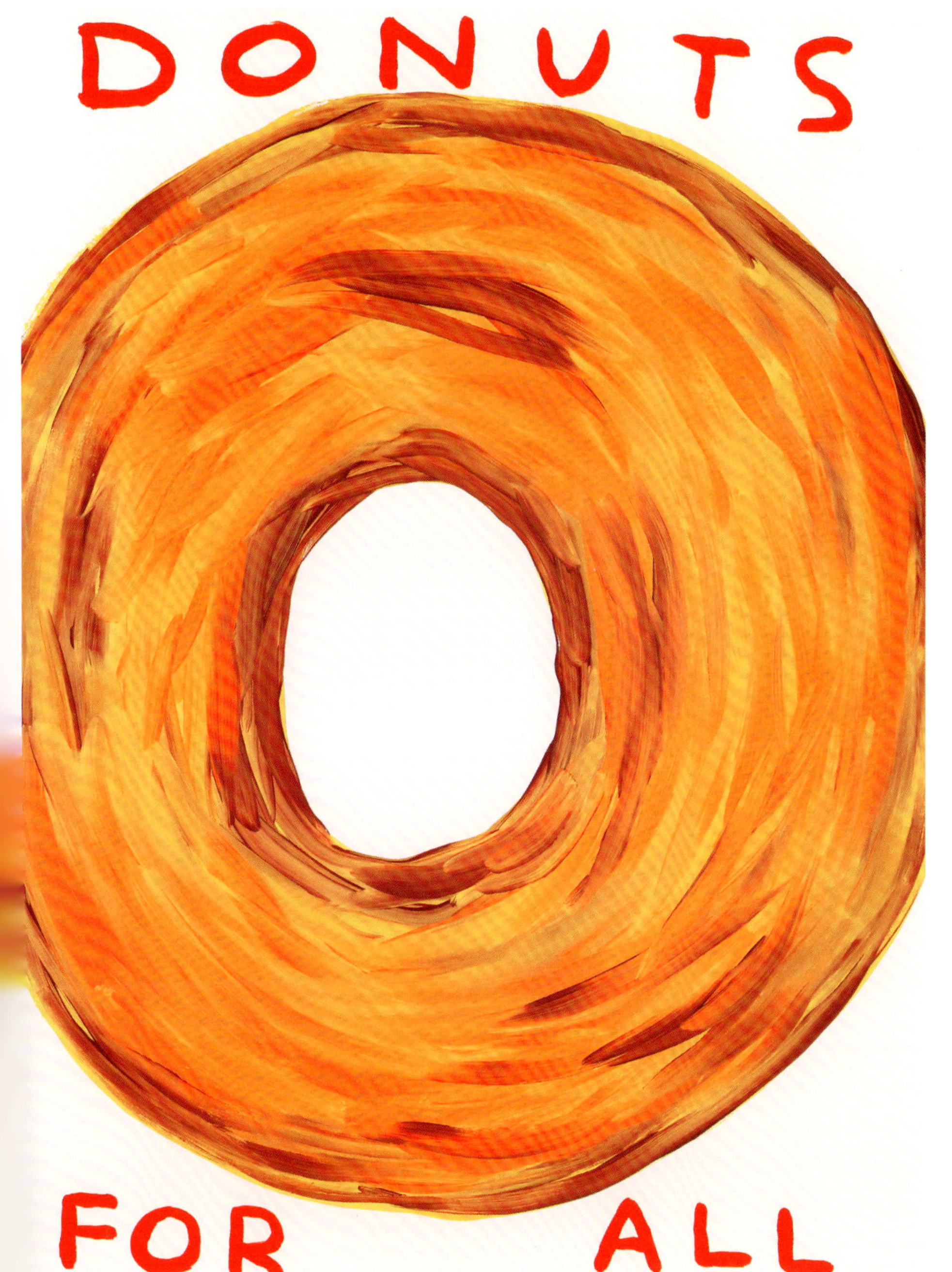
DONUTS
FOR ALL

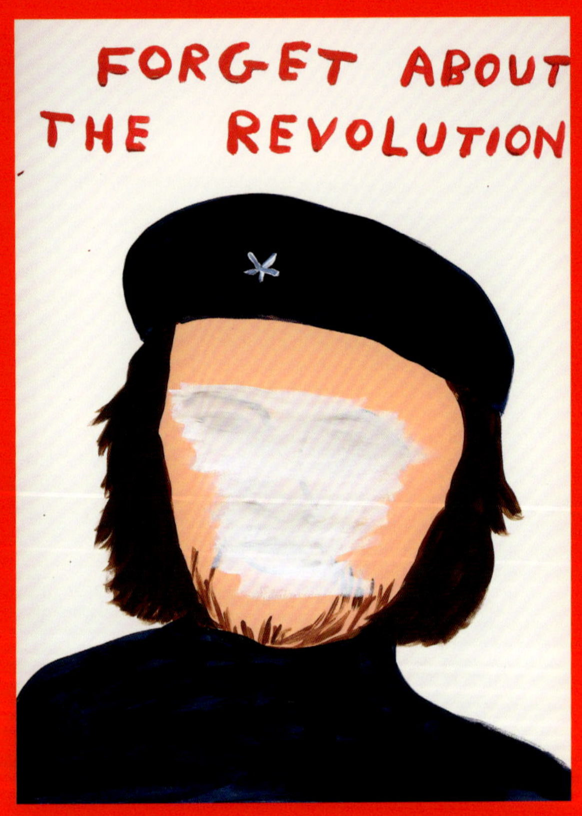
FORGET ABOUT
THE REVOLUTION

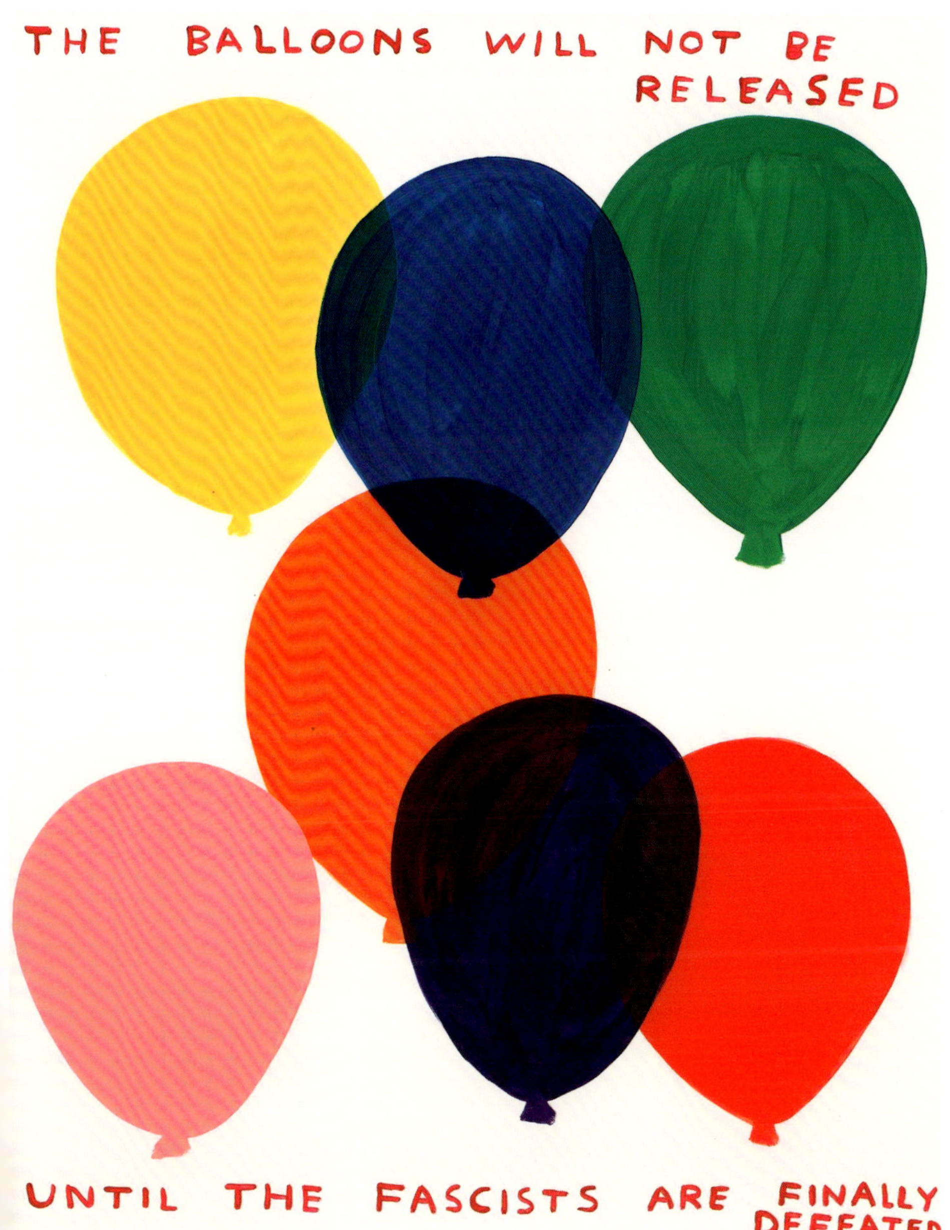
THE BALLOONS WILL NOT BE RELEASED
UNTIL THE FASCISTS ARE FINALLY DEFEATED

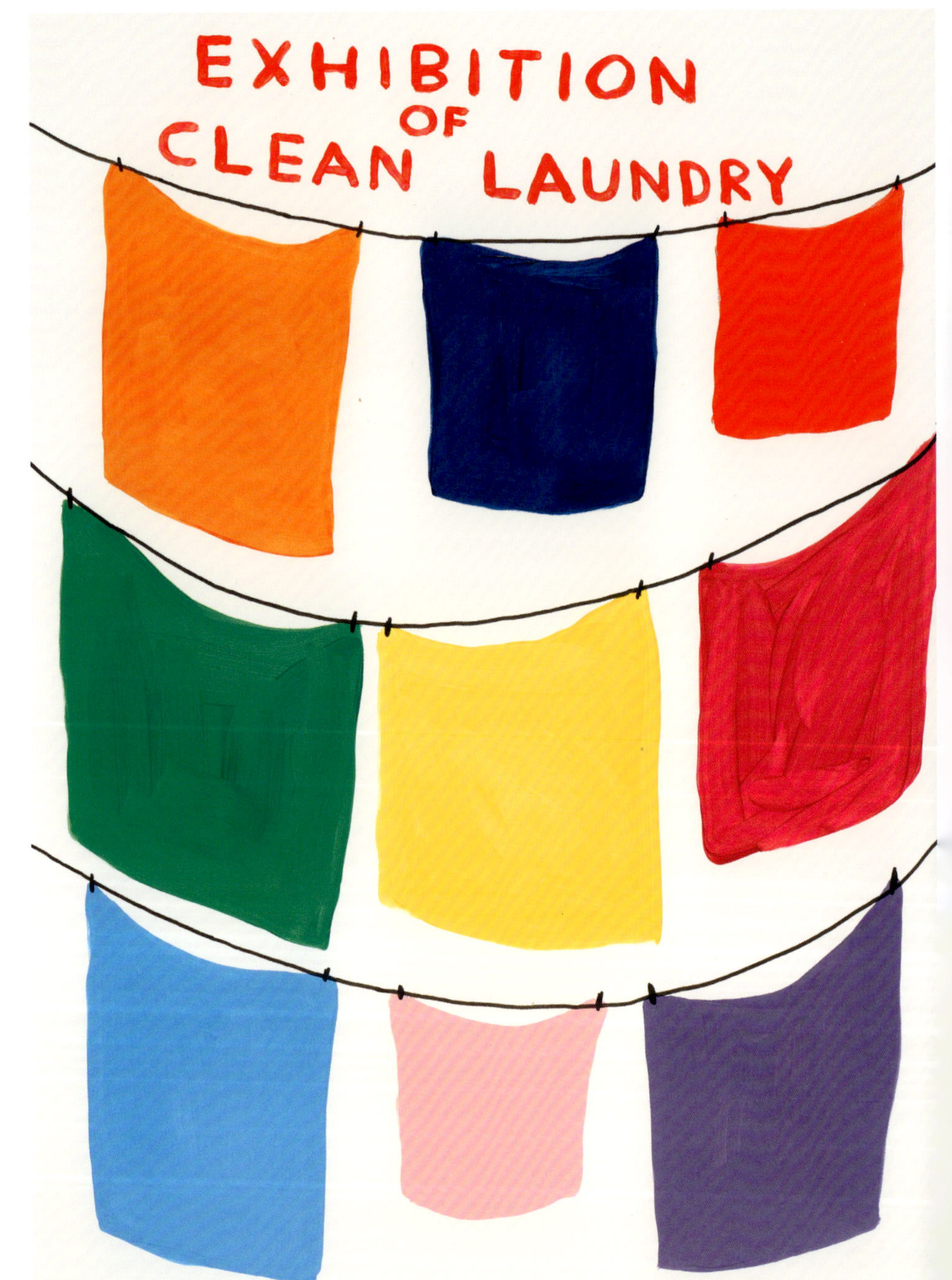
EXHIBITION
OF
CLEAN LAUNDRY

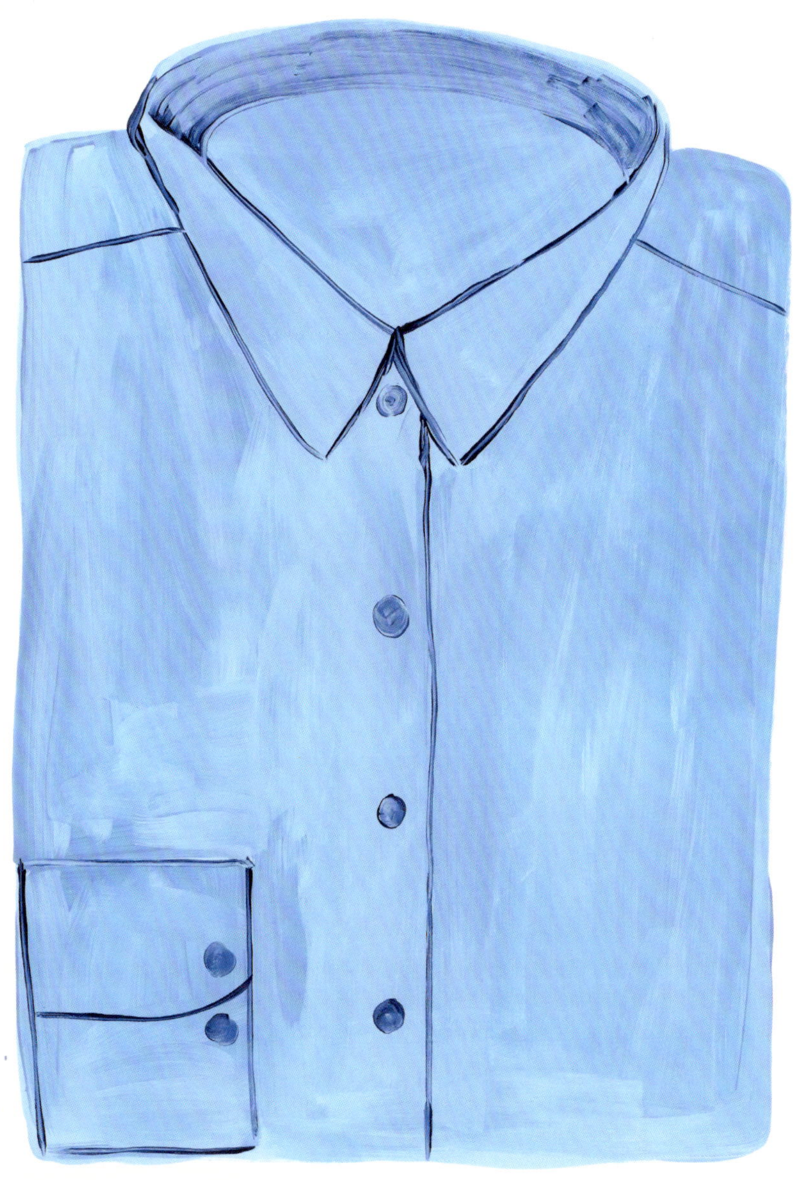

FAIRLY CLEAN

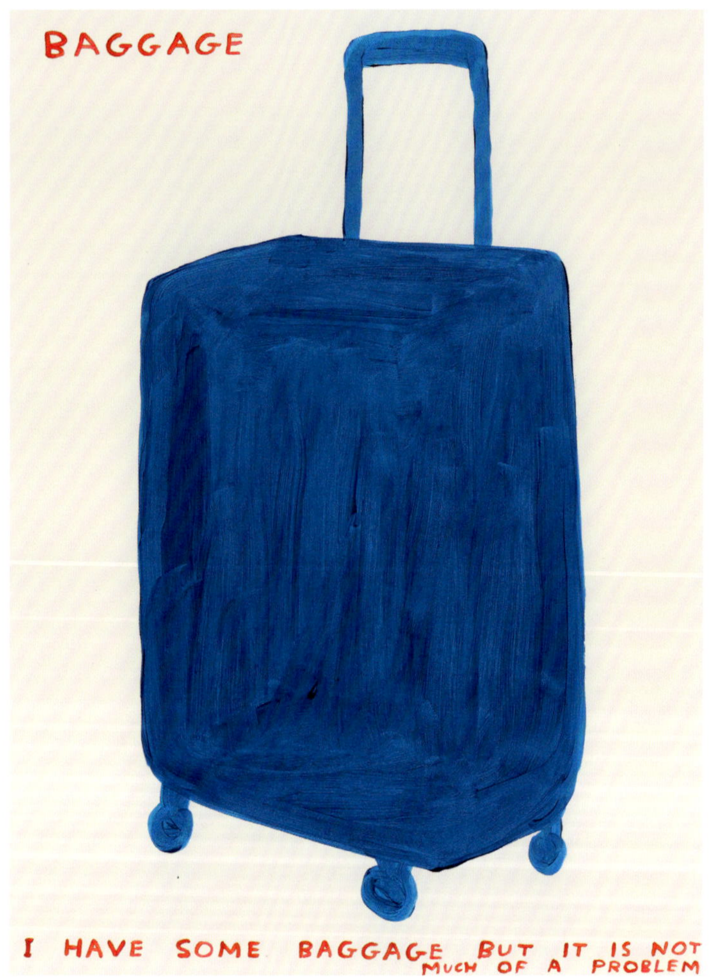
BAGGAGE
I HAVE SOME BAGGAGE BUT IT IS NOT MUCH OF A PROBLEM

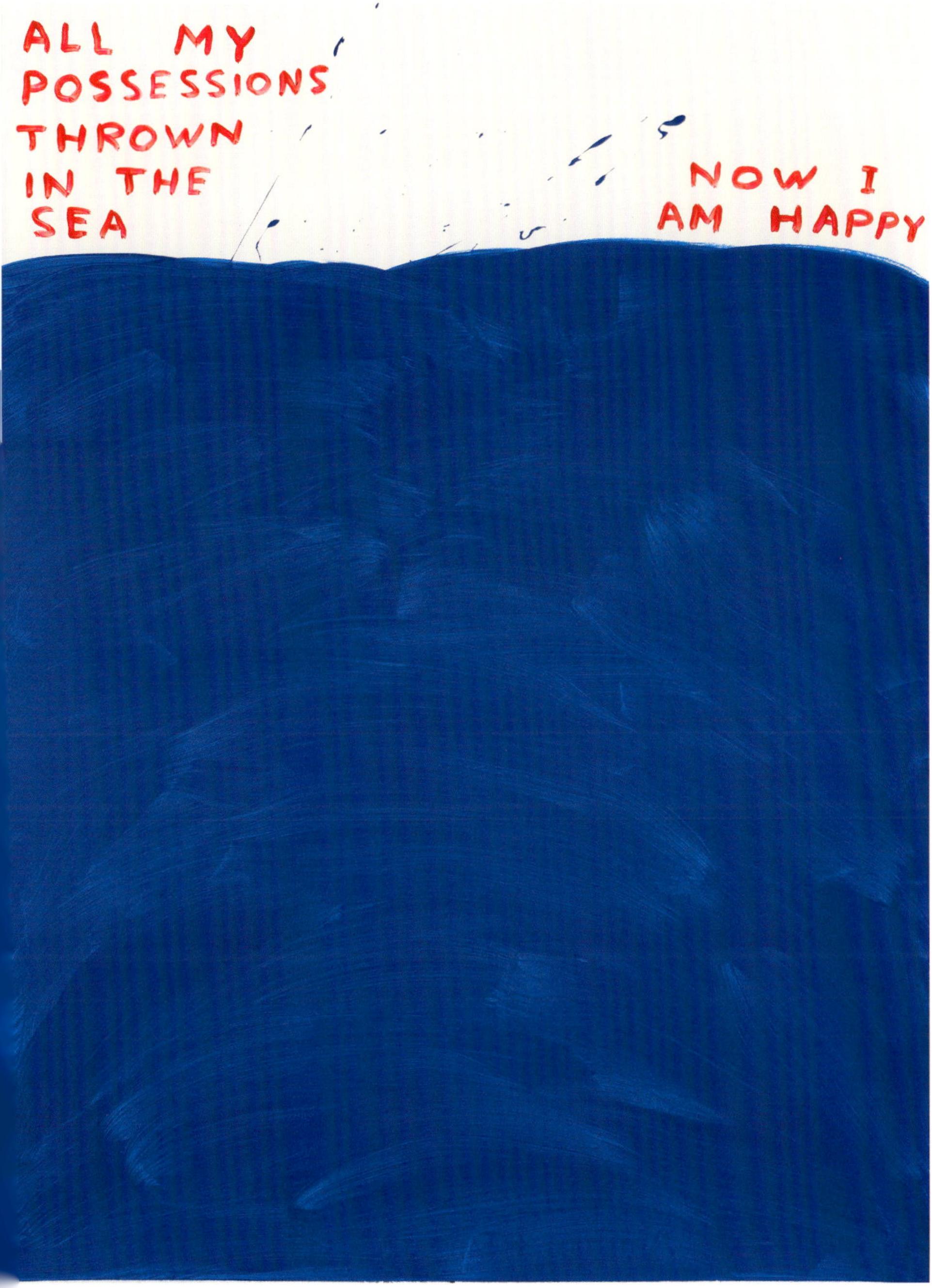

ALL MY POSSESSIONS THROWN IN THE SEA

NOW I AM HAPPY

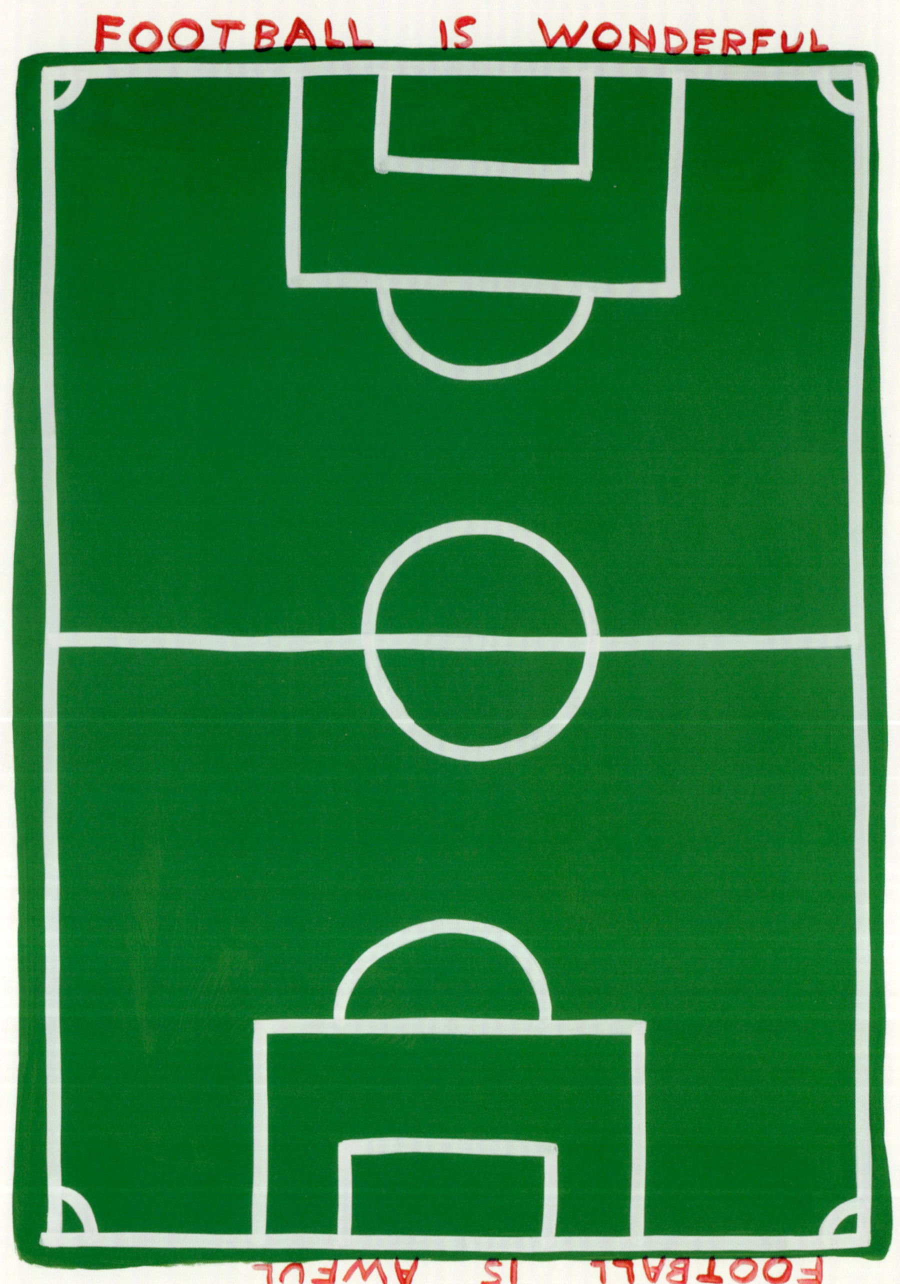
FOOTBALL IS WONDERFUL
FOOTBALL IS AWFUL

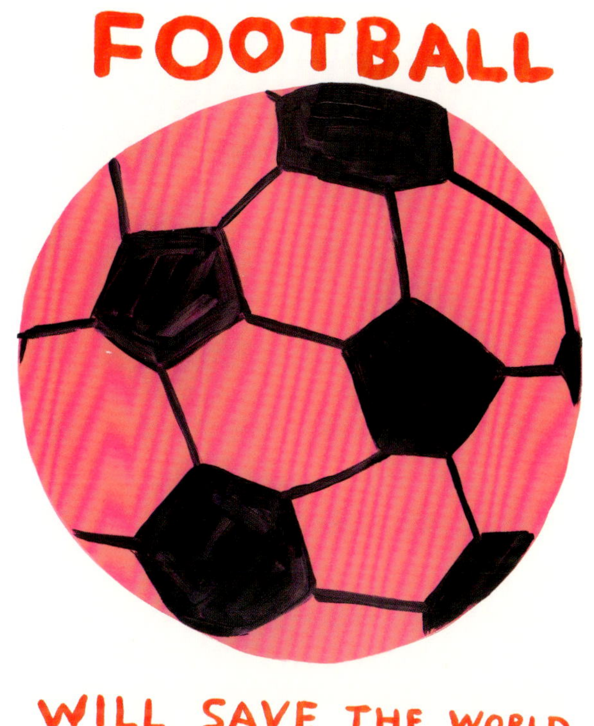
FOOTBALL
WILL SAVE THE WORLD

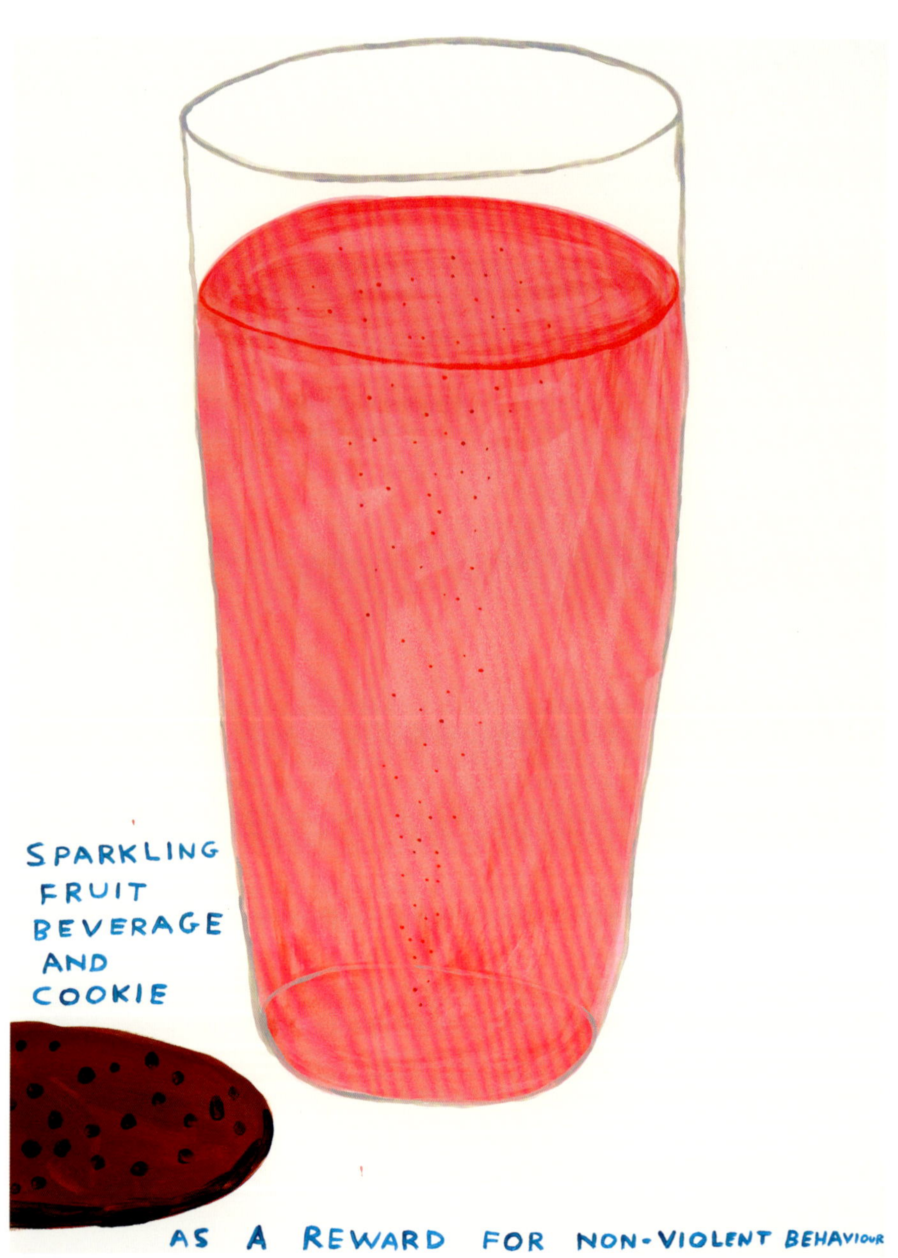
SPARKLING
FRUIT
BEVERAGE
AND
COOKIE
AS A REWARD FOR NON-VIOLENT BEHAVIOUR

STRAWBERRY MILK CURED MY INSANITY

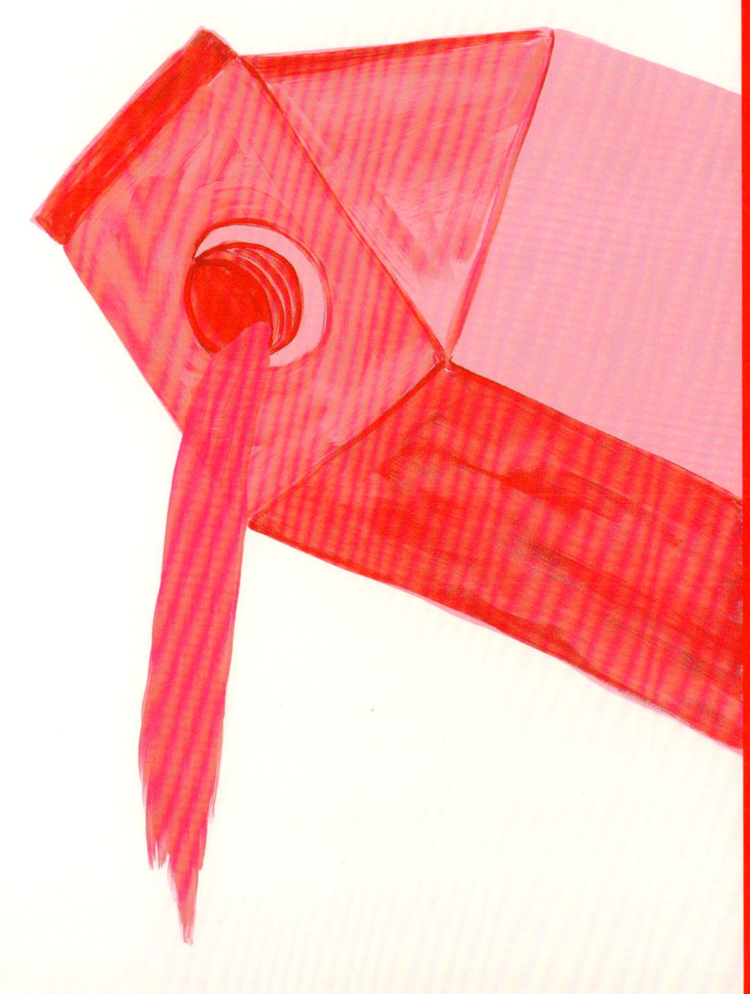

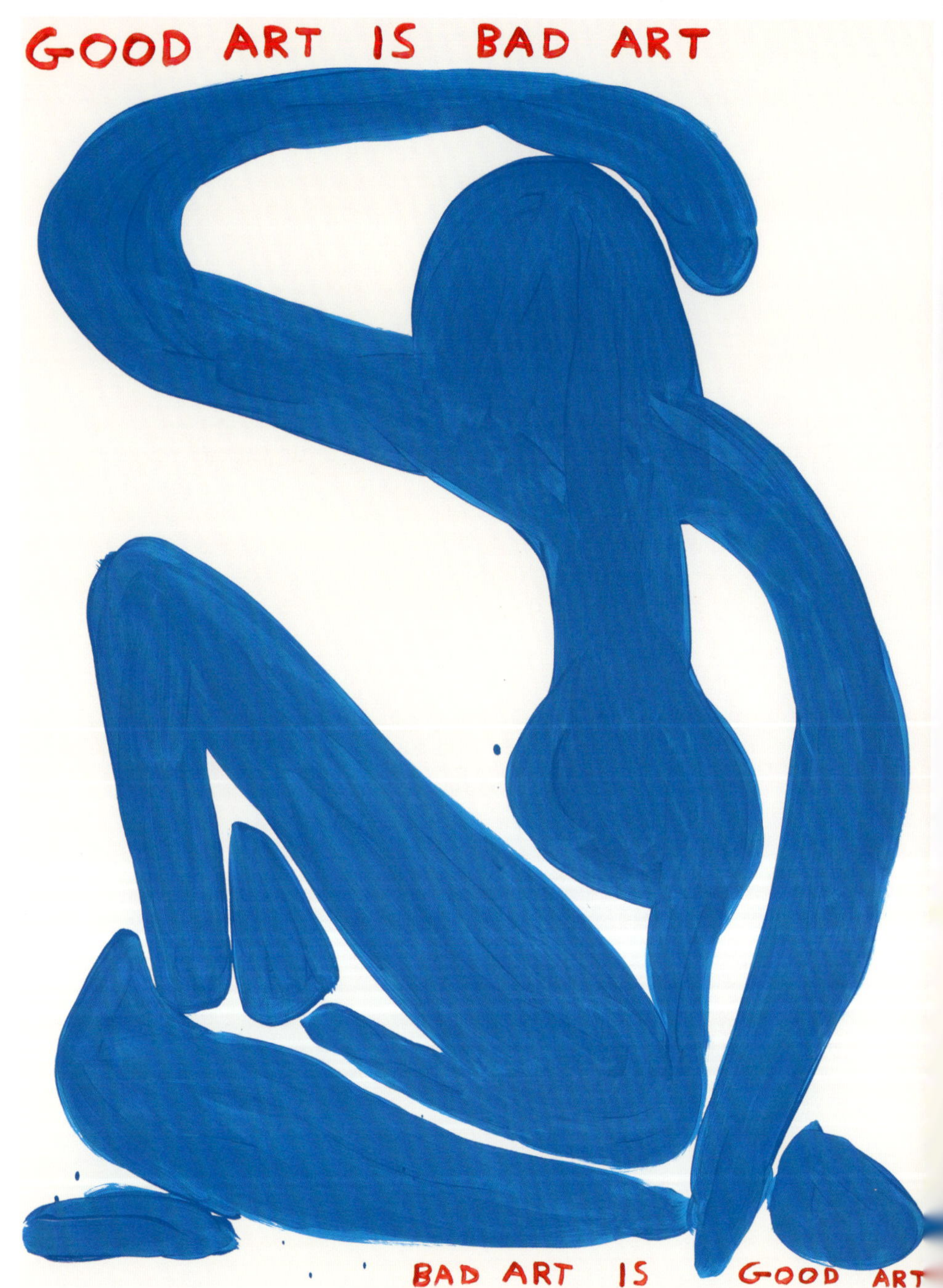
GOOD ART IS BAD ART
BAD ART IS GOOD ART

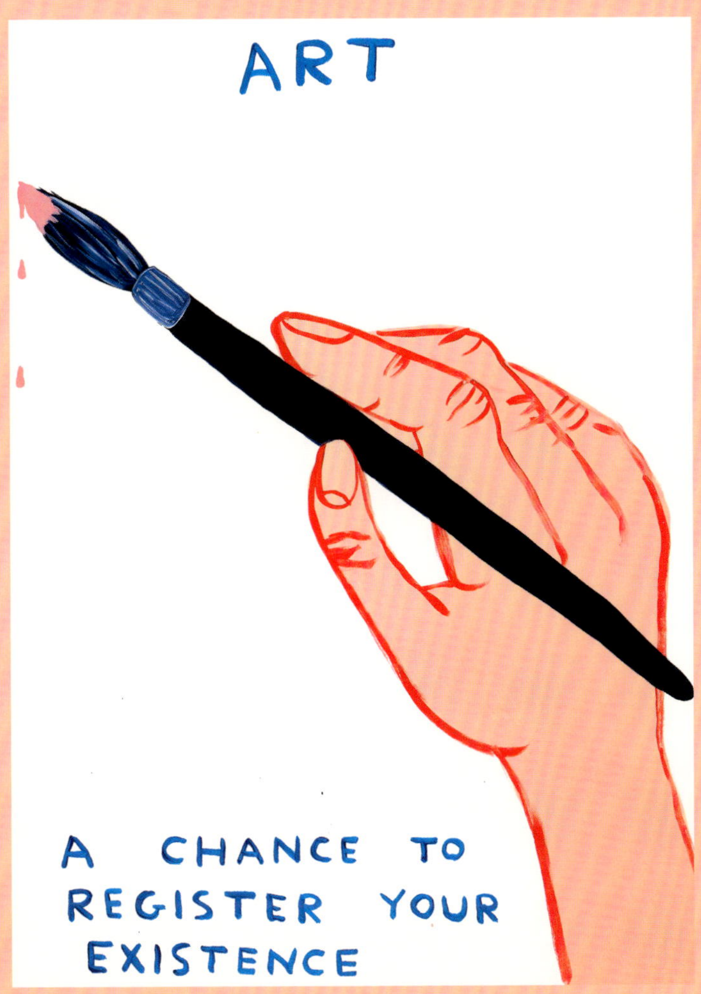
ART
A CHANCE TO
REGISTER YOUR
EXISTENCE

POND

WHAT IS AT THE END OF THE RAINBOW?
AT THE END OF THE RAINBOW THERE IS A POND
A POND?
YES
I THOUGHT THERE WOULD BE A POT OF GOLD?
NO, THERE IS A POND

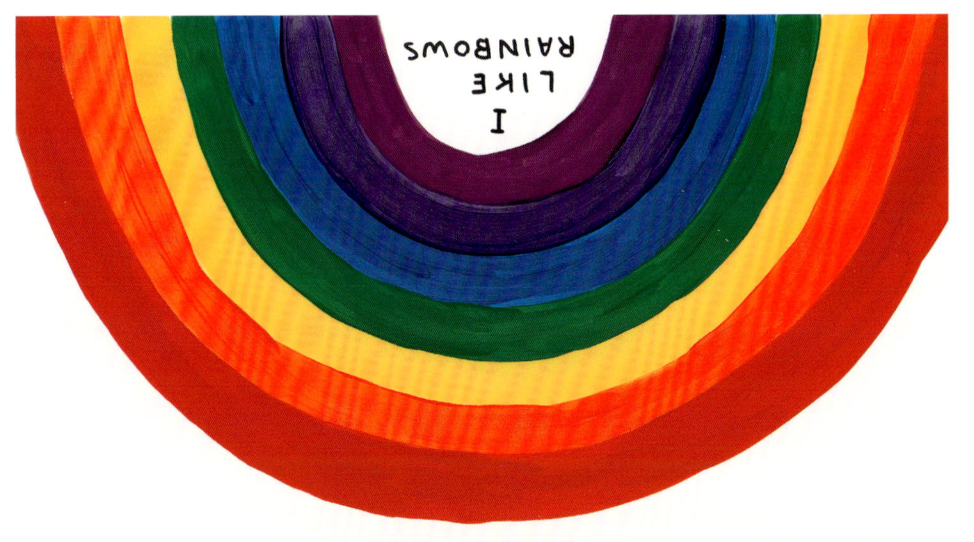
I
LIKE
RAINBOWS

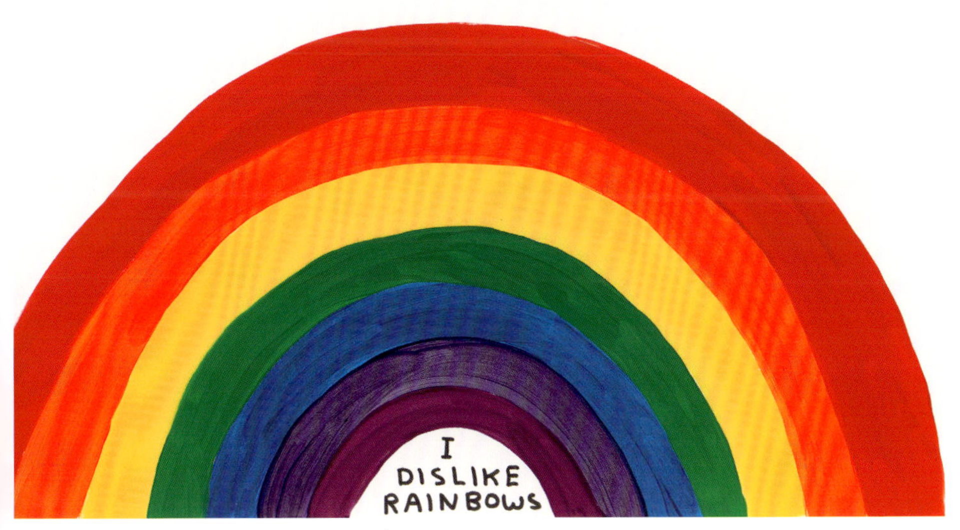
I
DISLIKE
RAINBOWS

WEATHER FORECAST

I AM A CLOUD
I AM FULL OF RAIN
I'M TELLING YOU THIS
OUT OF COURTESY

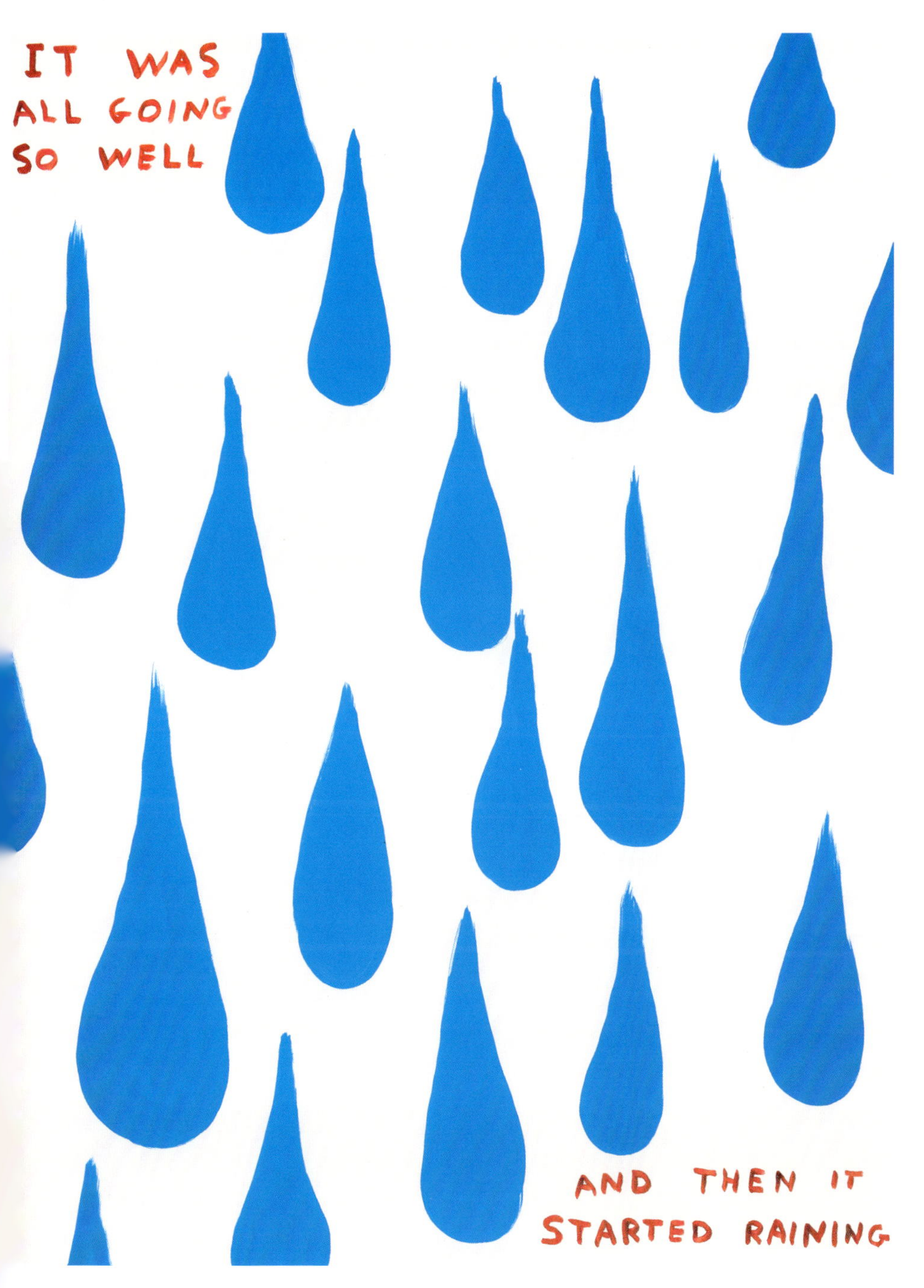
IT WAS
ALL GOING
SO WELL
AND THEN IT
STARTED RAINING

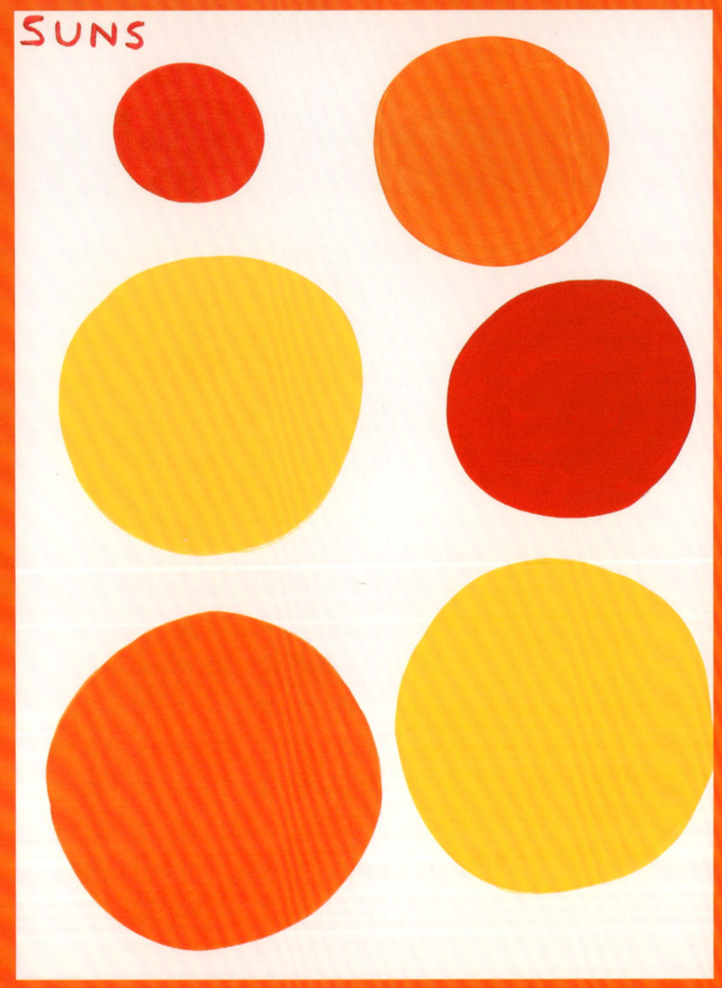
SUNS

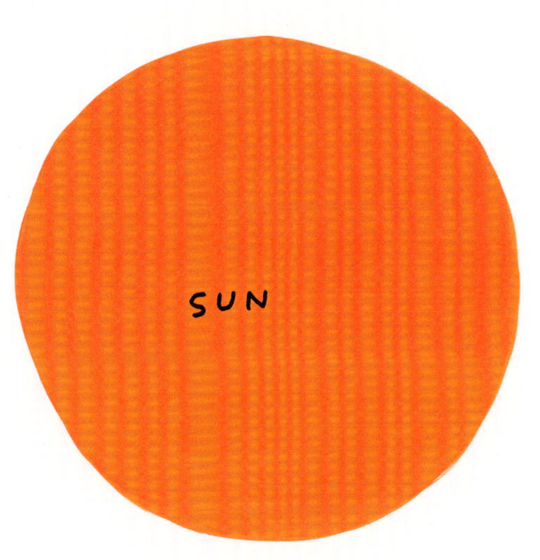
SUN

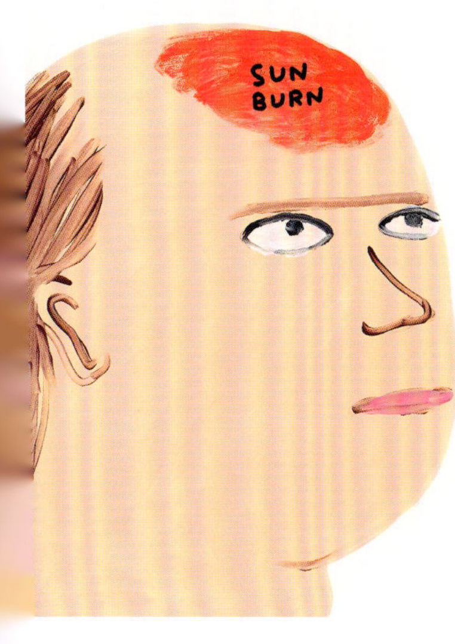
SUN
BURN

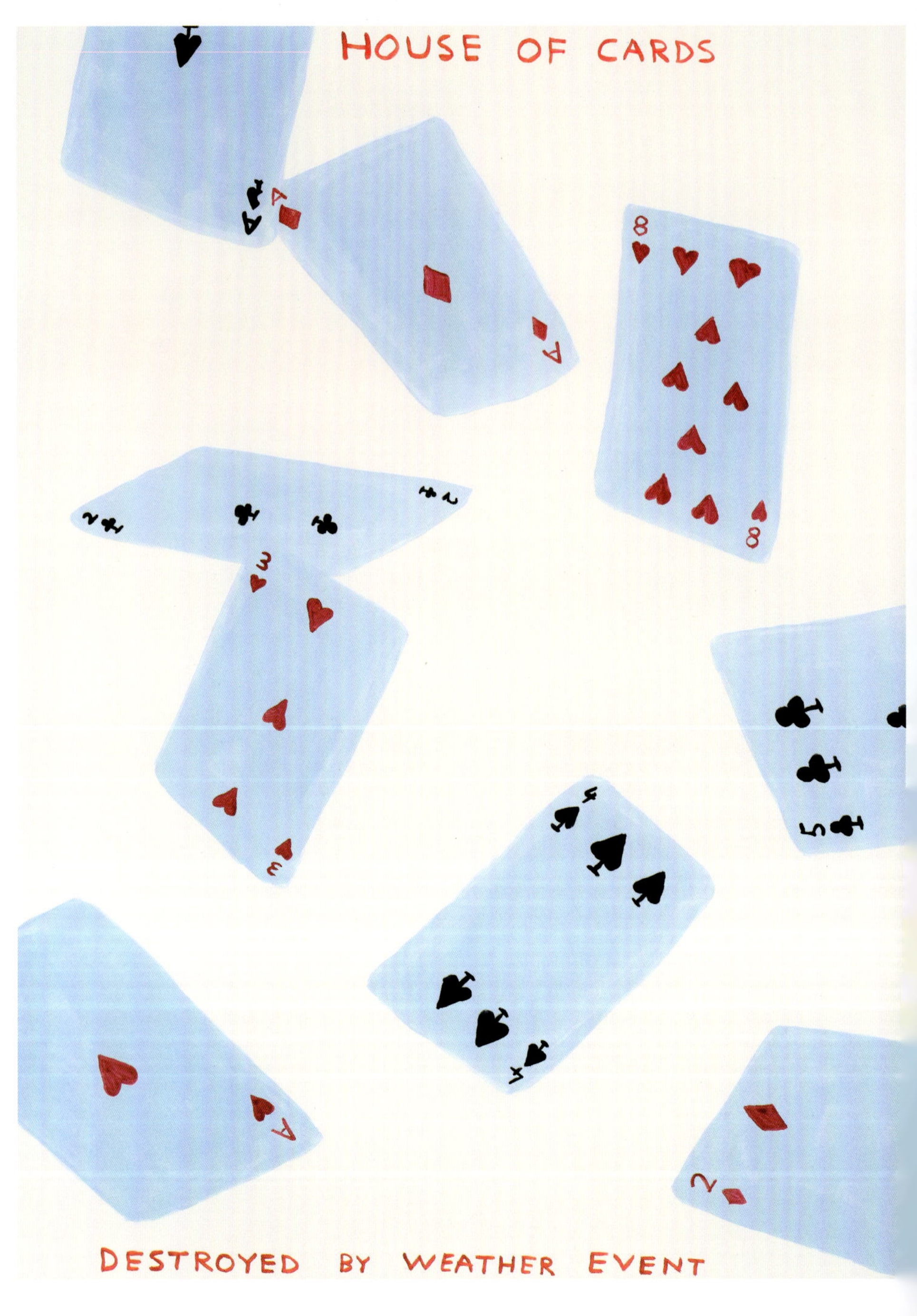
HOUSE OF CARDS
DESTROYED BY WEATHER EVENT

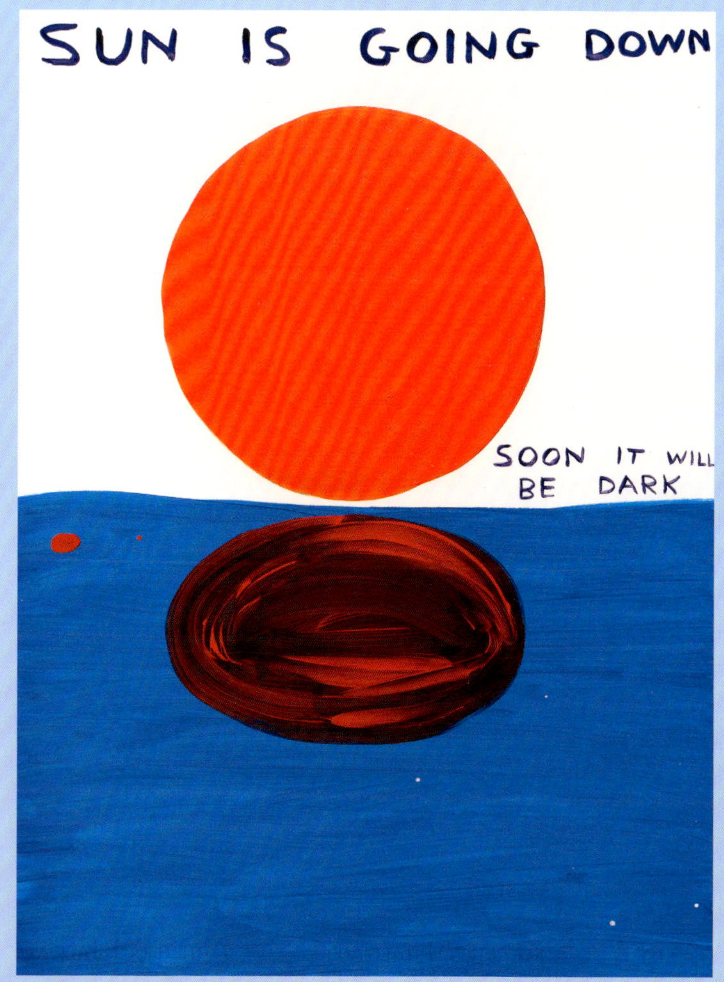
SUN IS GOING DOWN
SOON IT WILL
BE DARK

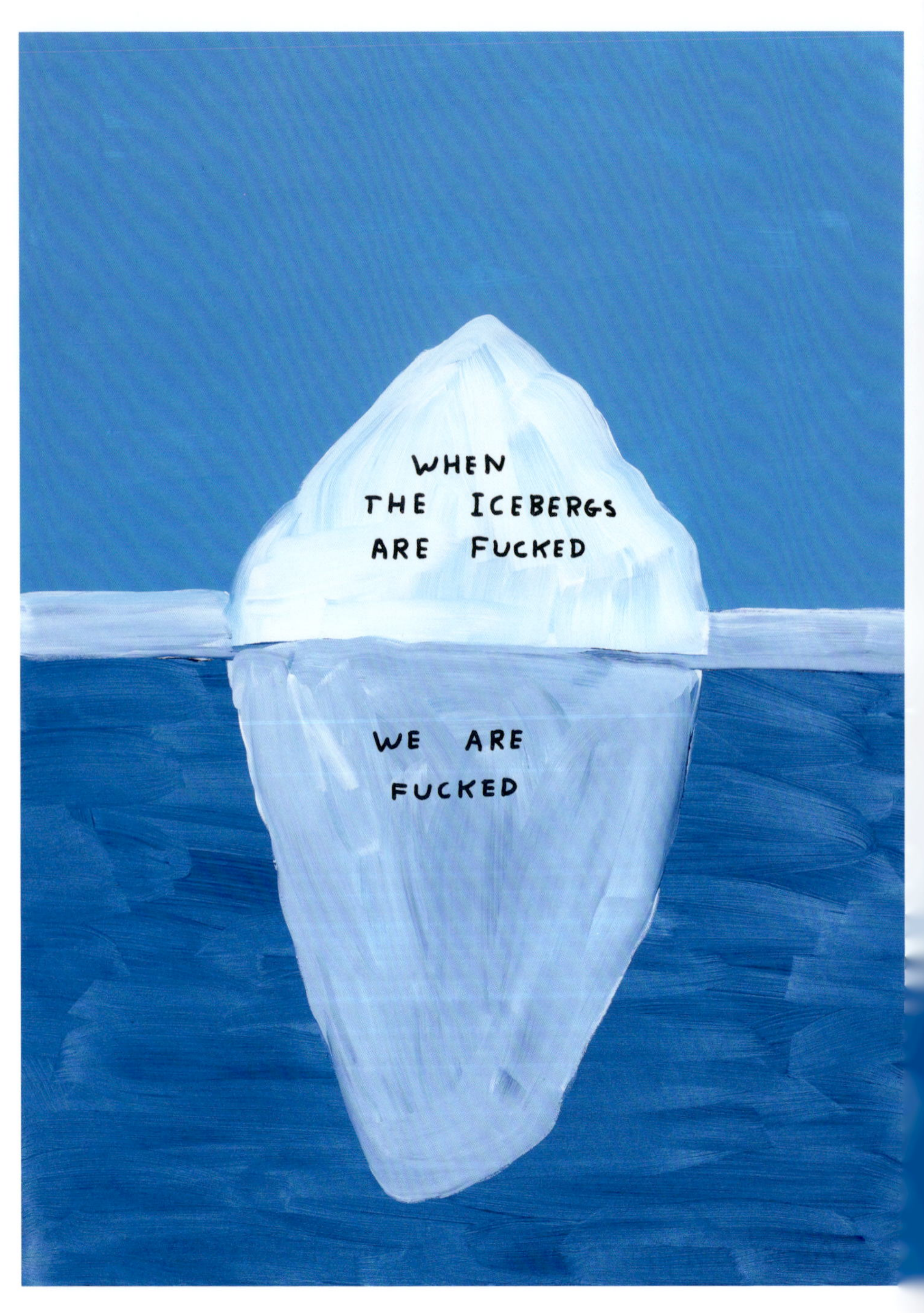
WHEN
THE ICEBERGS
ARE FUCKED
WE ARE
FUCKED

TO HELL WITH ZOOS

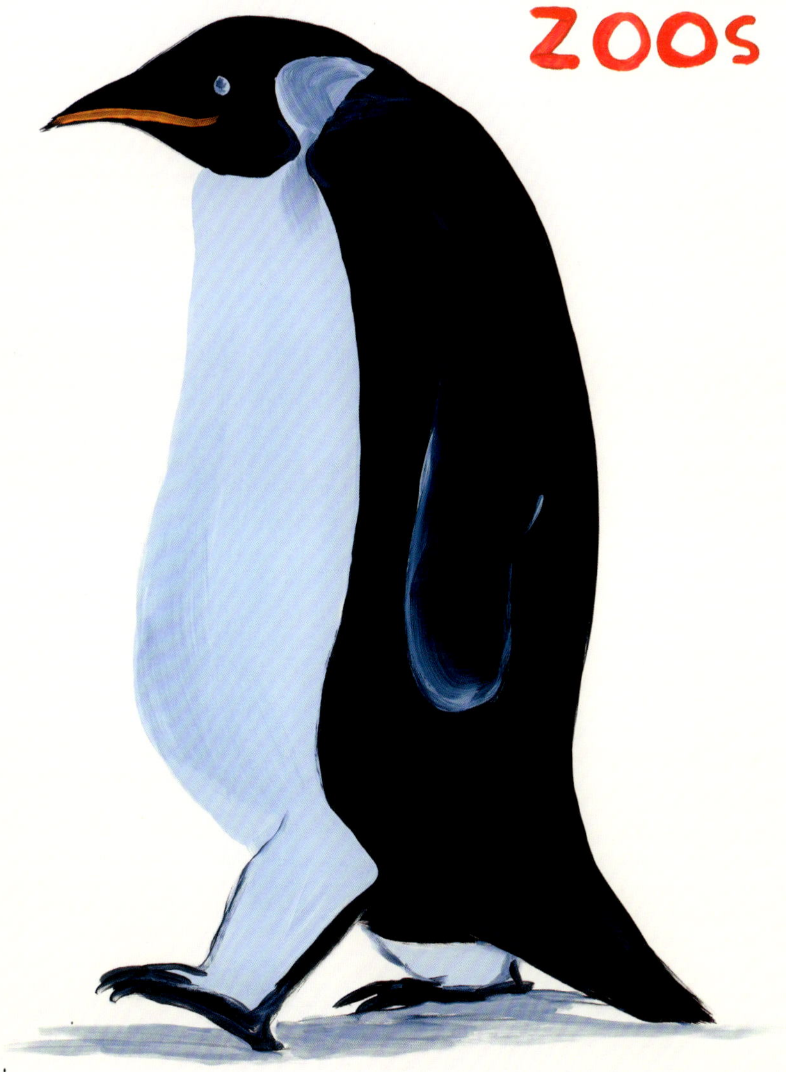

FREE THE PENGUINS FIRST

WHALES

WHALES ARE HUGE CREATURES THAT
LIVE IN THE SEA
THEY ARE MAMMALS
I'M NOT SURE WHAT THAT MEANS
I THINK IT MEANS THAT THEY
HAVE LUNGS
THEY EAT TINY SEA CREATURES
THEY ARE KILLED FOR THEIR
BLUBBER
BLUBBER IS FAT
I'M NOT SURE WHAT THEY DO
WITH BLUBBER
I THINK THEY MAKE CANDLES

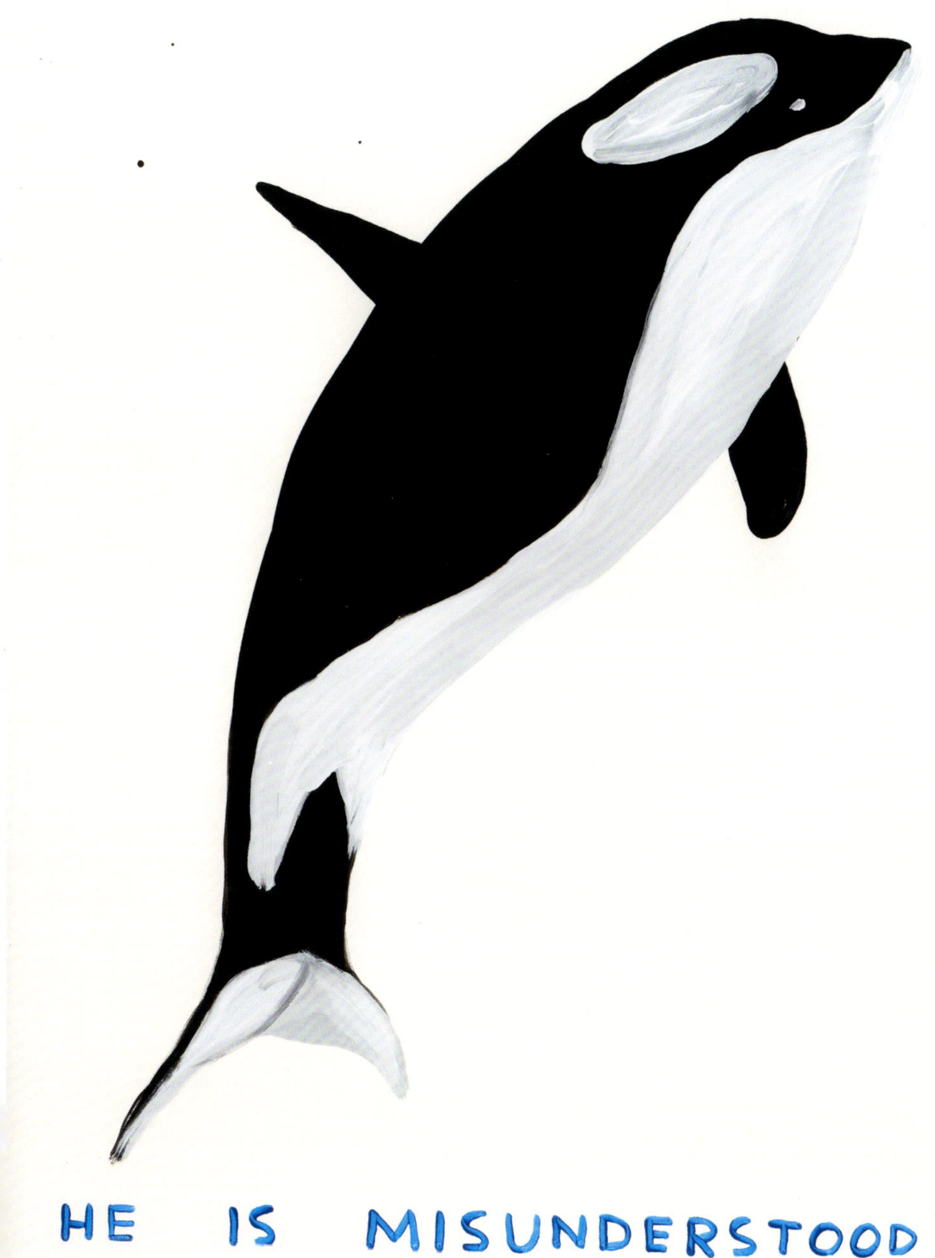

HE IS MISUNDERSTOOD

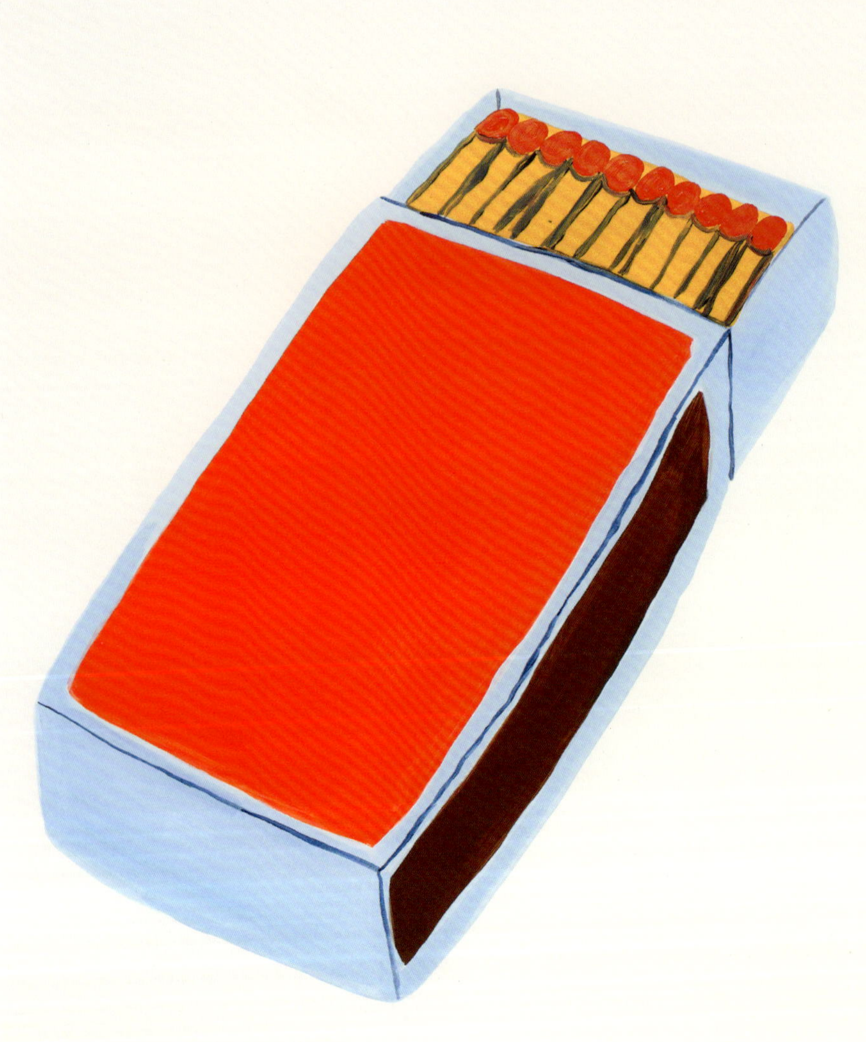

I DON'T REMEMBER ASKING YOU TO BURN DOWN MY HOUSE

DO NOT EXTINGUISH MY FIRE

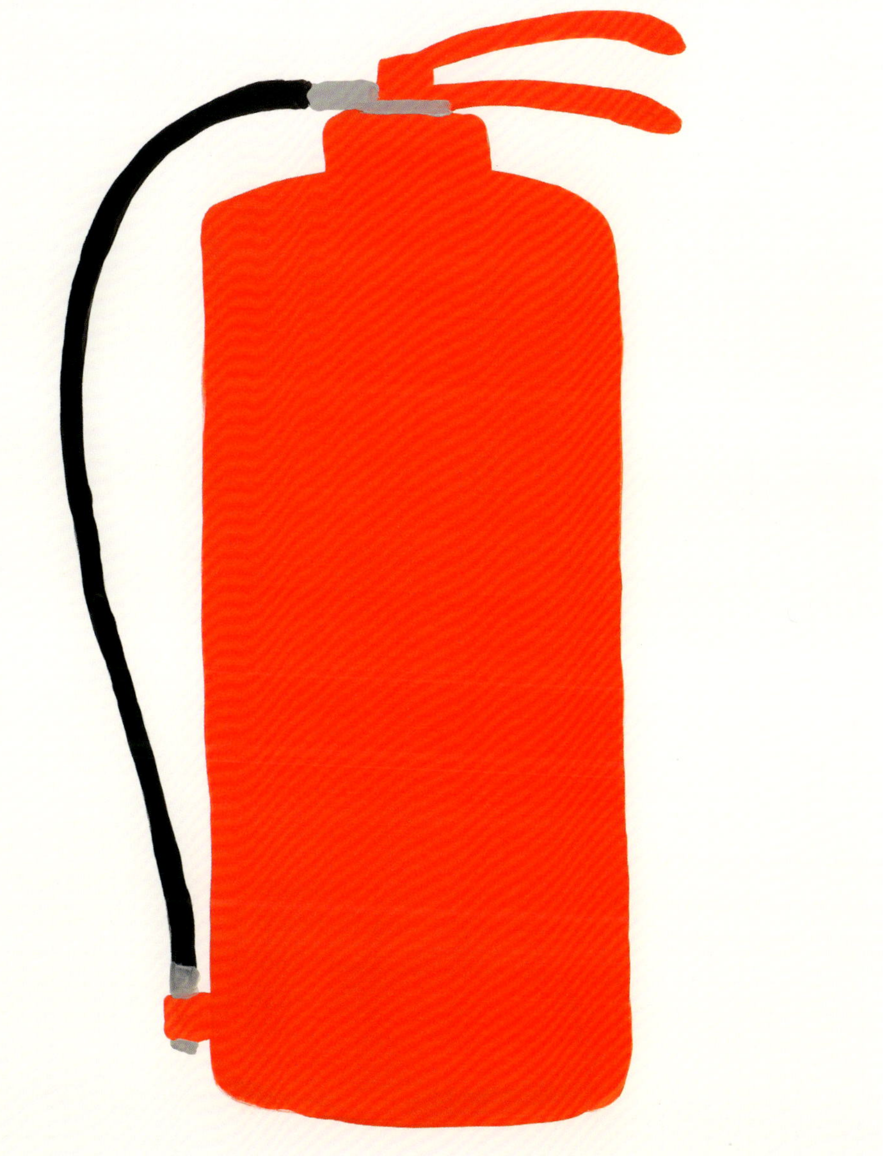

PLEASE DO NOT EXTINGUISH MY FIRE

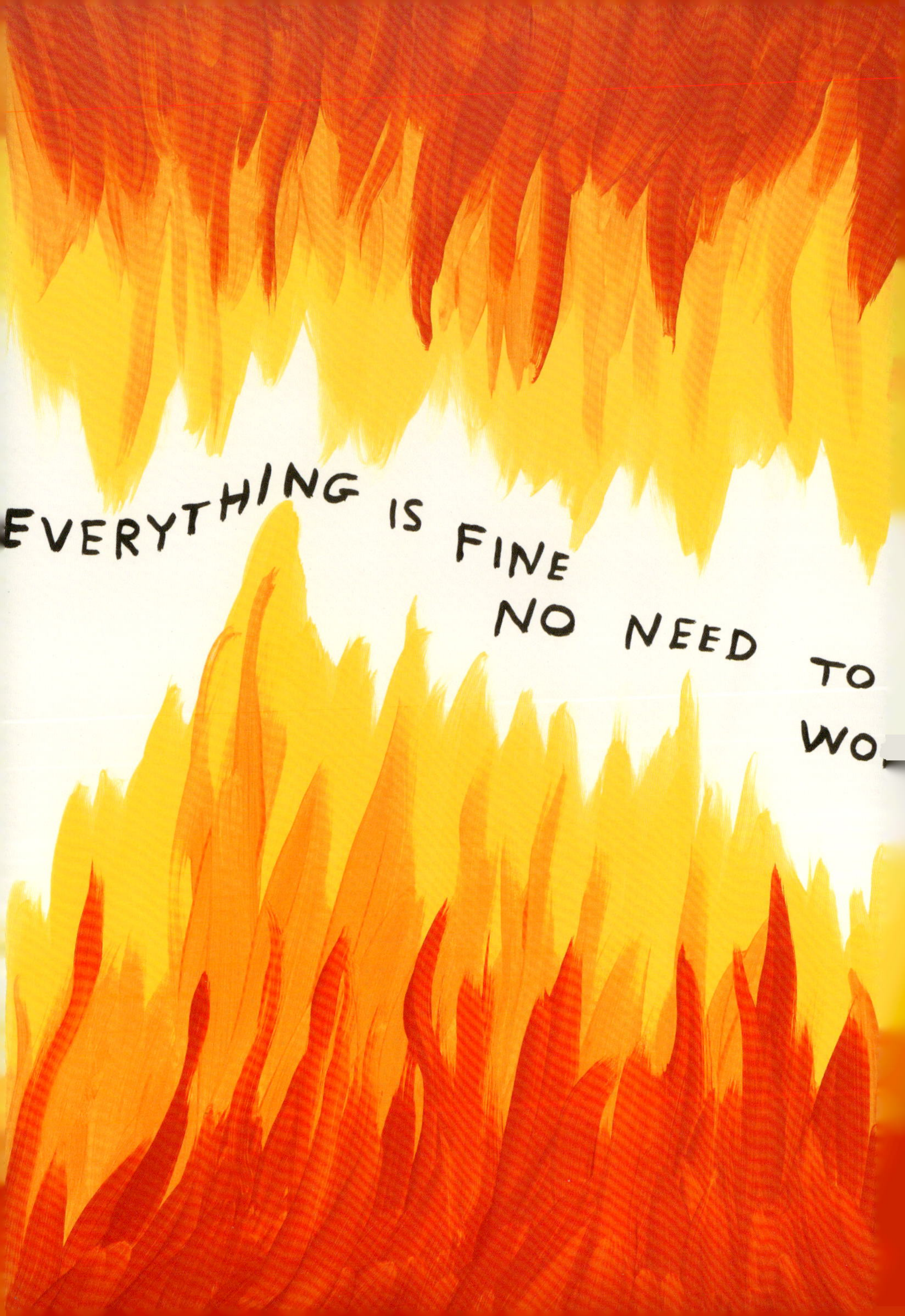
EVERYTHING IS FINE
NO NEED TO
WO

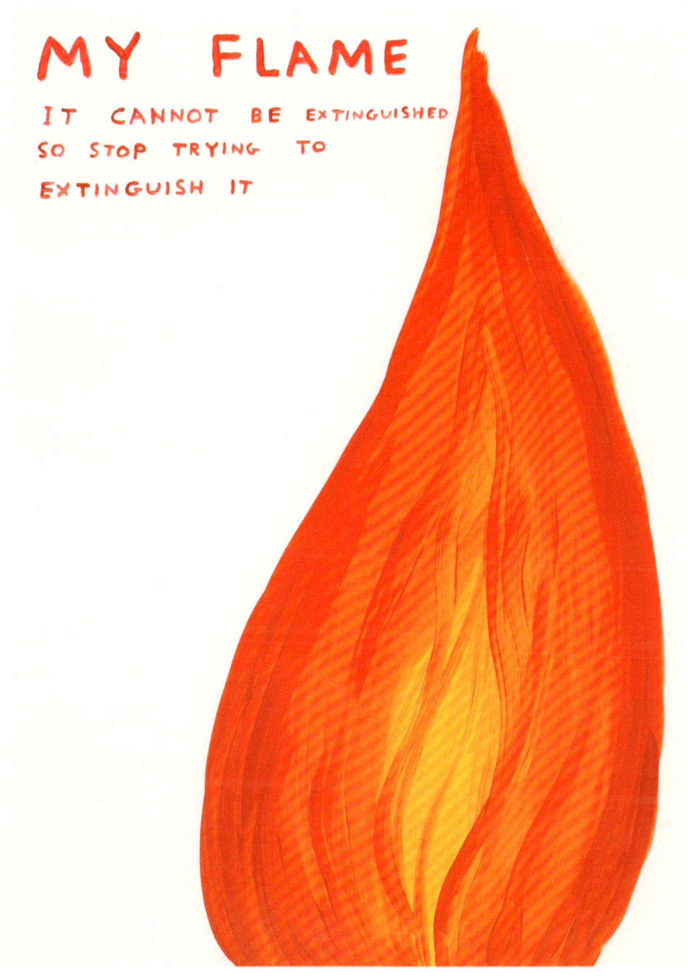
MY FLAME
IT CANNOT BE EXTINGUISHED
SO STOP TRYING TO
EXTINGUISH IT

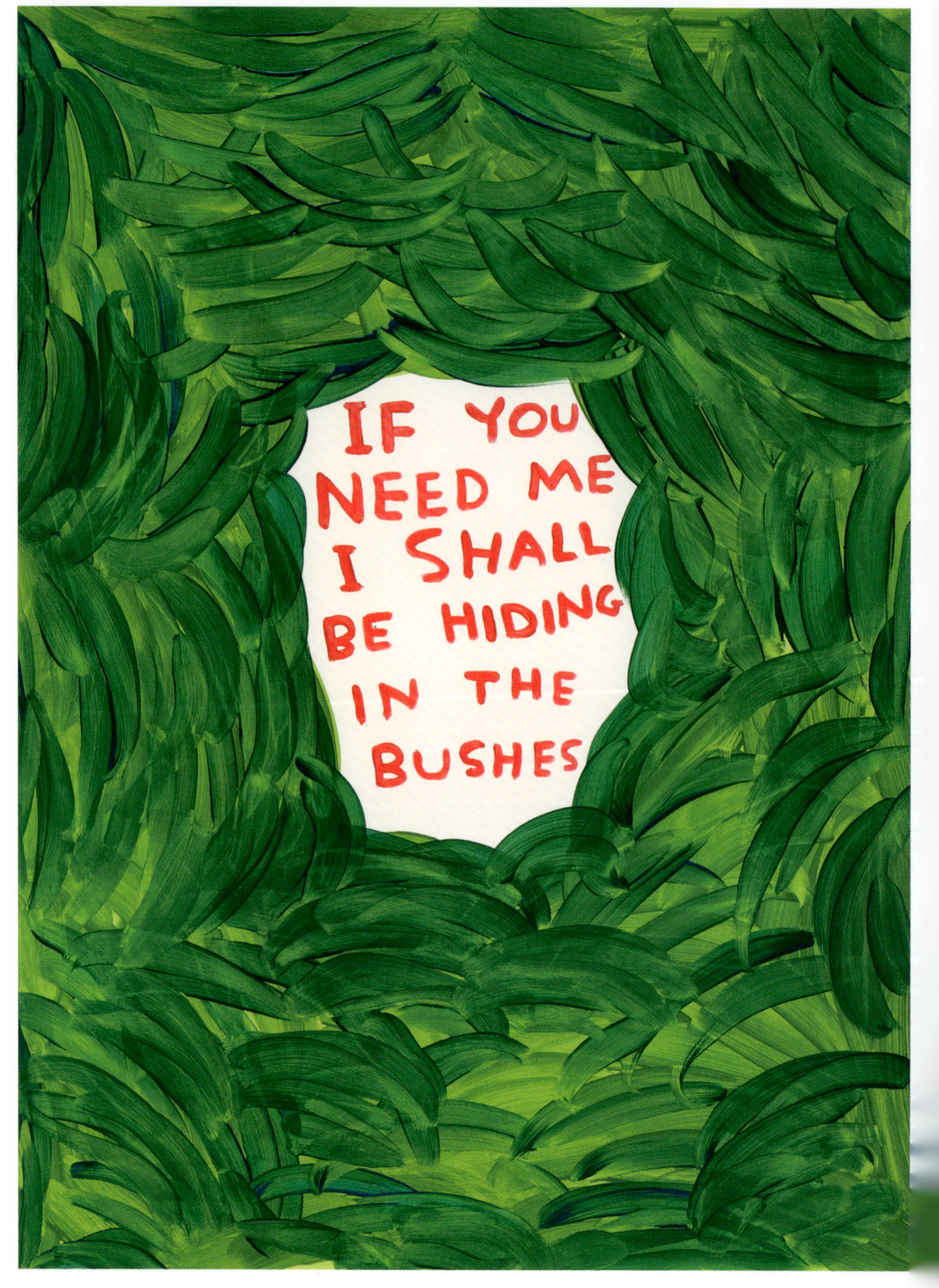
IF YOU
NEED ME
I SHALL
BE HIDING
IN THE
BUSHES

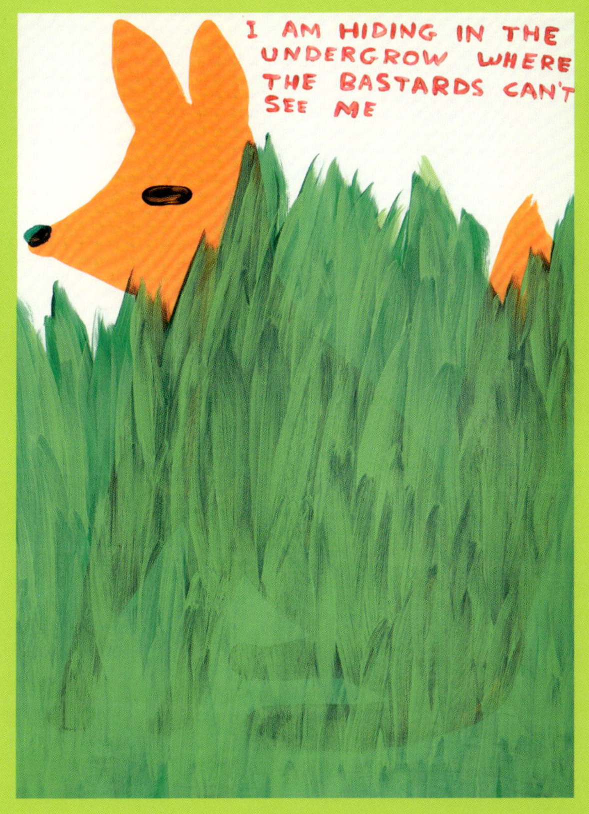
I AM HIDING IN THE
UNDERGROW WHERE
THE BASTARDS CAN'T
SEE ME

WARBLING

WILL YOU PLEASE STOP WARBLING
WARBLING IS UNDIGNIFIED
AND YOU ARE ANNOYING ME AND
THE OTHER BIRDS

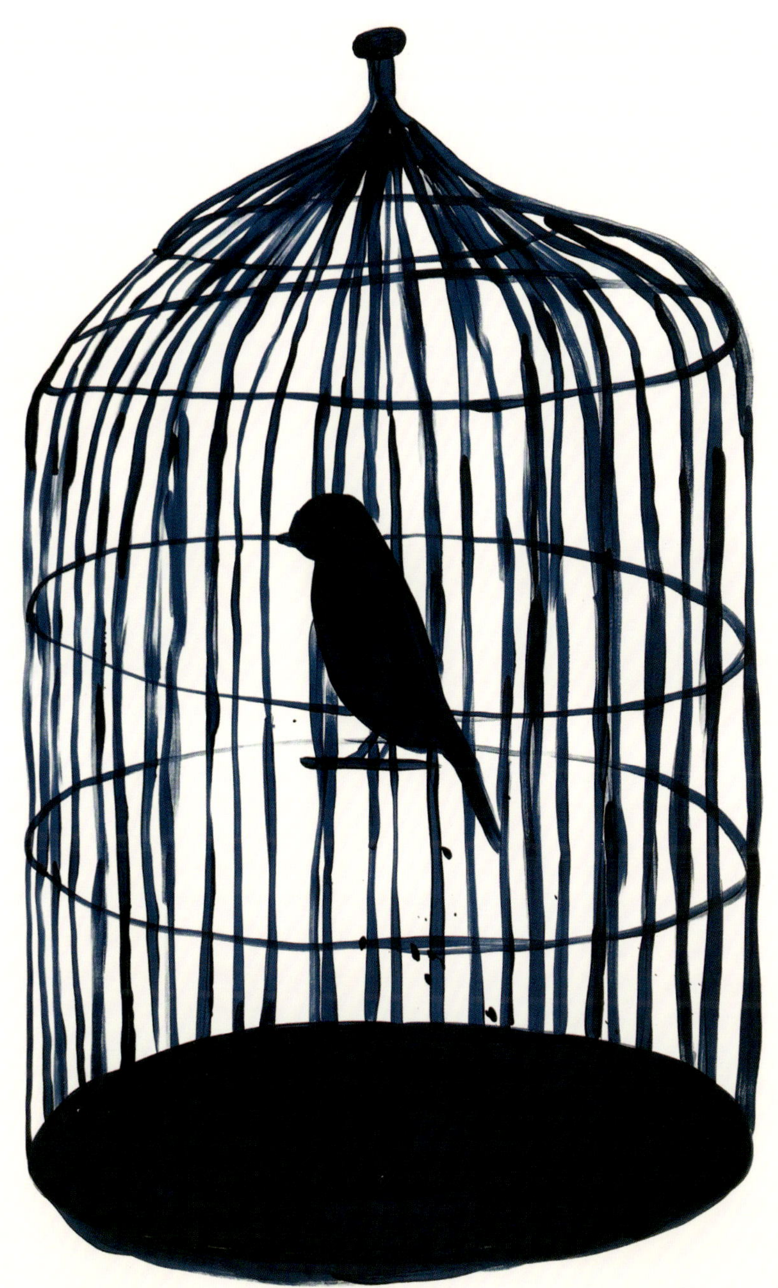
YOU CANNOT KNOW WHAT IT IS LIKE TO BE ME

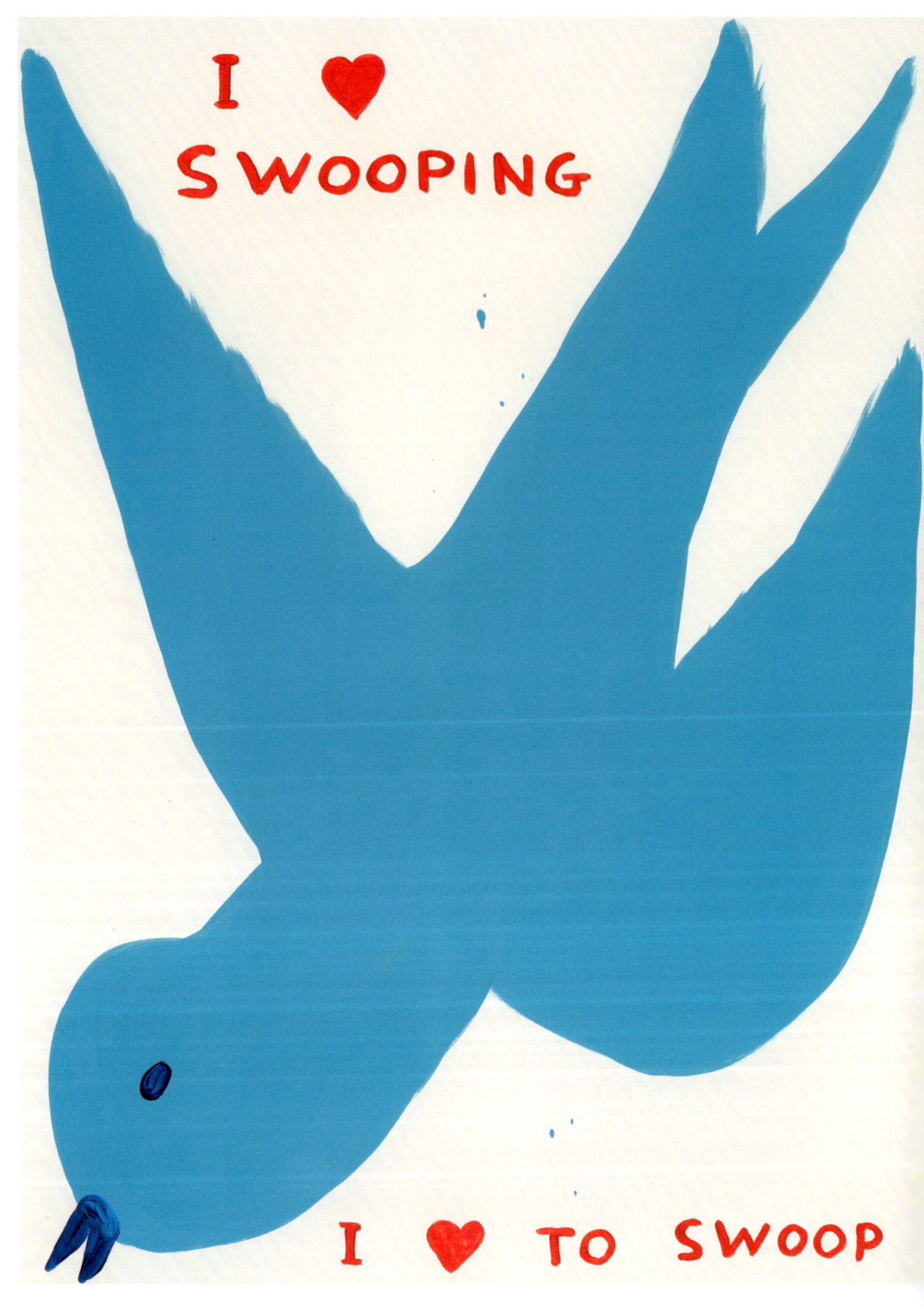
I ♥
SWOOPING
I ♥ TO SWOOP

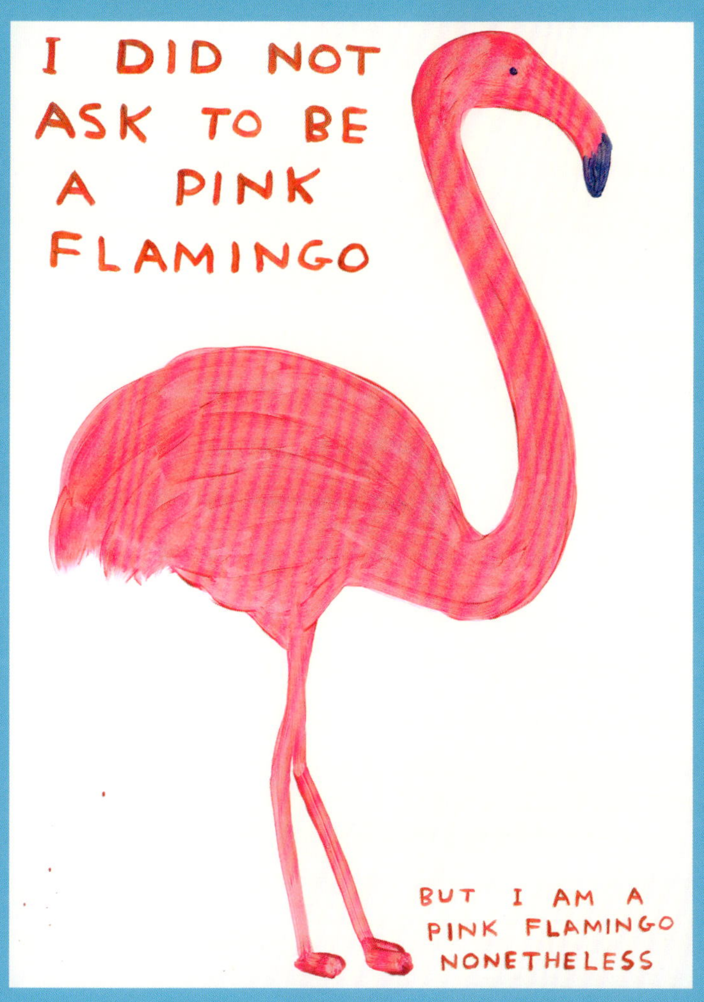
I DID NOT
ASK TO BE
A PINK
FLAMINGO
BUT I AM A
PINK FLAMINGO
NONETHELESS

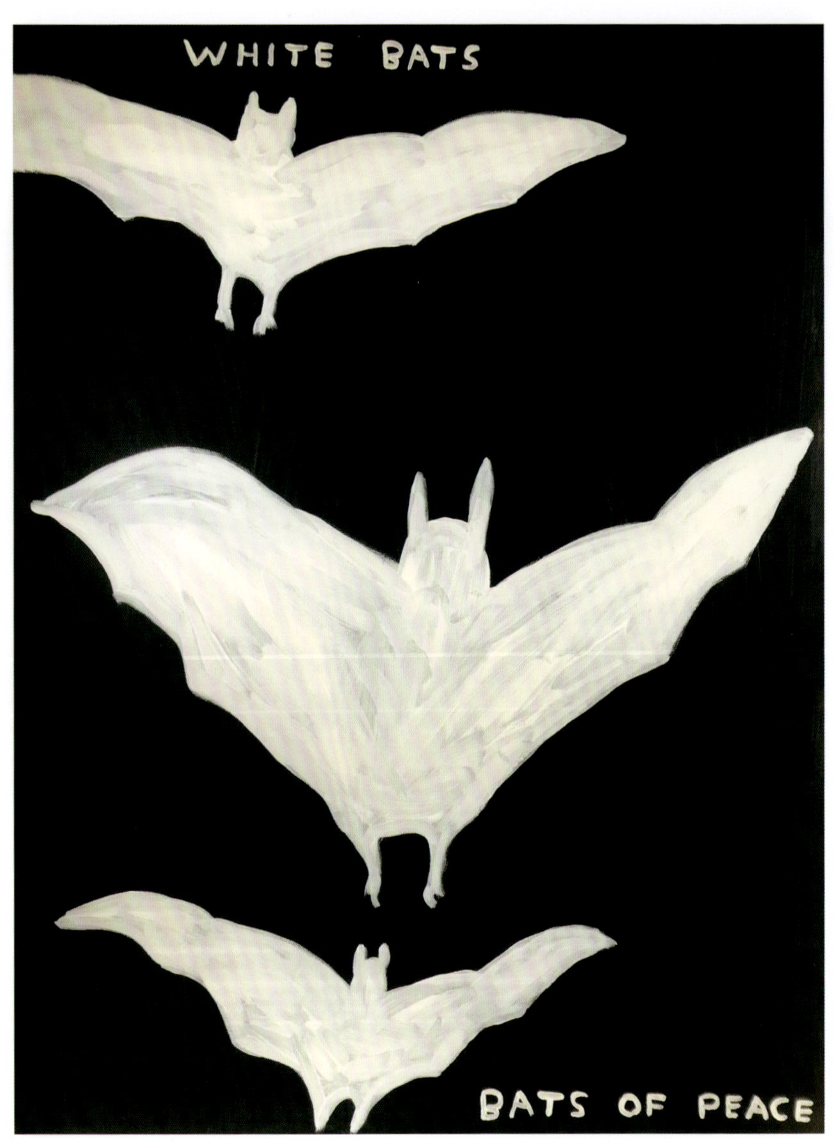
WHITE BATS
BATS OF PEACE

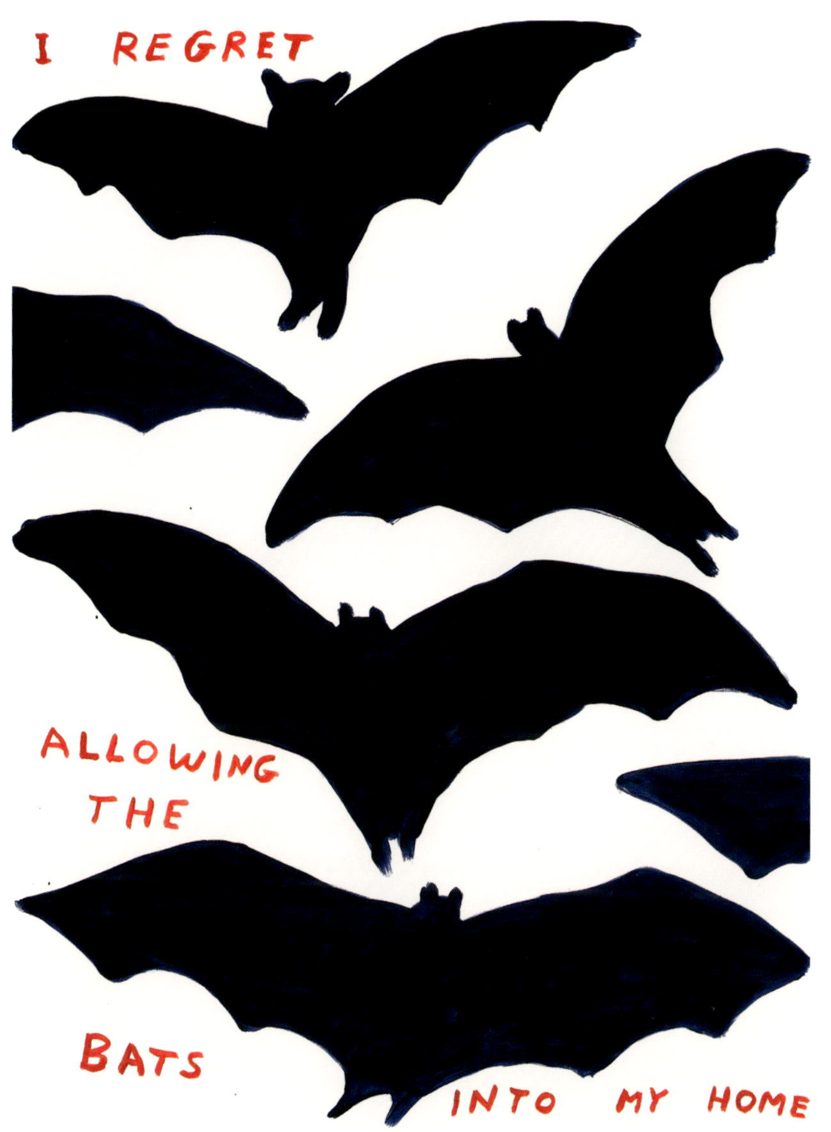
I REGRET
ALLOWING
THE
BATS
INTO MY HOME

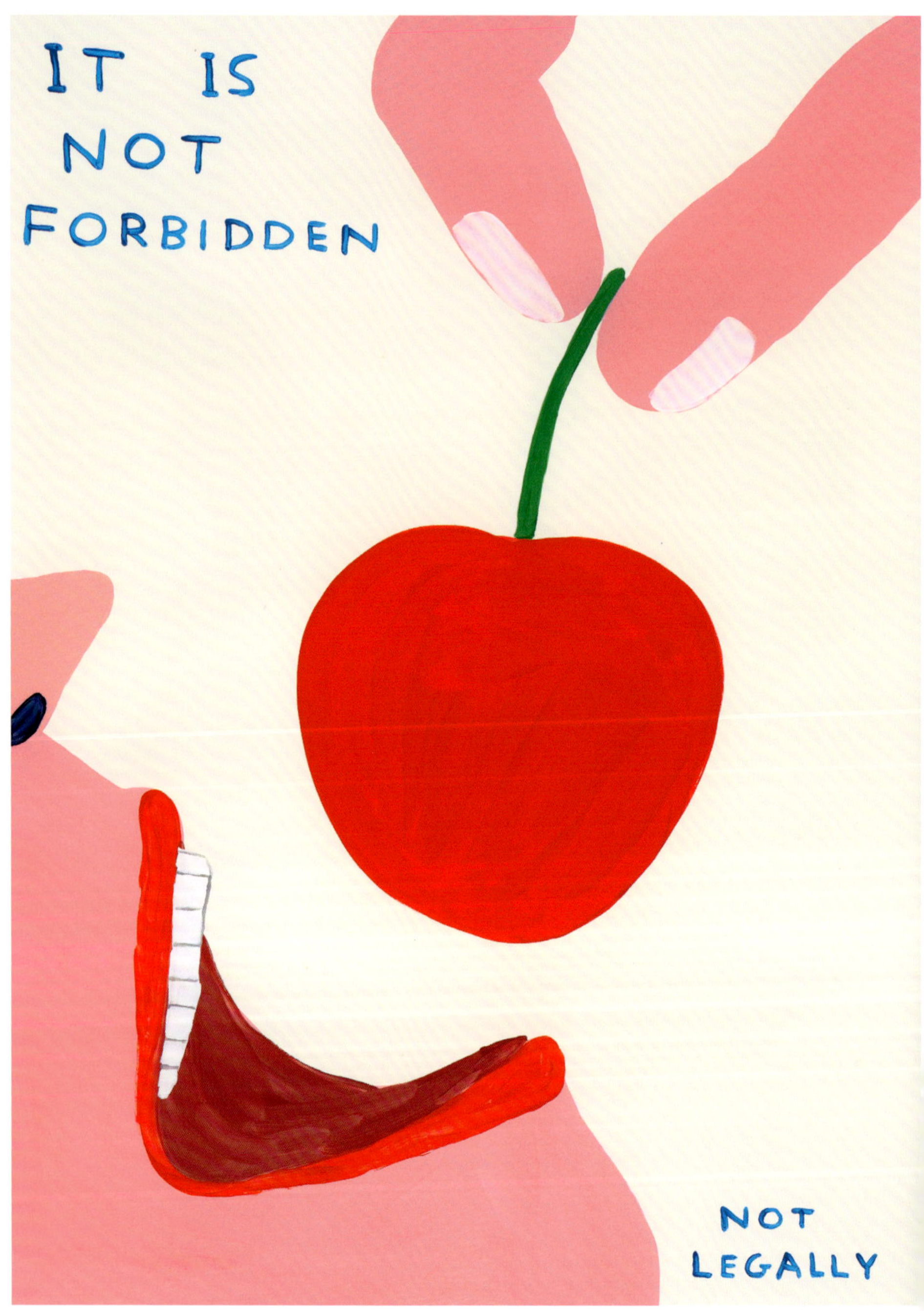
IT IS
NOT
FORBIDDEN
NOT
LEGALLY

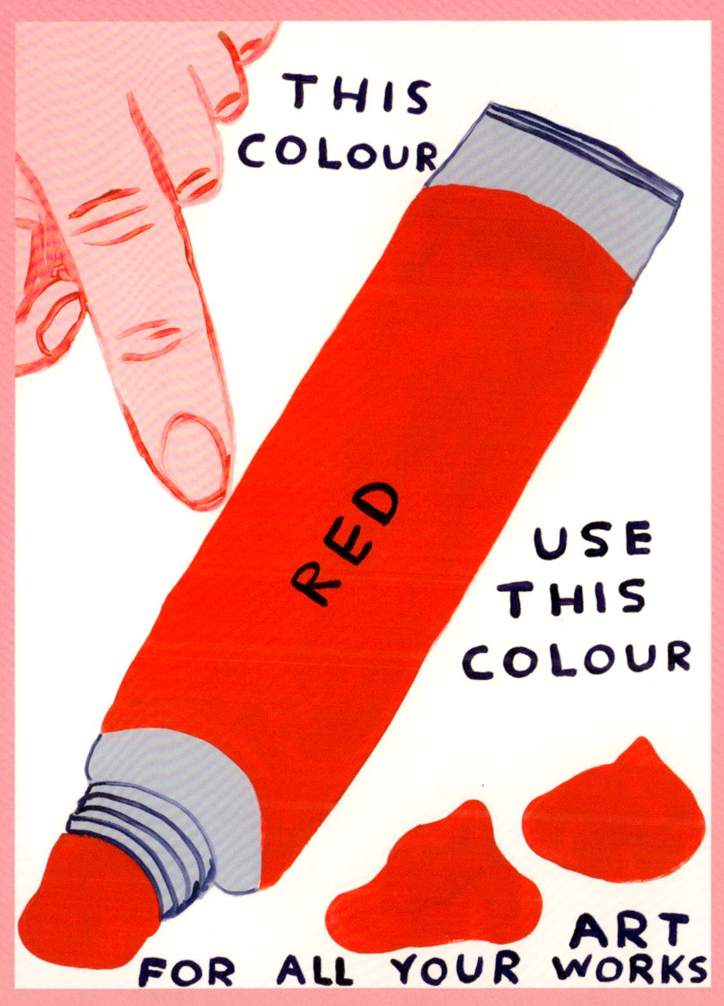
THIS
COLOUR
RED
USE
THIS
COLOUR
FOR ALL YOUR ART WORKS

ADVICE TO PASSENGERS

DON'T GET IN A CAR WITH
SOMEONE YOU DON'T KNOW
YOU MAY WELL COME TO REGRET
IT
THEY MIGHT TAKE YOU AWAY AND
HARM YOU
OR EVEN KILL YOU
OR THEY MIGHT BE A VERY
BAD DRIVER
AND CRASH INTO A WALL

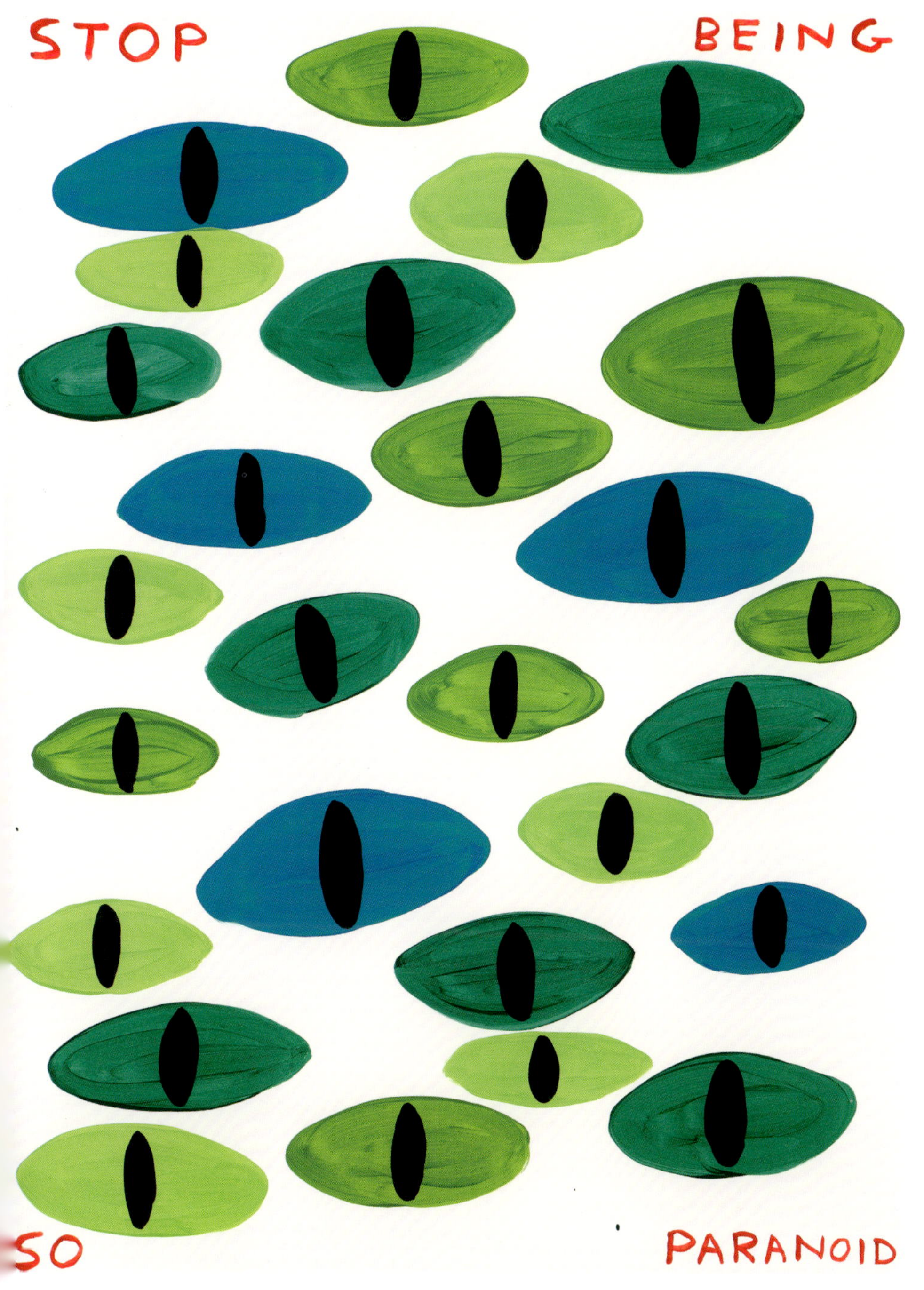
STOP
BEING
SO
PARANOID

IT'S
OK

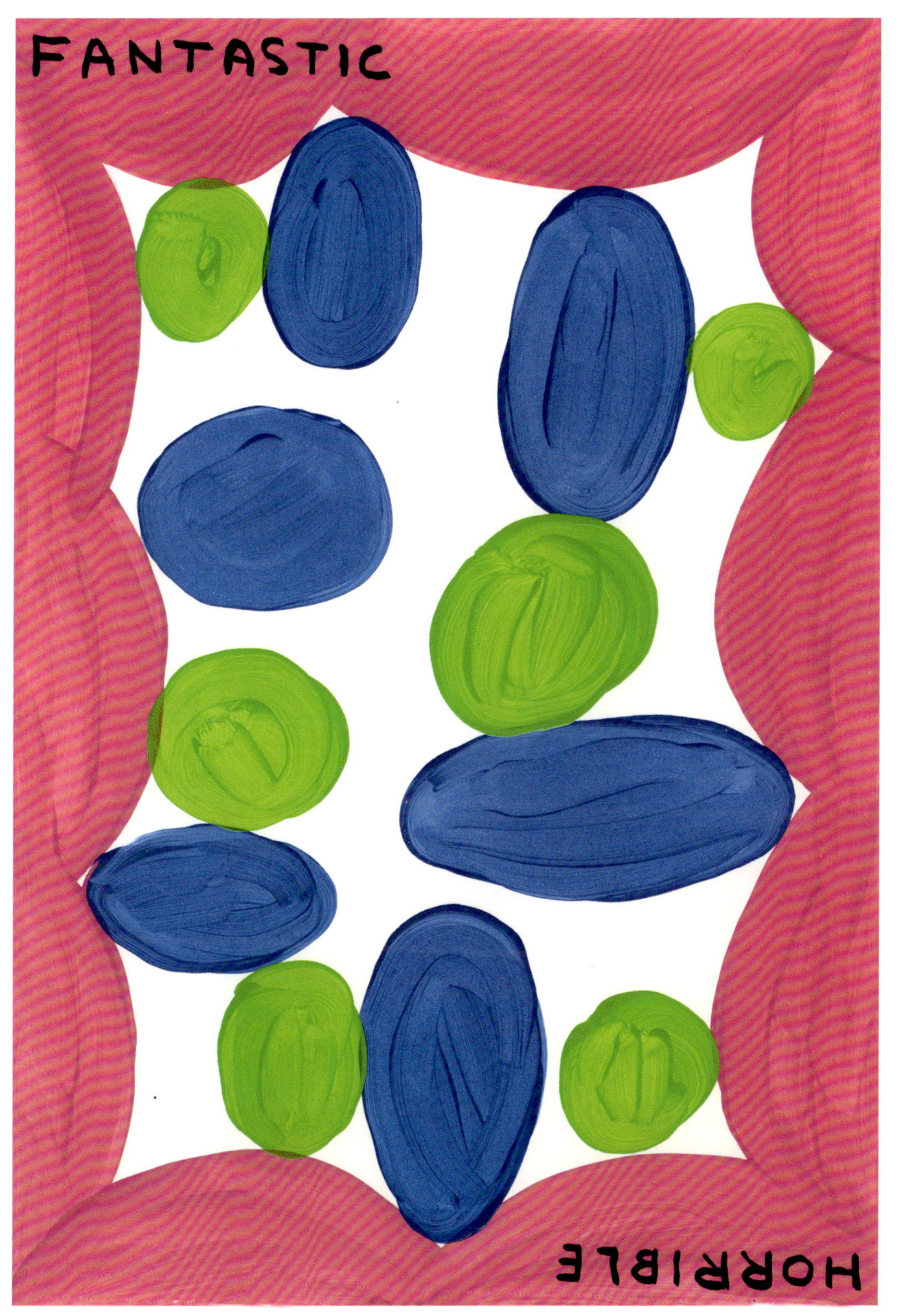
FANTASTIC
HORRIBLE

IT'S OK

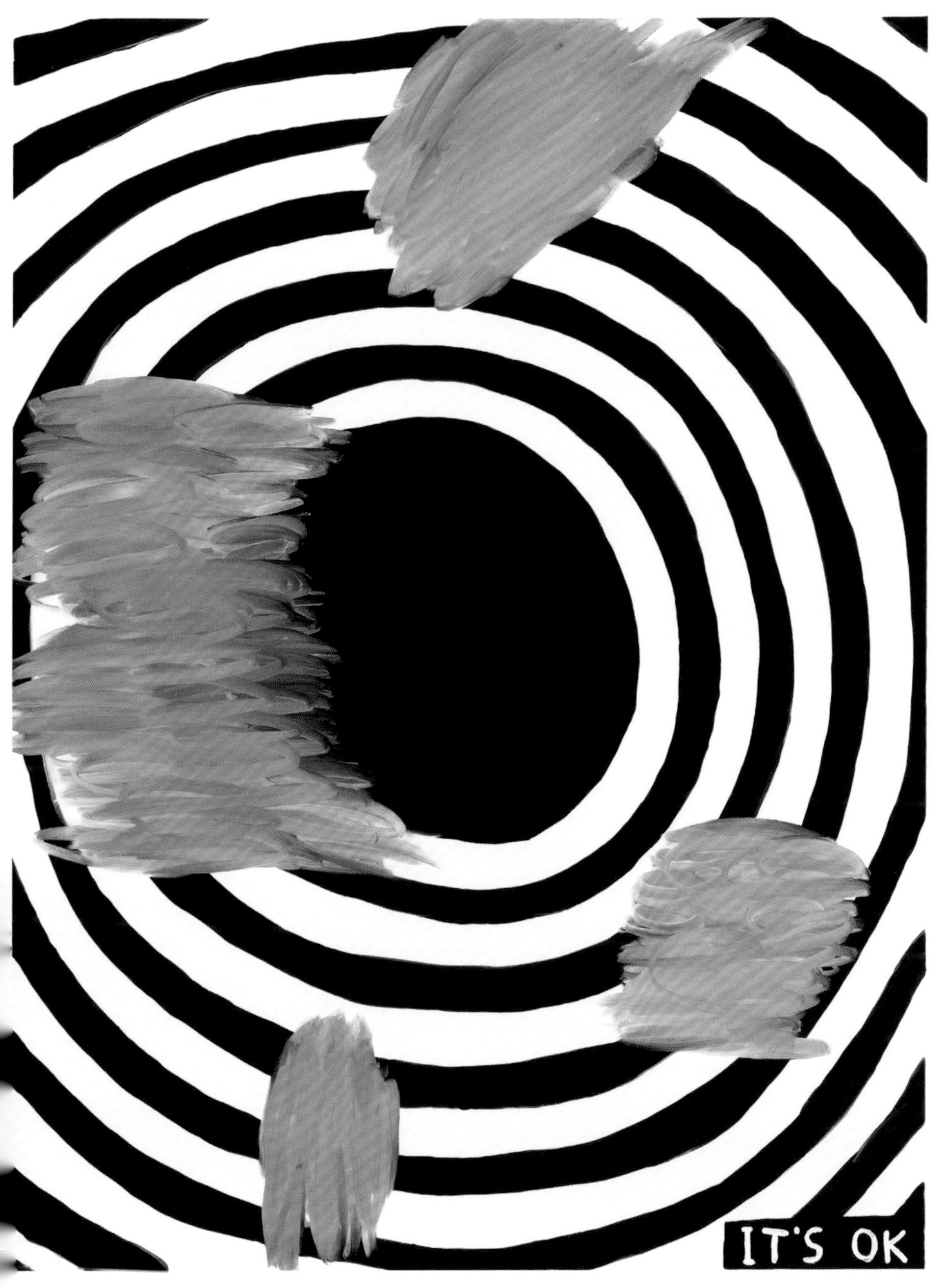
IT'S OK

DONKEYS

- WHAT USE ARE DONKEYS?

DONKEYS ARE BEASTS OF BURDEN:
THEY PULL THINGS AND CARRY
THINGS
SO WE DON'T HAVE TO

- I HATE DONKEYS

THAT IS YOUR CHOICE

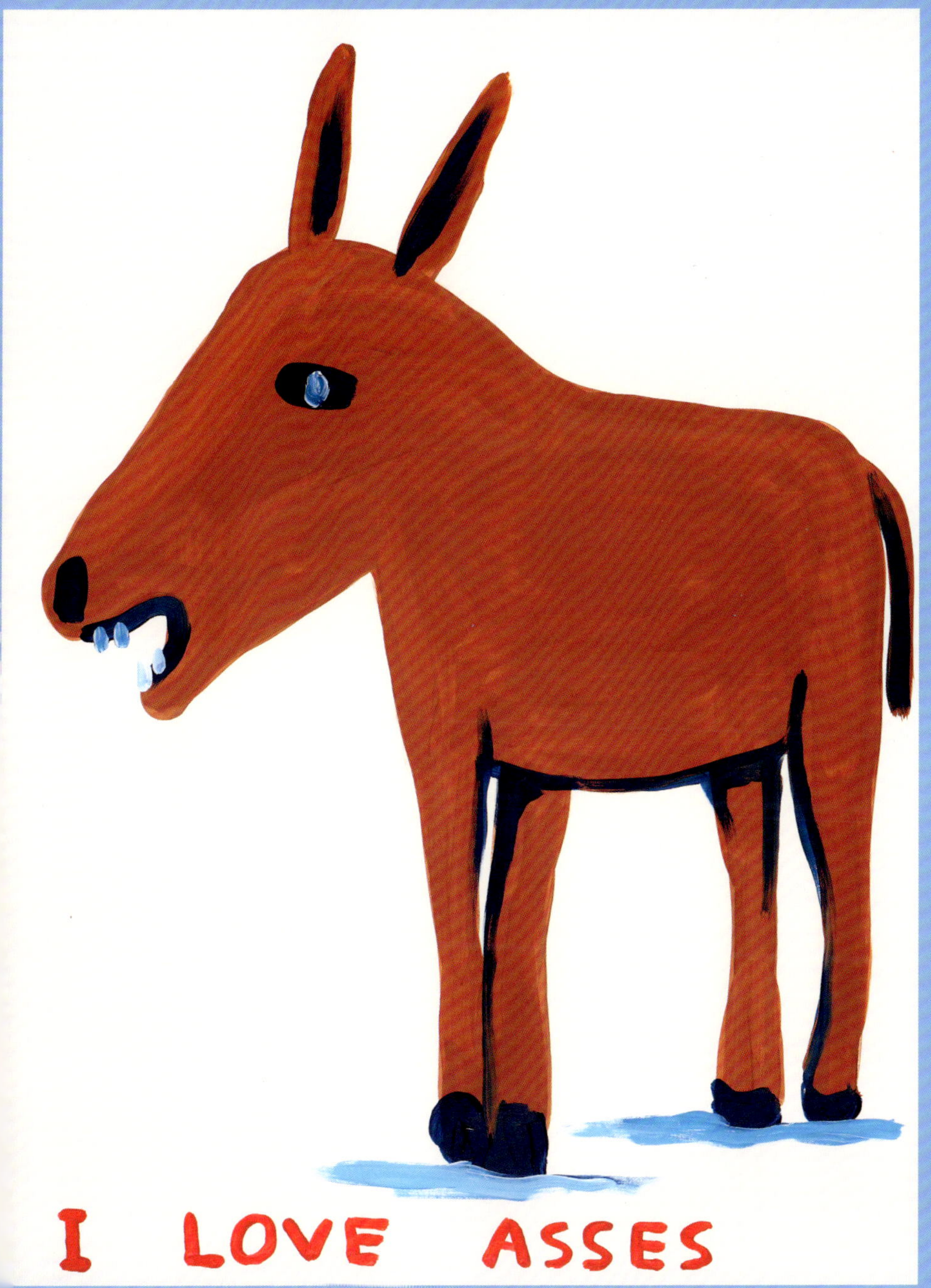
I LOVE ASSES

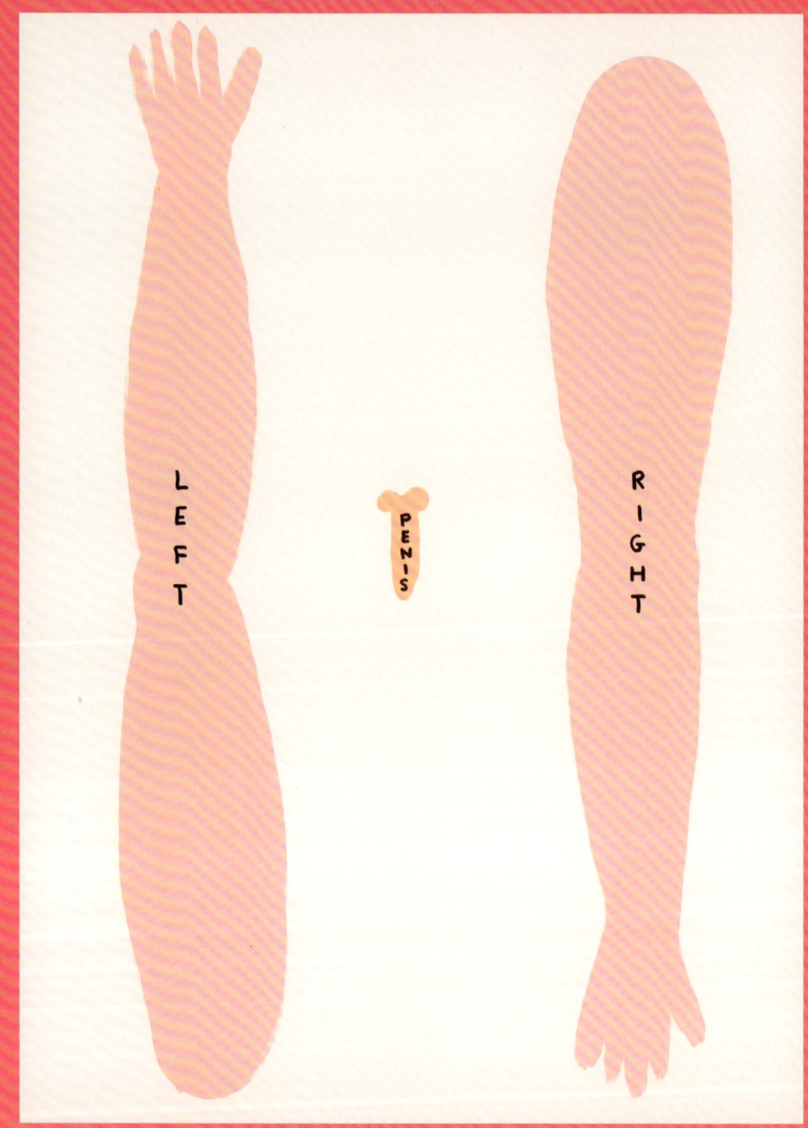
LEFT
PENIS
RIGHT

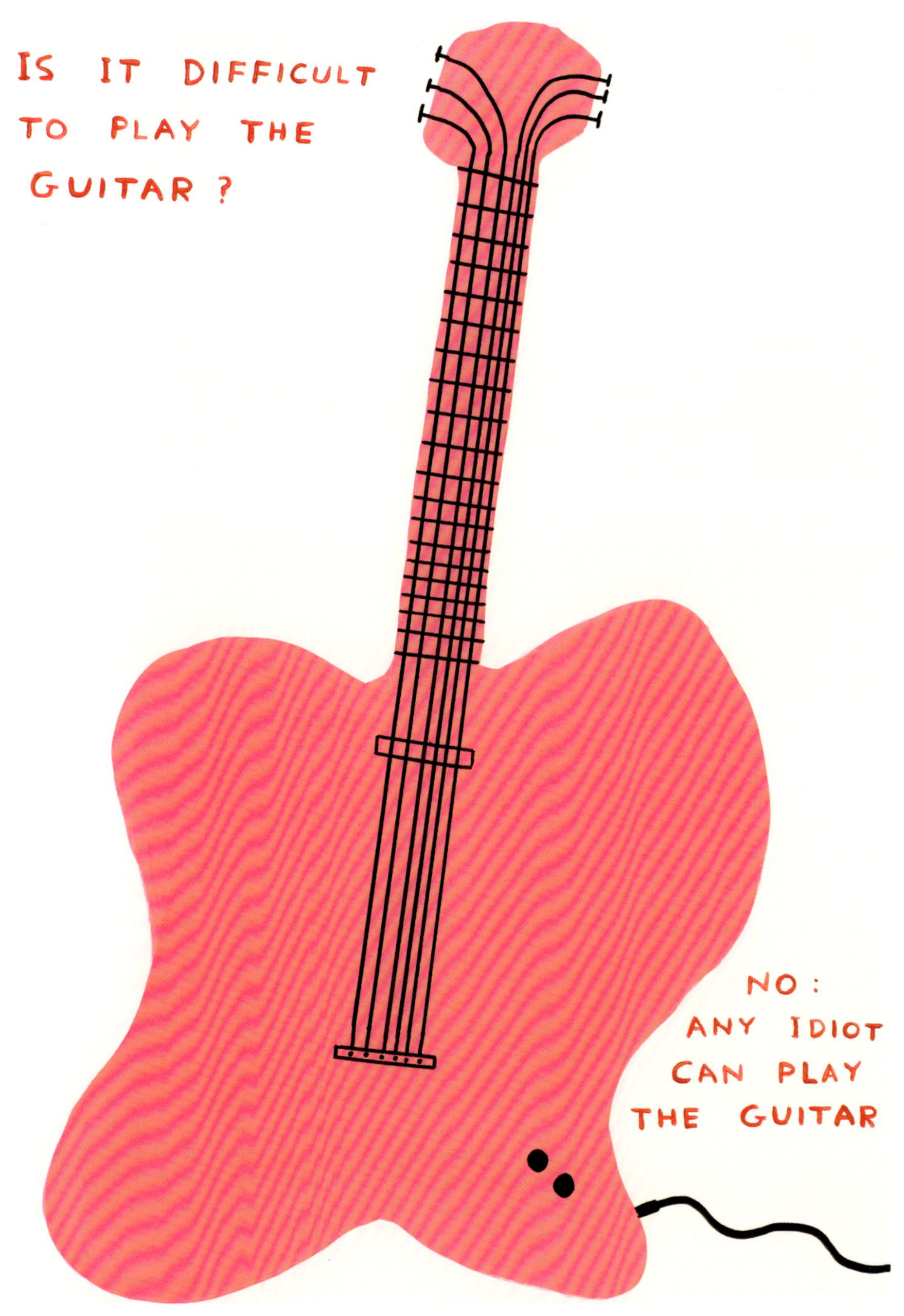
IS IT DIFFICULT TO PLAY THE GUITAR ?
NO : ANY IDIOT CAN PLAY THE GUITAR

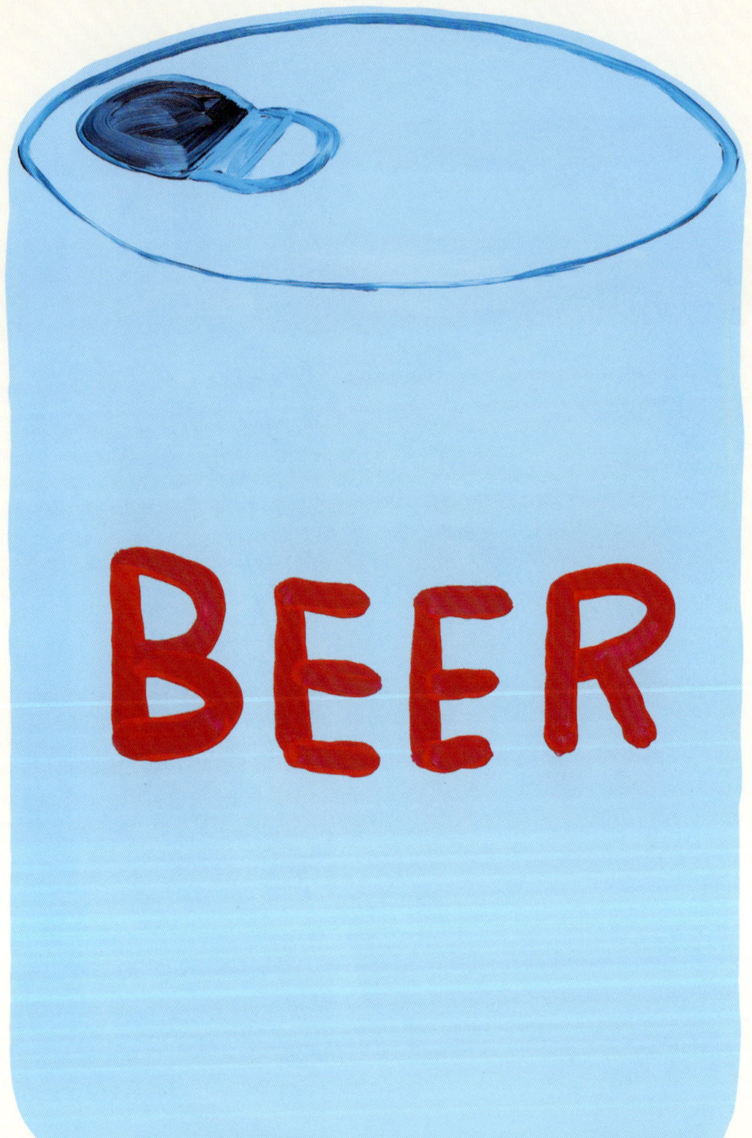
GOD DAMN THAT TERRIBLE BEER
BEER
IT MADE ME DRUNK
IT MADE ME OH SO VER
DRUN

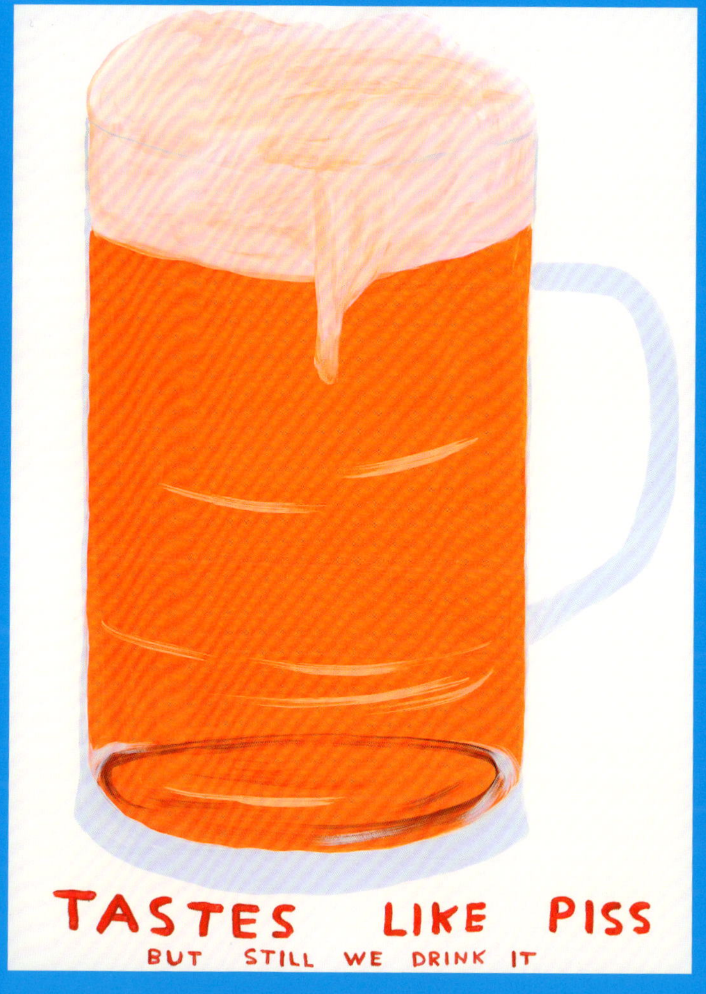
TASTES LIKE PISS
BUT STILL WE DRINK IT

DO NOT MARRY
A PSYCHOPATH

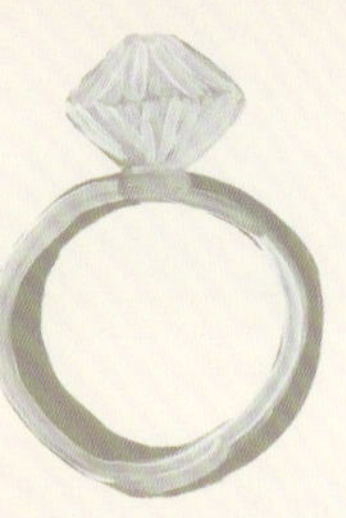

YOU WILL REGRET I
IF YOU MARRY A
PSYCHOPATH

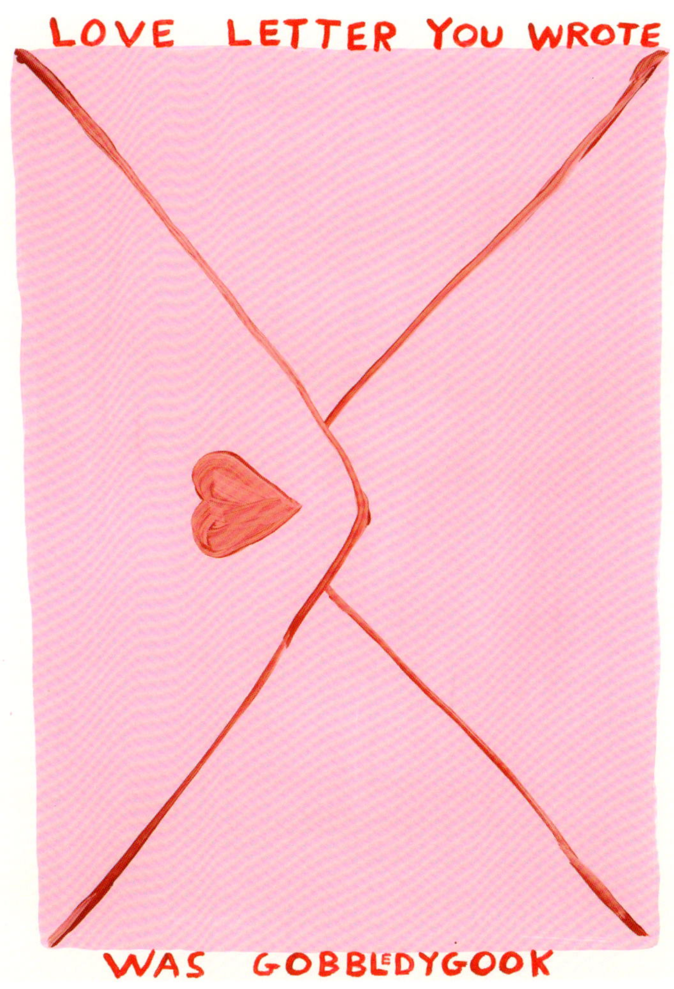
LOVE LETTER YOU WROTE
WAS GOBBLEDYGOOK

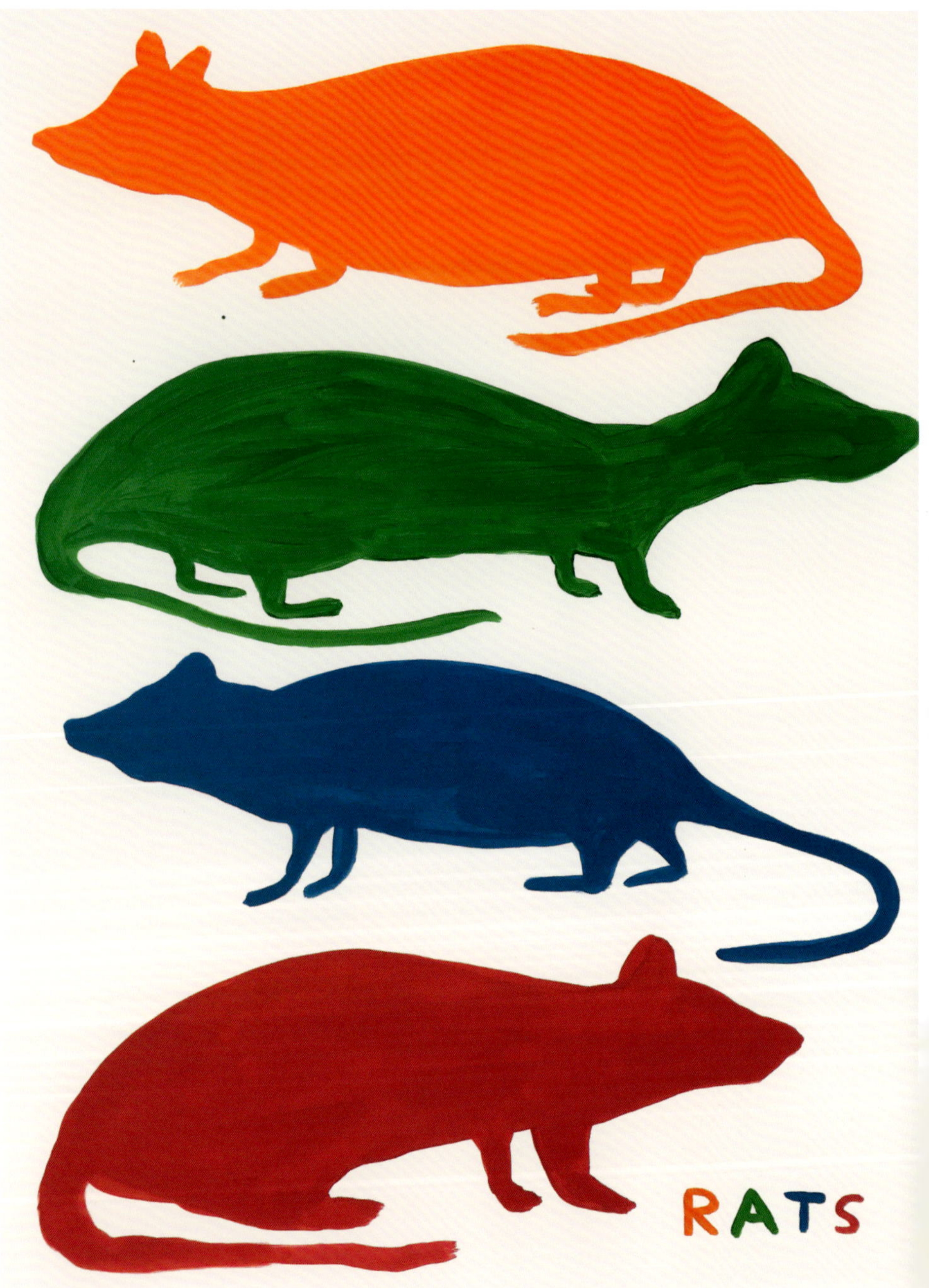
RATS

MY CASE WAS FULL OF RODENTS

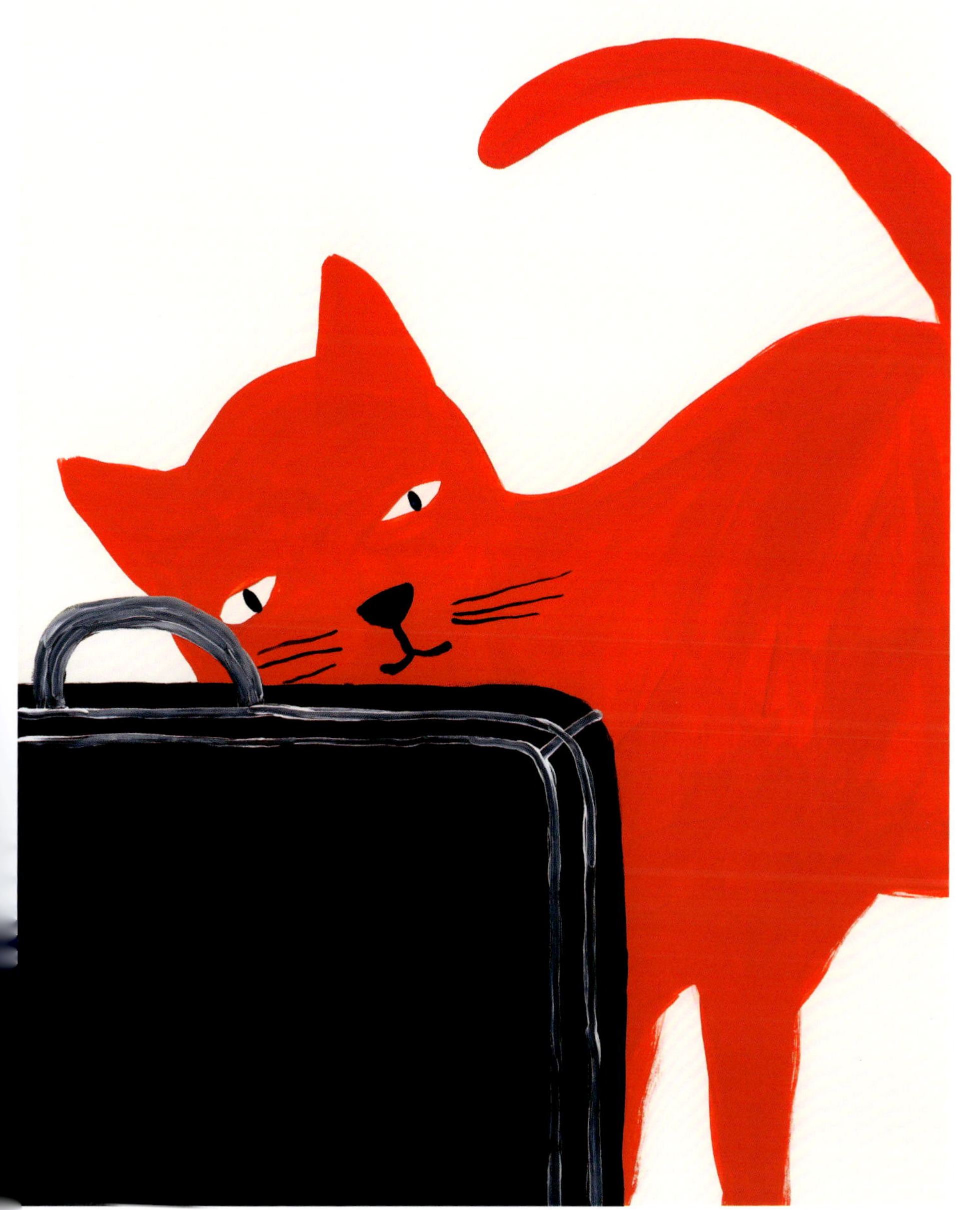

OTHERS

DO UNTO OTHERS
WHAT YOU WOULD HAVE THEM DO
UNTO YOU
UNLESS YOU ARE SOME KIND OF
WEIRD PERVERT
WHO LIKES GETTING STABBED, ETC.

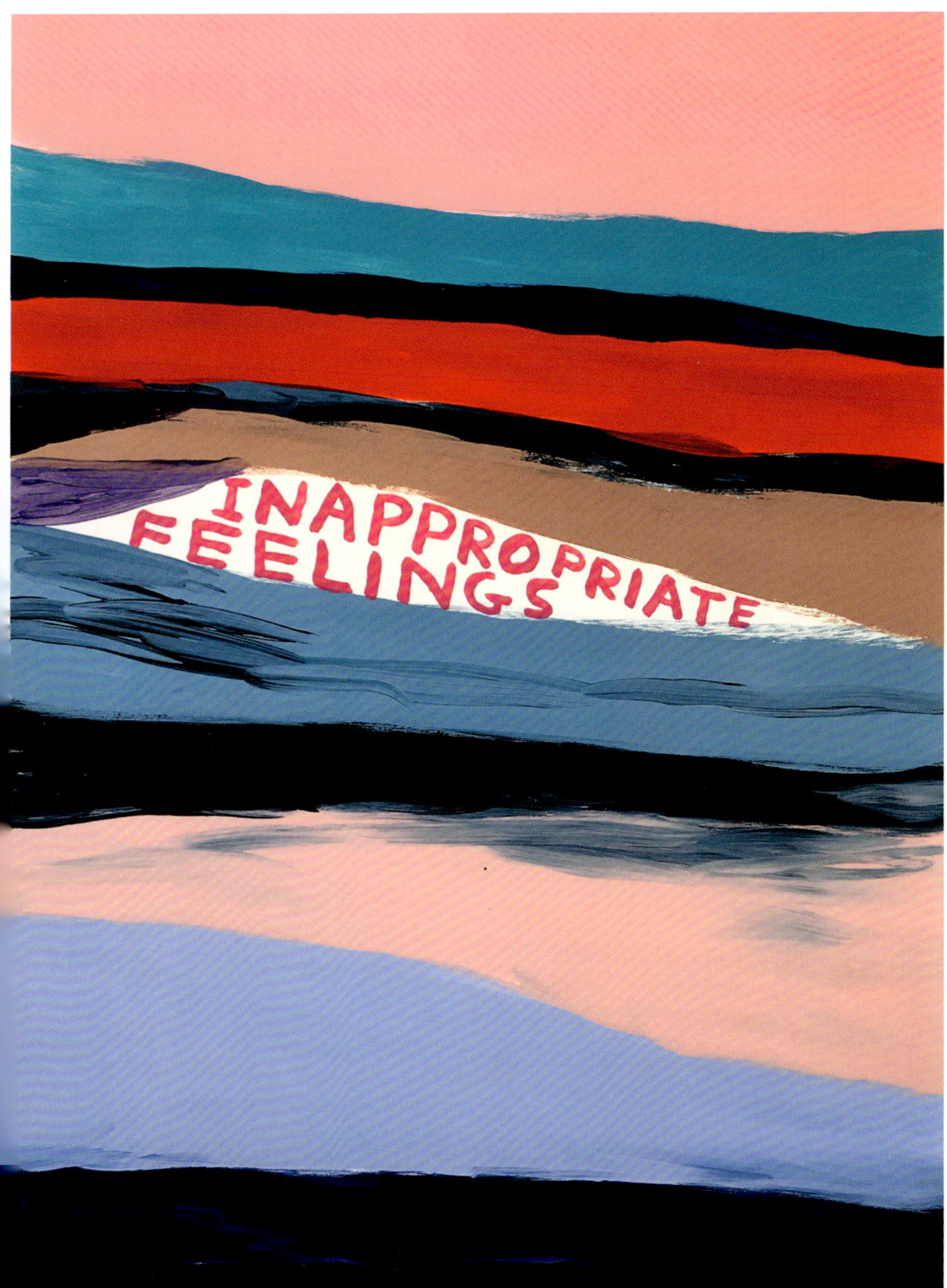
INAPPROPRIATE
FEELINGS

I TOOK ACID
BUT IT MADE
NO DIFFERENCE

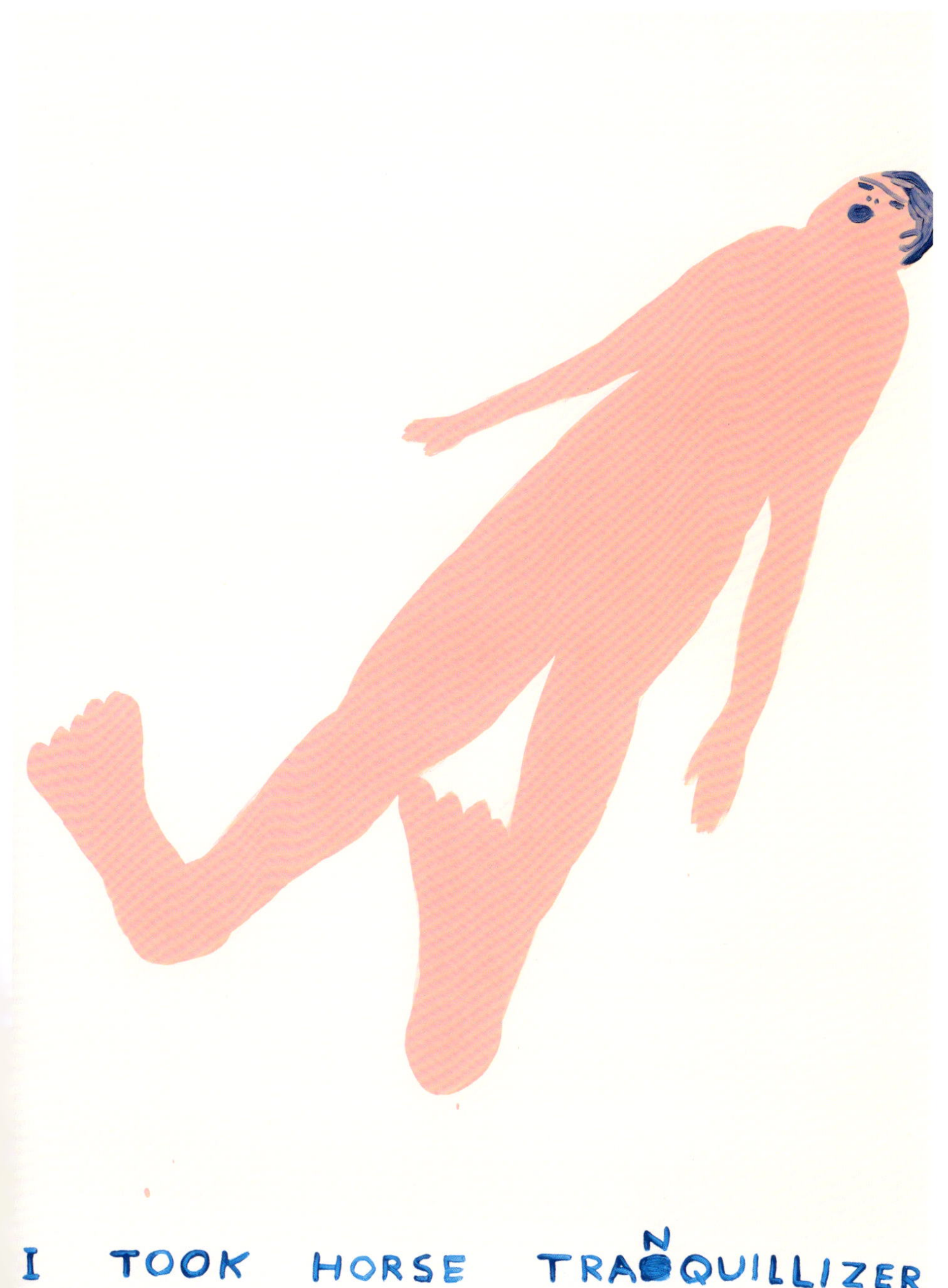
I TOOK HORSE TRANQUILLIZER

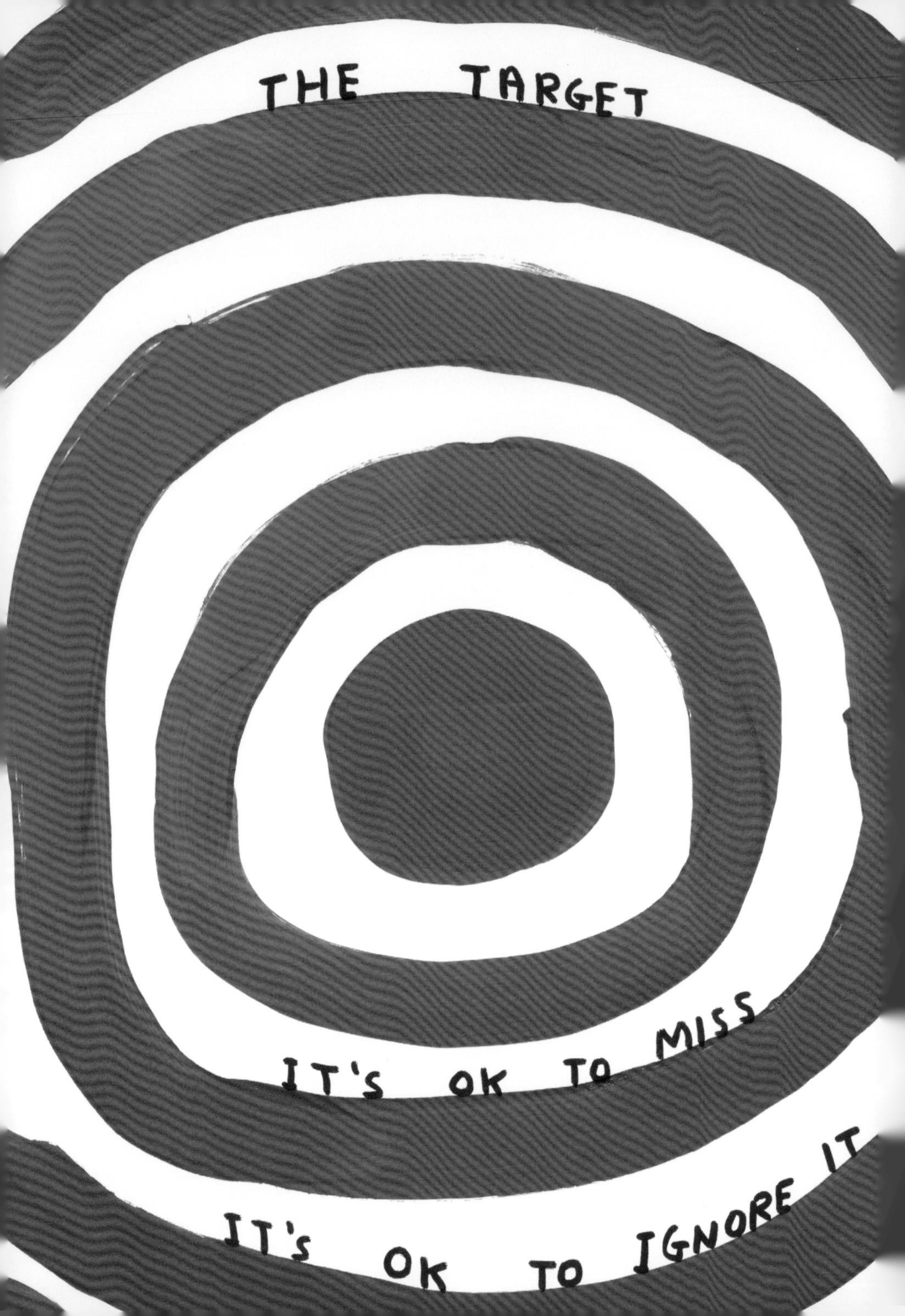

THE TARGET

IT'S OK TO MISS

IT'S OK TO IGNORE IT

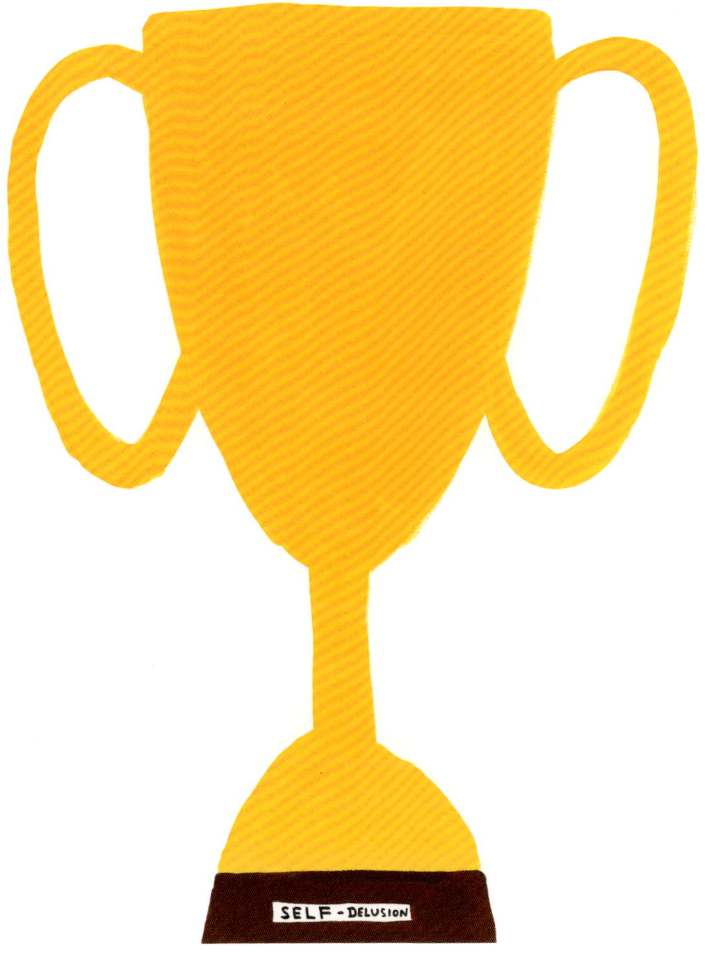
SELF-DELUSION

NO WORDS

NO WORDS
WRITTEN DOWN
ON THE PAGE
THE AUTHOR
HAD NO WORDS
IN HIS HEAD
HIS MIND WAS
EMPTY OF WORDS
HE MADE A DRAWING
I SHAN'T TELL YOU
WHAT THE DRAWING WAS OF
YOU CAN PROBABLY
GUESS

I NEED SPACE

KNOW THIS

KNOW THIS:
IT COMETH
YOU CANNOT
STOP IT.
YOU MUST ACCEPT IT

DEAR CLOCK

I AM YOUR LOYAL SERVANT

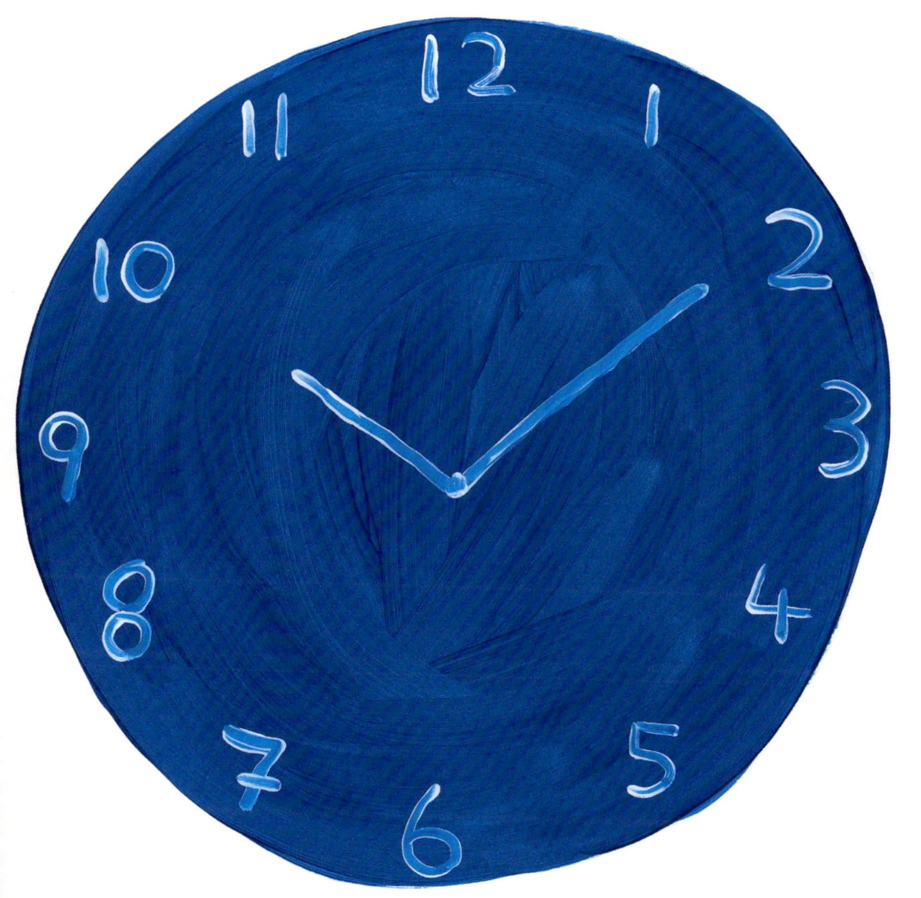

BUT NOW I HUMBLY ASK
YOU TO RELEASE ME
I MUST BE FREE

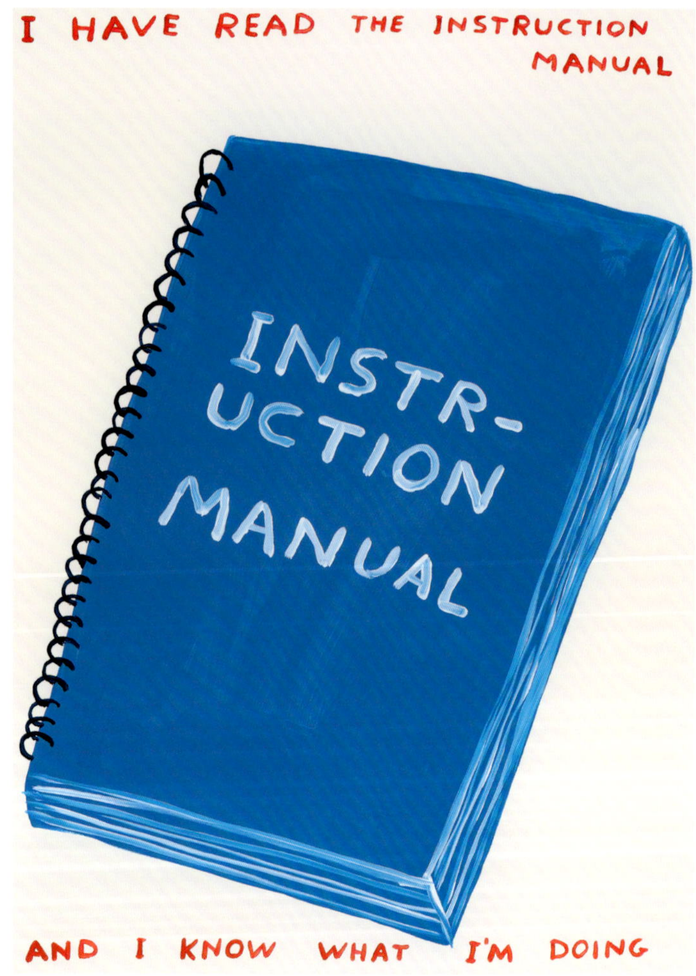
I HAVE READ THE INSTRUCTION MANUAL
INSTR-
UCTION
MANUAL
AND I KNOW WHAT I'M DOING

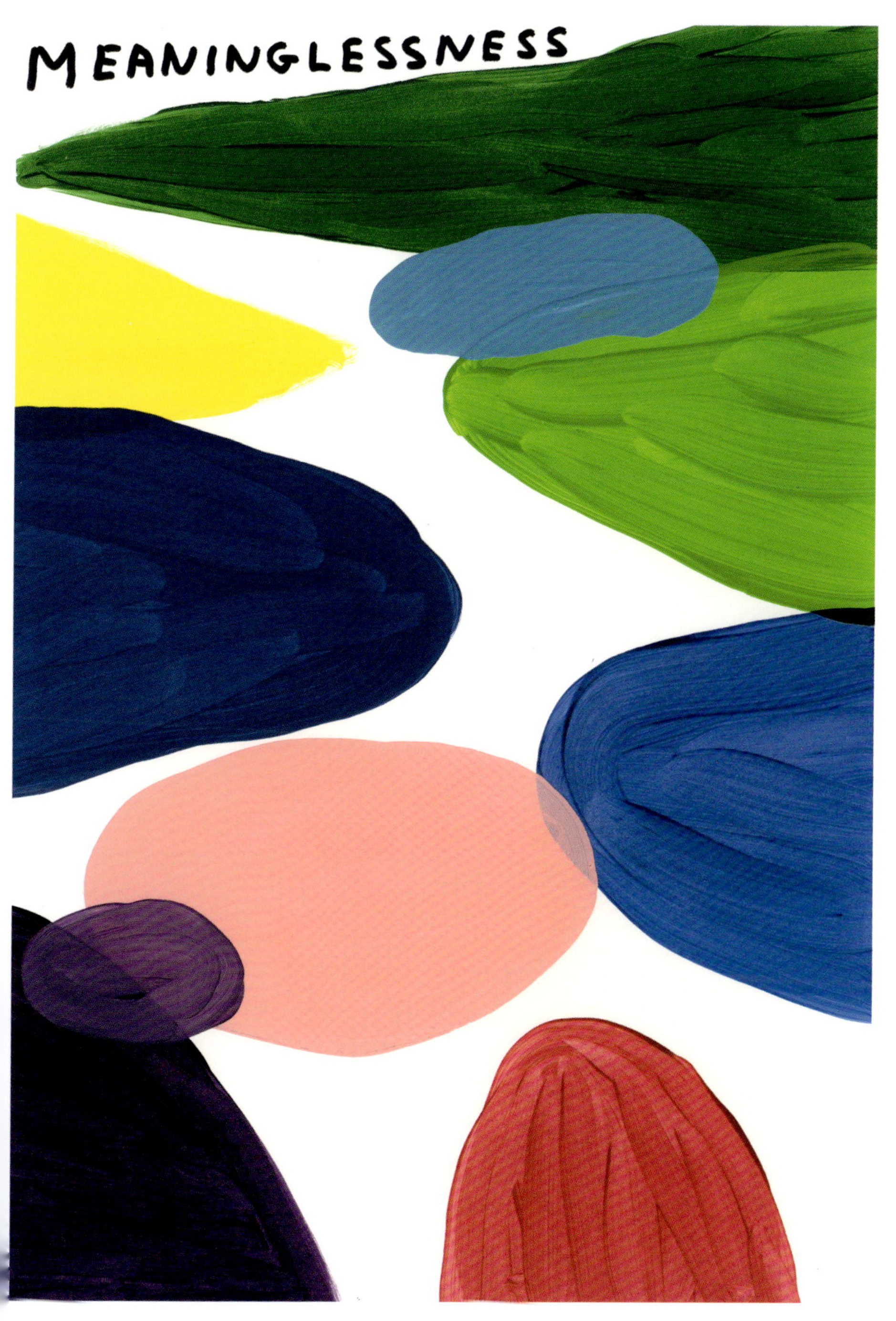
MEANINGLESSNESS

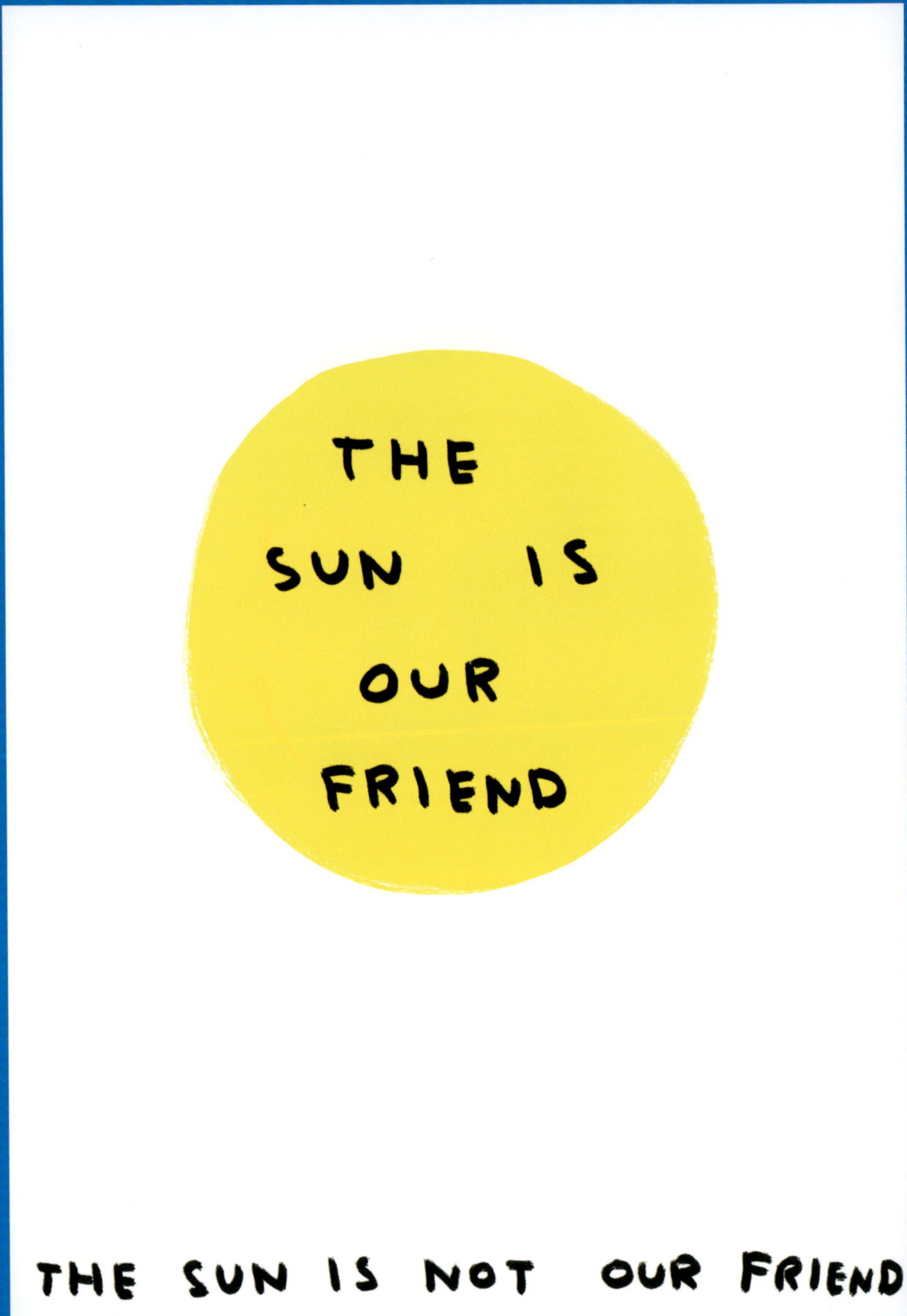

THE SUN IS OUR FRIEND

THE SUN IS NOT OUR FRIEND

IF YOU NEED ME I SHALL
BE AT THE BOTTOM OF
THE POND

THE DIAMOND-ENCRUSTED SKULL

I WANT THAT FUCKING THING
I WANT IT SO BADLY
GIVE IT TO ME
OR I'M GOING TO COME OVER
AND TAKE IT FROM YOU

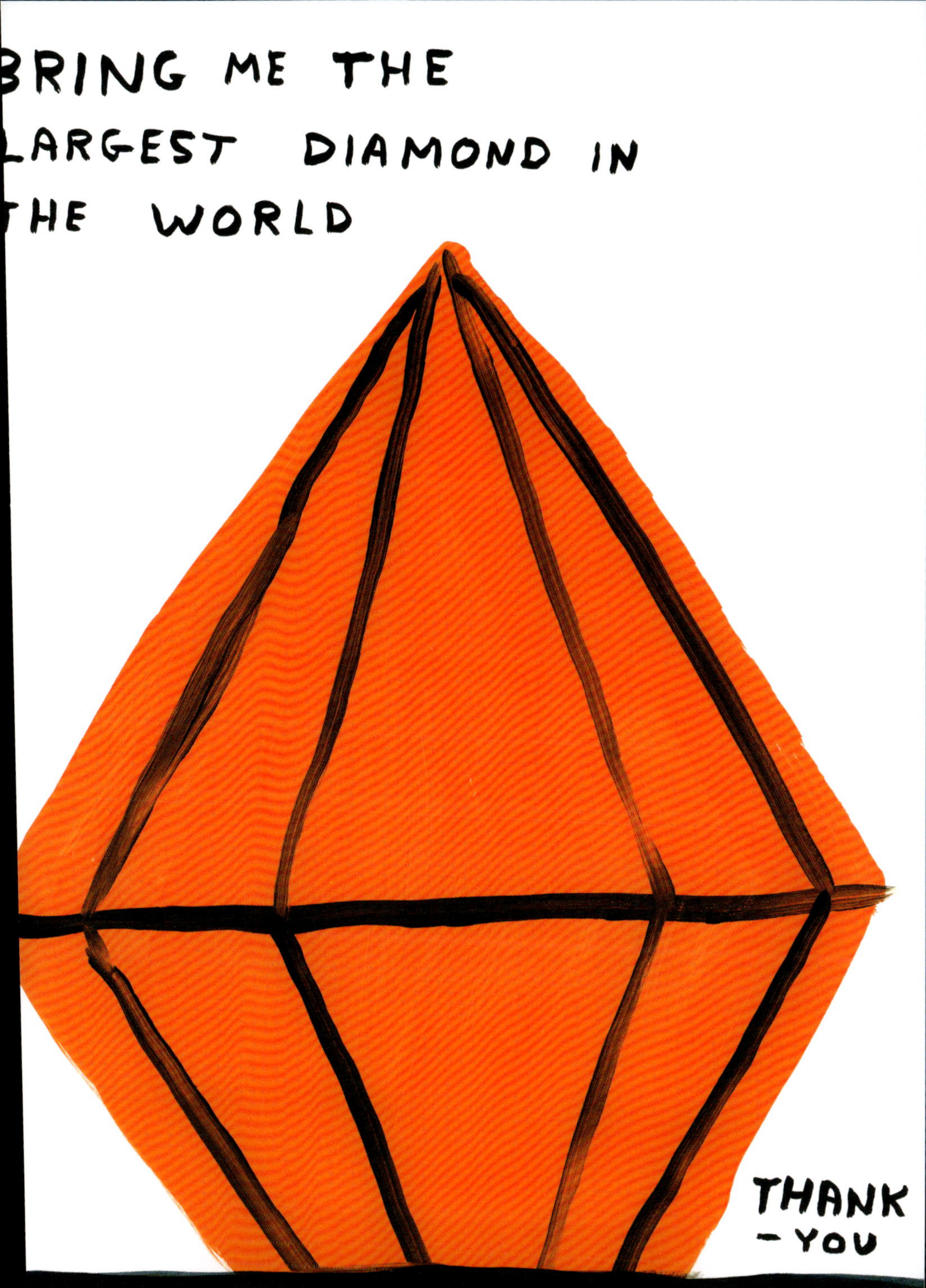

BRING ME THE
LARGEST DIAMOND IN
THE WORLD

THANK
- YOU

SHOPPING

SIFTING THROUGH PILES OF JUNK
TRYING TO FIND SOMETHING THAT
YOU WANT
BUT YOU CAN'T FIND ANYTHING
THAT YOU WANT

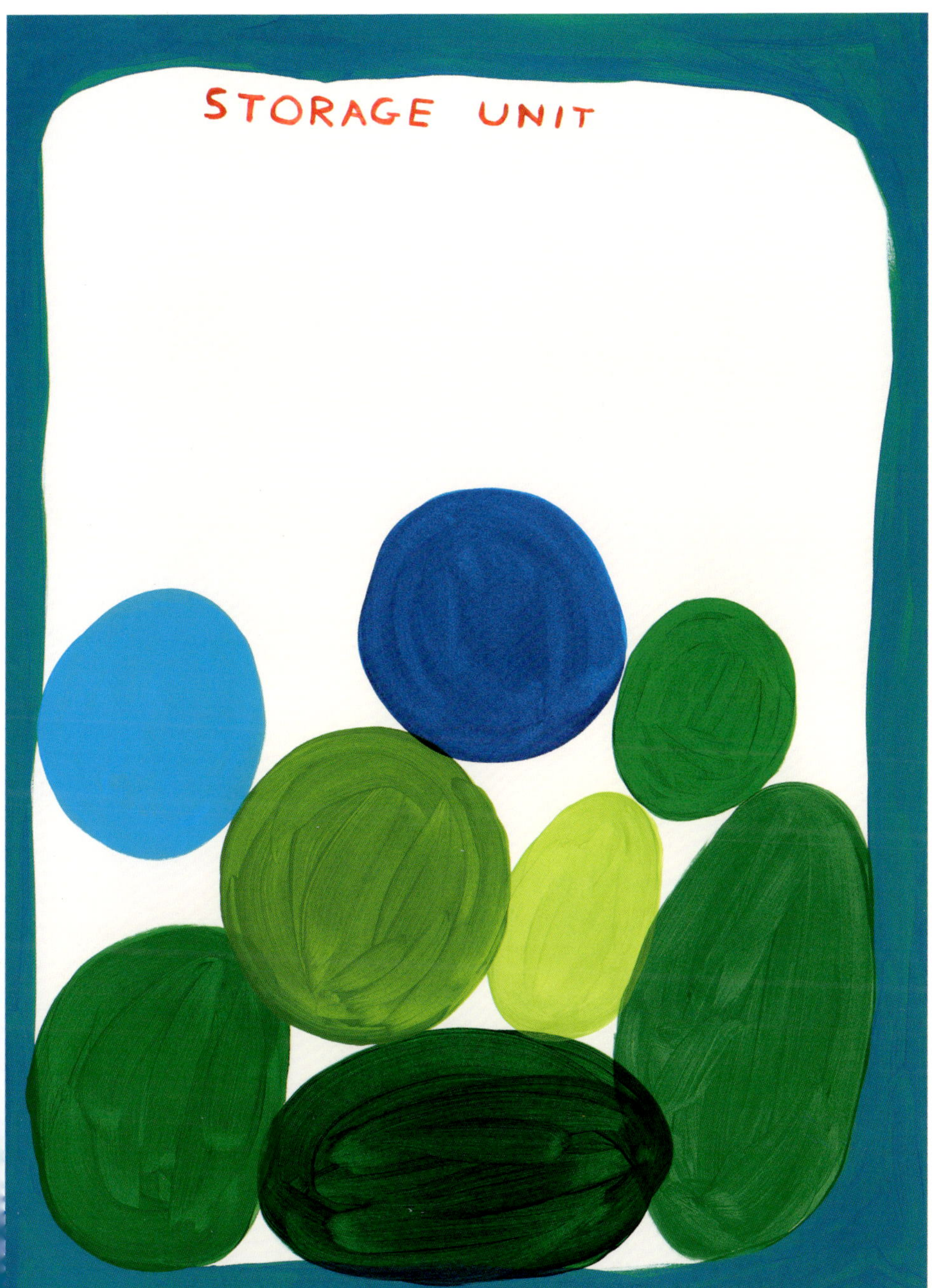
STORAGE UNIT

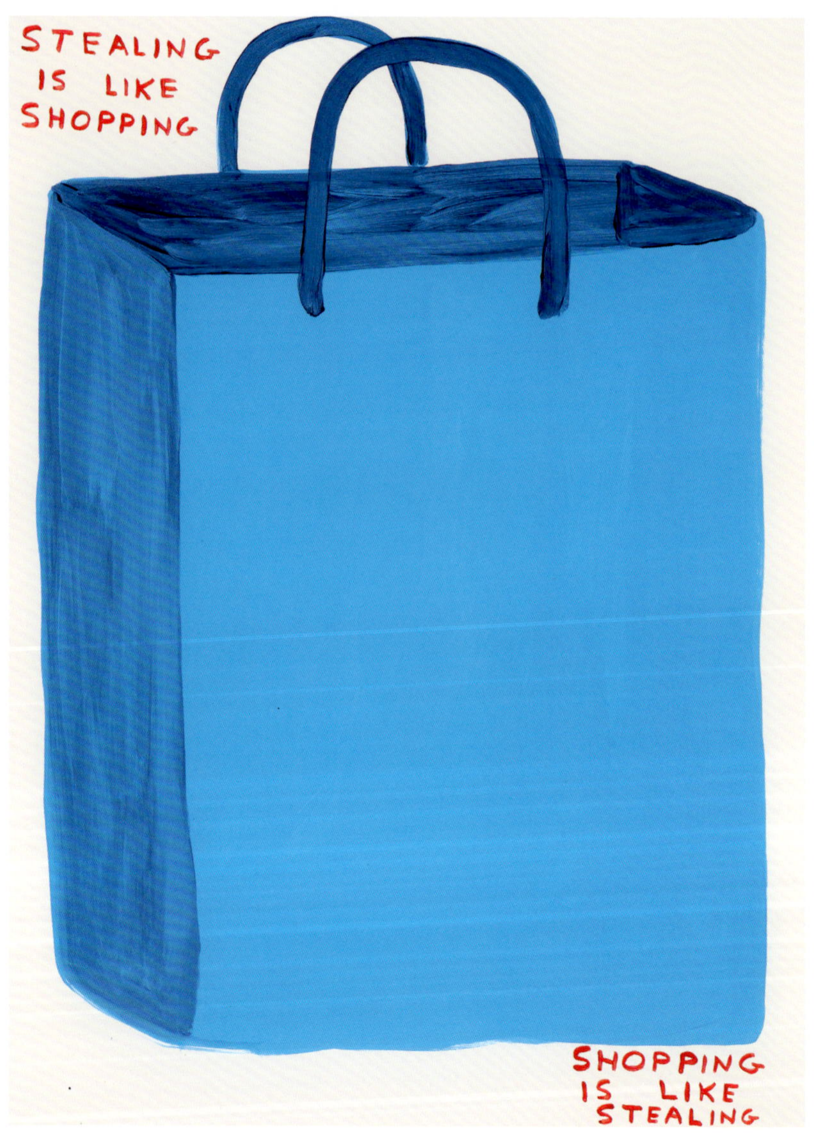
STEALING
IS LIKE
SHOPPING
SHOPPING
IS LIKE
STEALING

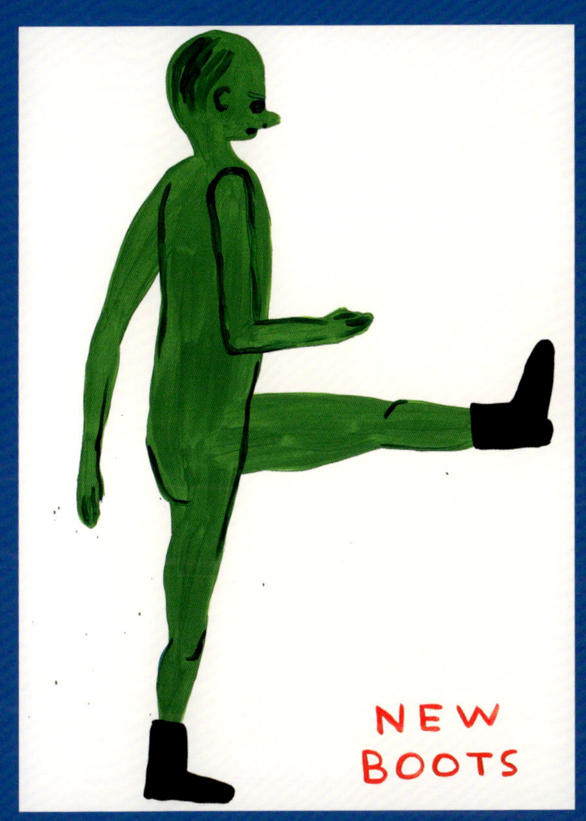
NEW
BOOTS

GLUE

GLUE IS NOW ILLEGAL
YOU CAN'T BUY IT IN THE SHOPS
ANYMORE

IF THEY FIND YOU GLUEING THINGS
THEN YOU'LL GET INTO TROUBLE
THEY DON'T WANT YOU TO FIX
THINGS
WHEN THINGS BREAK
THEY WANT YOU TO THROW THEM
AWAY

YOU CAN MAKE YOUR OWN GLUE
IN SECRET
AND USE IT
BUT IT'S A RISK

I AM BROKEN AND I SHALL NEVER WORK AGAIN

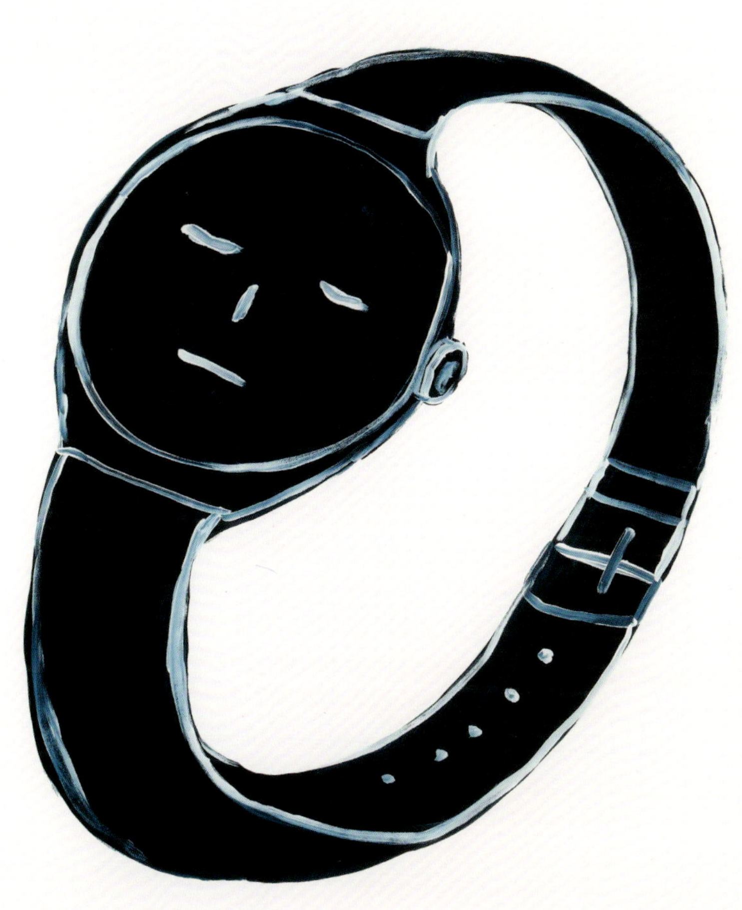

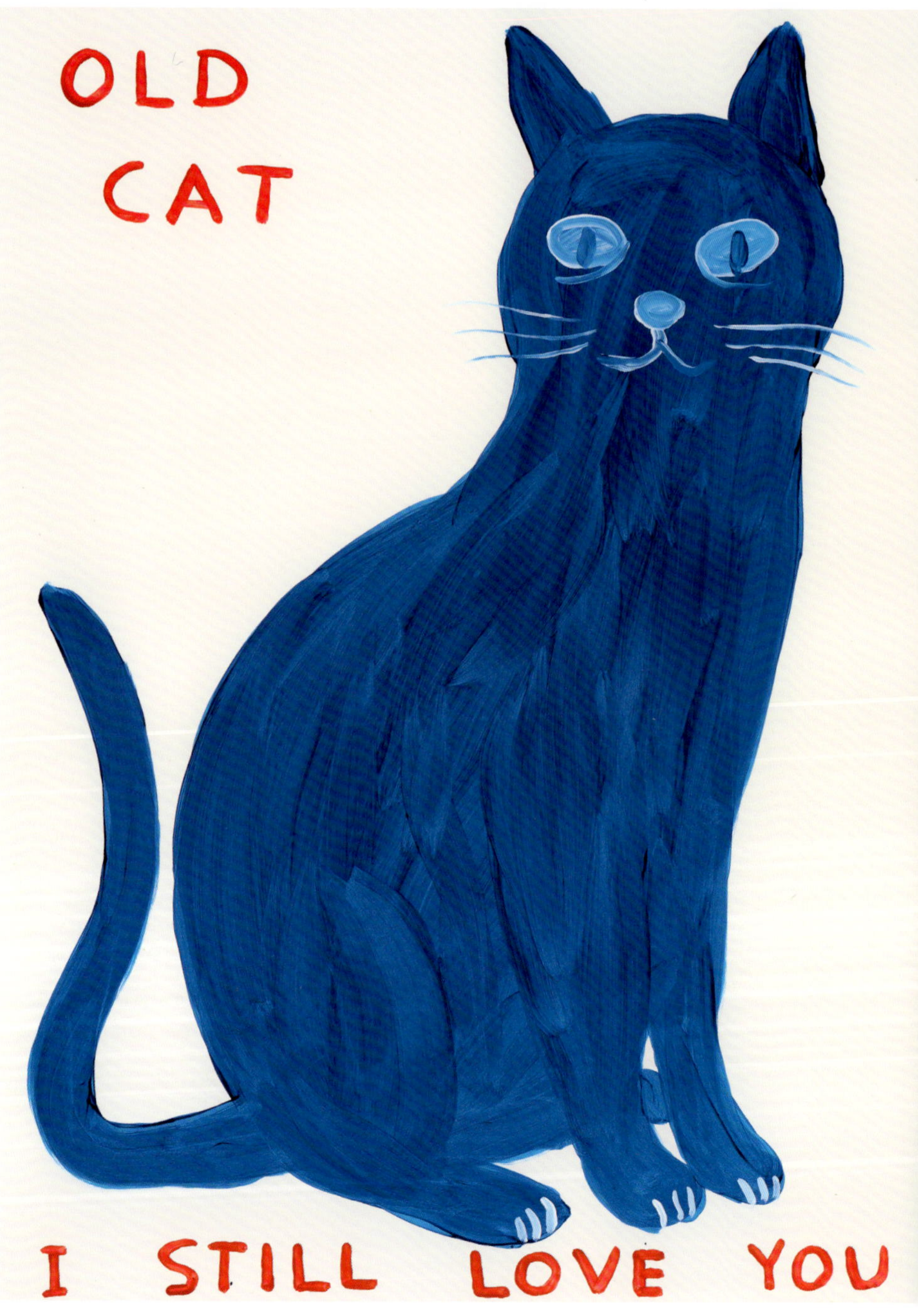
OLD
CAT
I STILL LOVE YOU

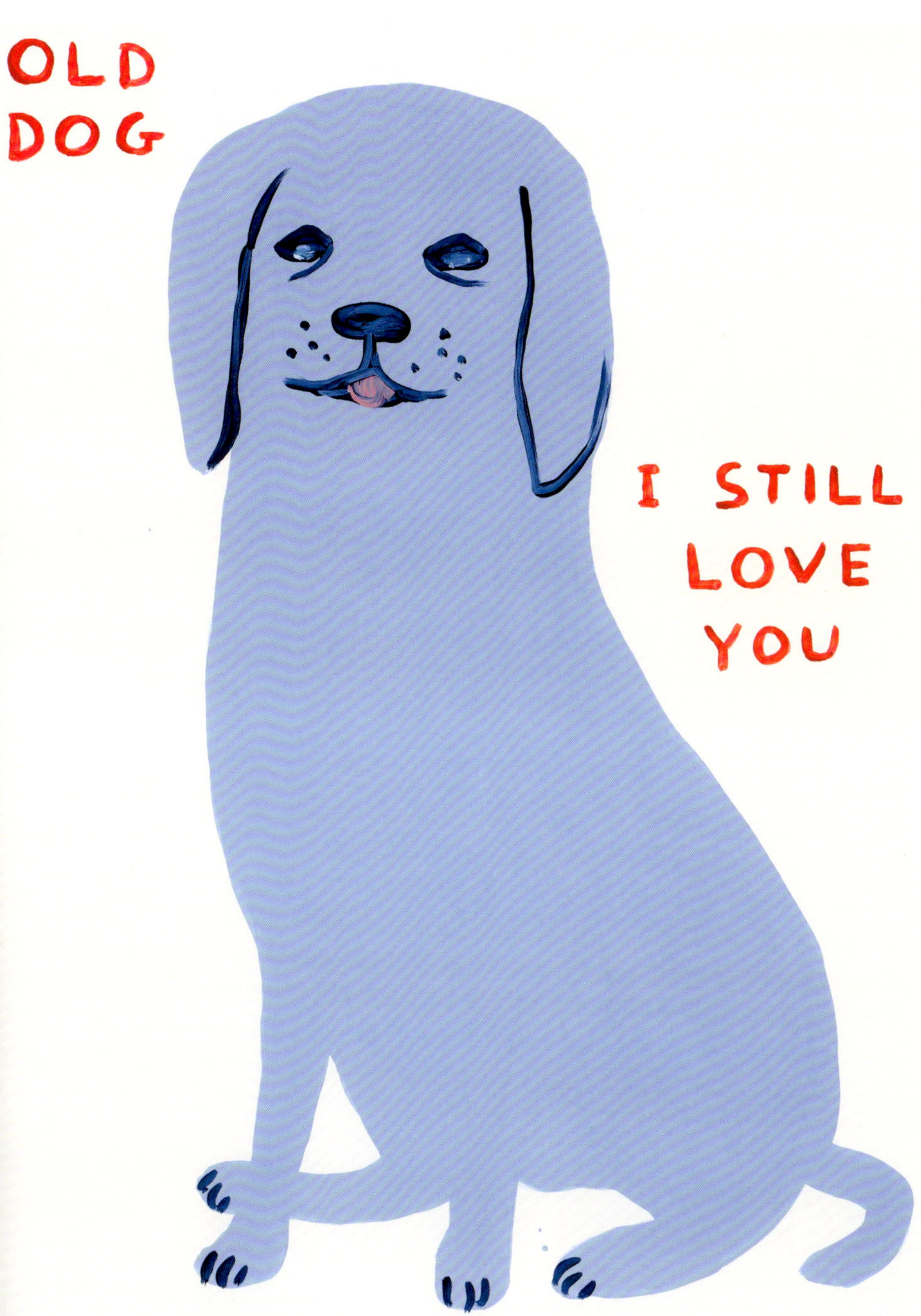
OLD DOG
I STILL LOVE YOU

DOG'S NAME

YOU BUY A DOG
YOU GIVE IT A NAME
THE SAME NAME AS ONE OF YOUR FRIENDS
THE FRIEND IS OFFENDED
TO HELL WITH HER!
SHE IS NO LONGER YOUR FRIEND

SHE SLEEPS
ON THE BED

WE SLEEP
ON THE FLOOR

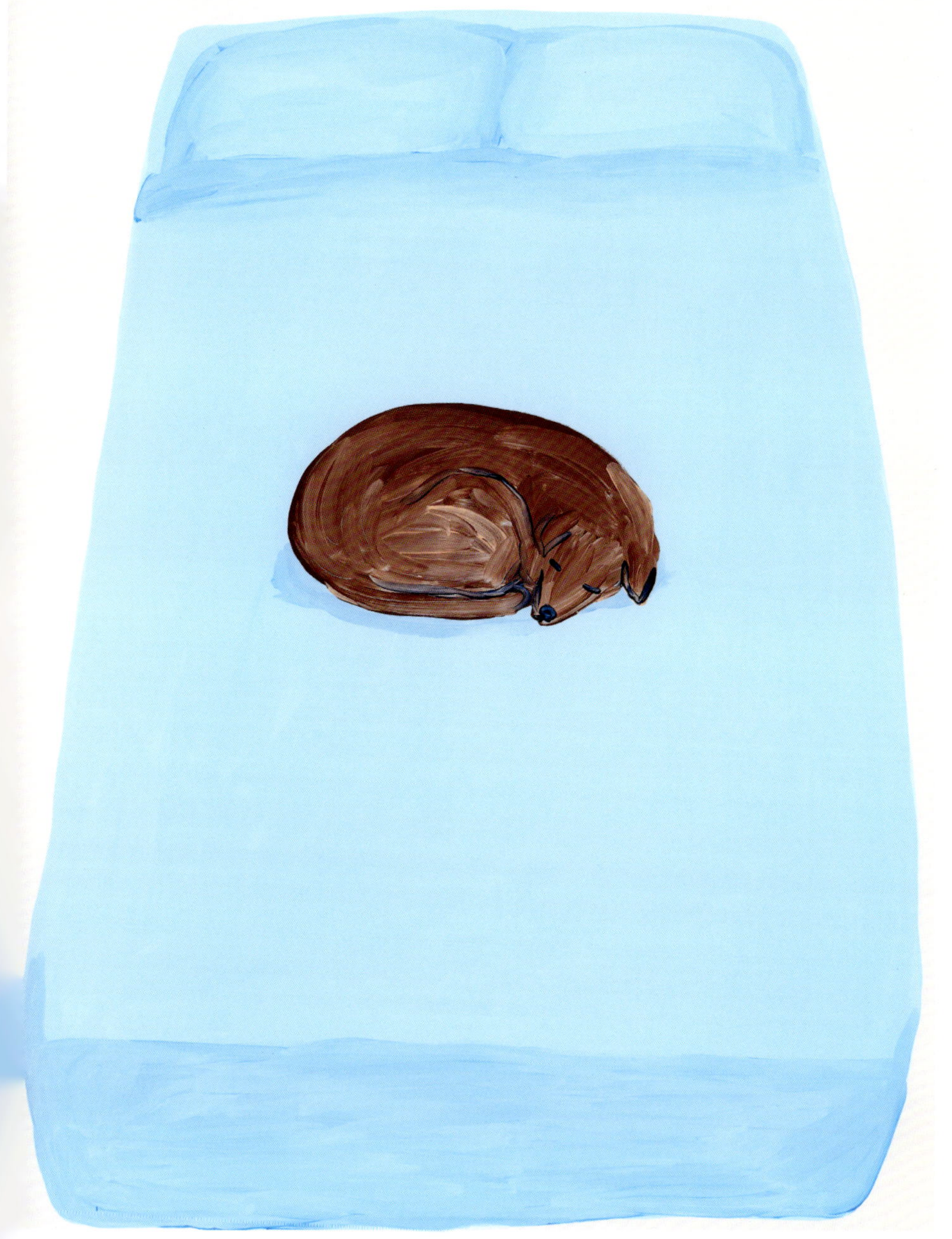

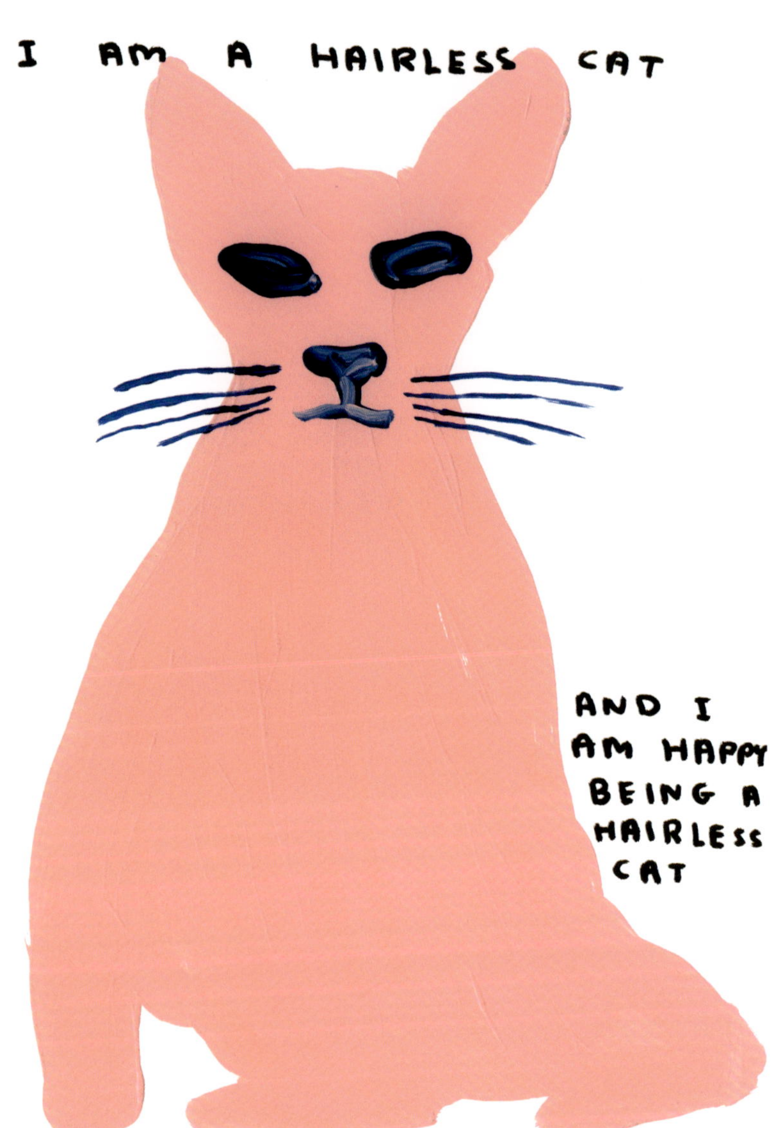
I AM A HAIRLESS CAT
AND I
AM HAPPY
BEING A
HAIRLESS
CAT

PINK PAINT

IT WAS THE ONLY
COLOUR I HAD

AND EVEN THEN
I DID NOT HAVE ENOUGH

THE PROCEDURE

I AM CARRYING OUT A PROCEDURE
IT REQUIRES CONCENTRATION
AND DILIGENCE
AND FOR ME TO BE HAPPY AND CALM
PLEASE RESPECT MY ATTEMPT
TO CARRY OUT THE PROCEDURE
AND STOP LAUGHING AT ME

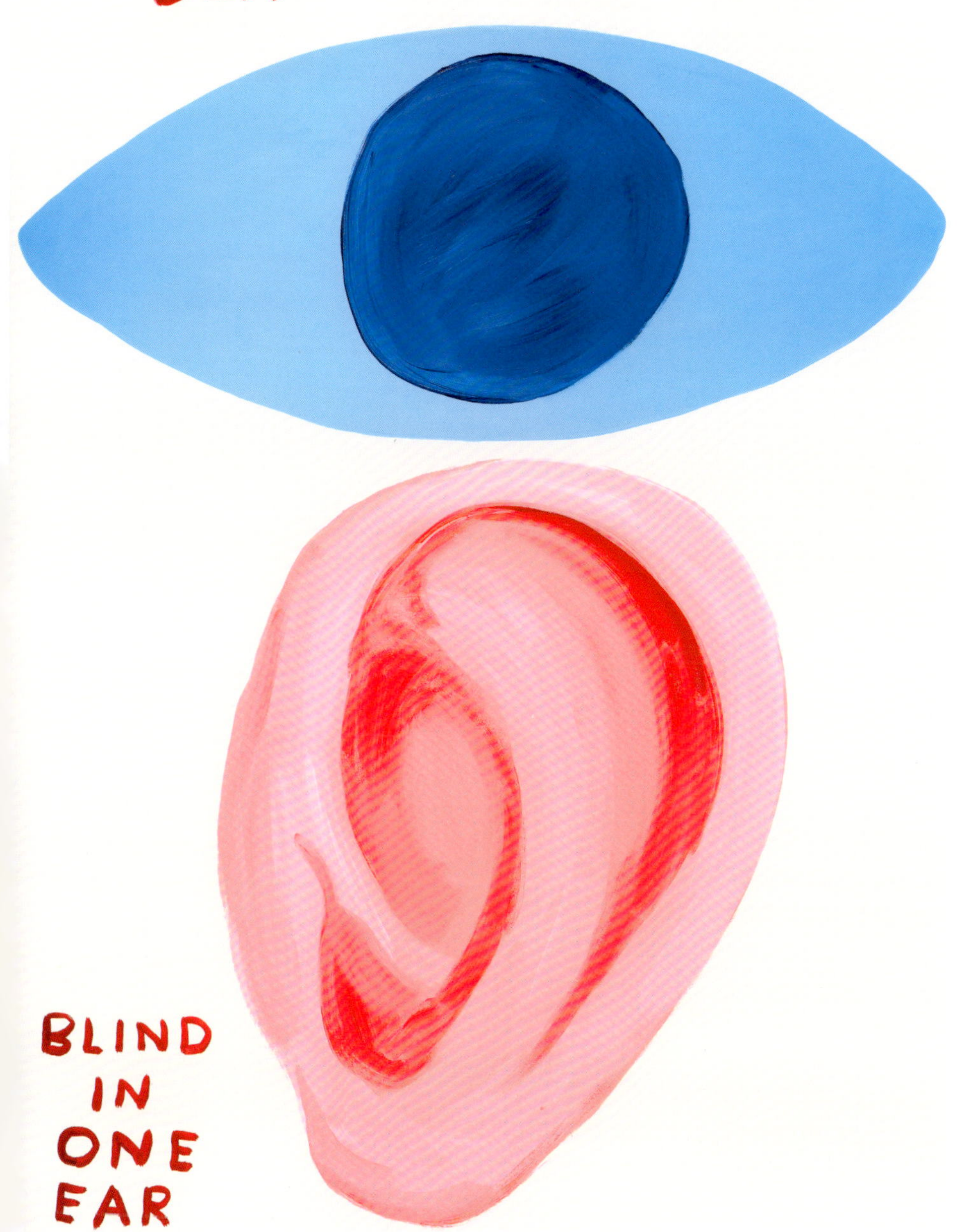
DEAF IN ONE EYE
BLIND
IN
ONE
EAR

EACH PRODUCT IS DIFFERENT

EACH PRODUCT IS THE SAME

TRY TO
CONCEN
-TRATE

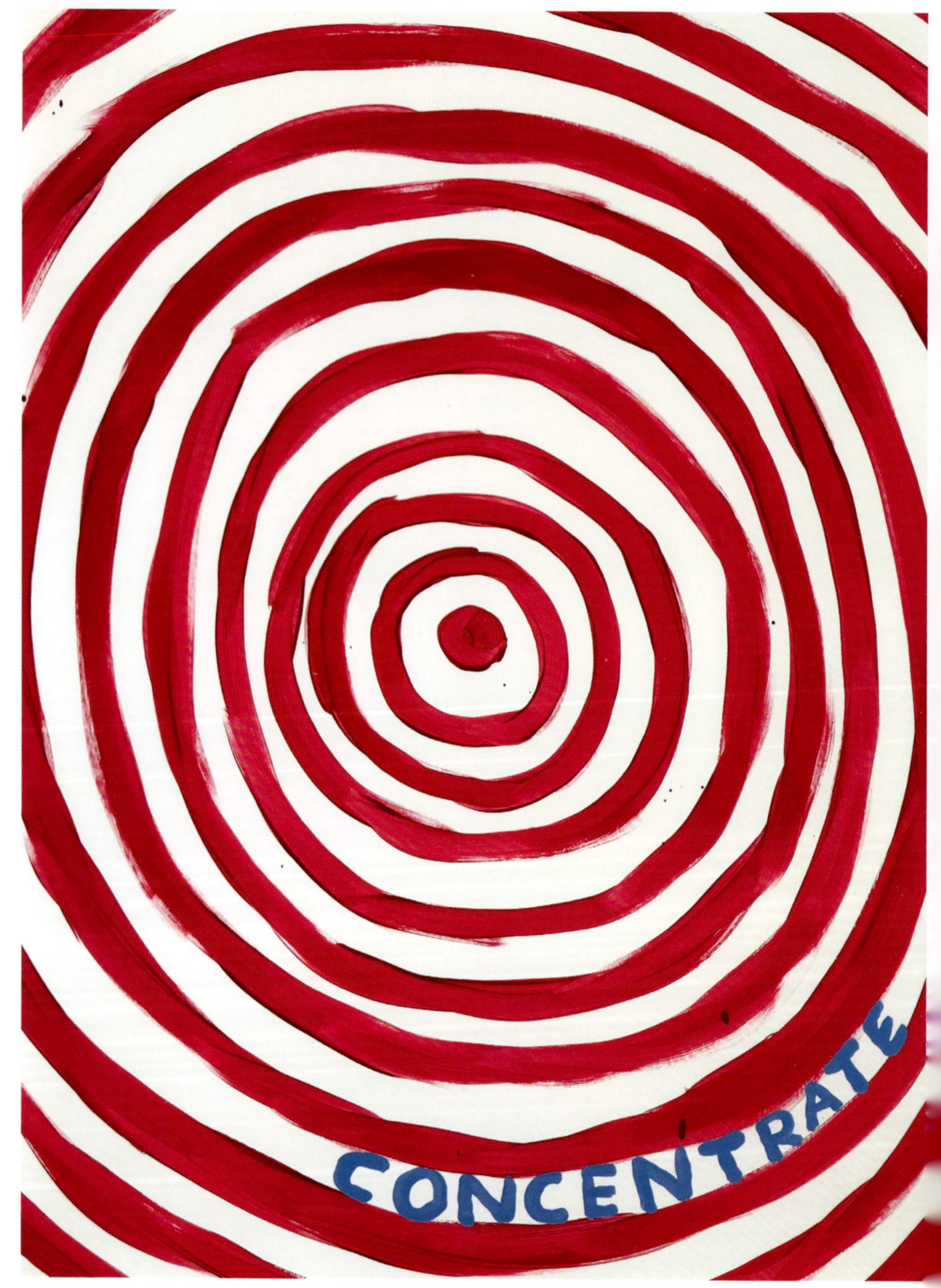
CONCENTRATE

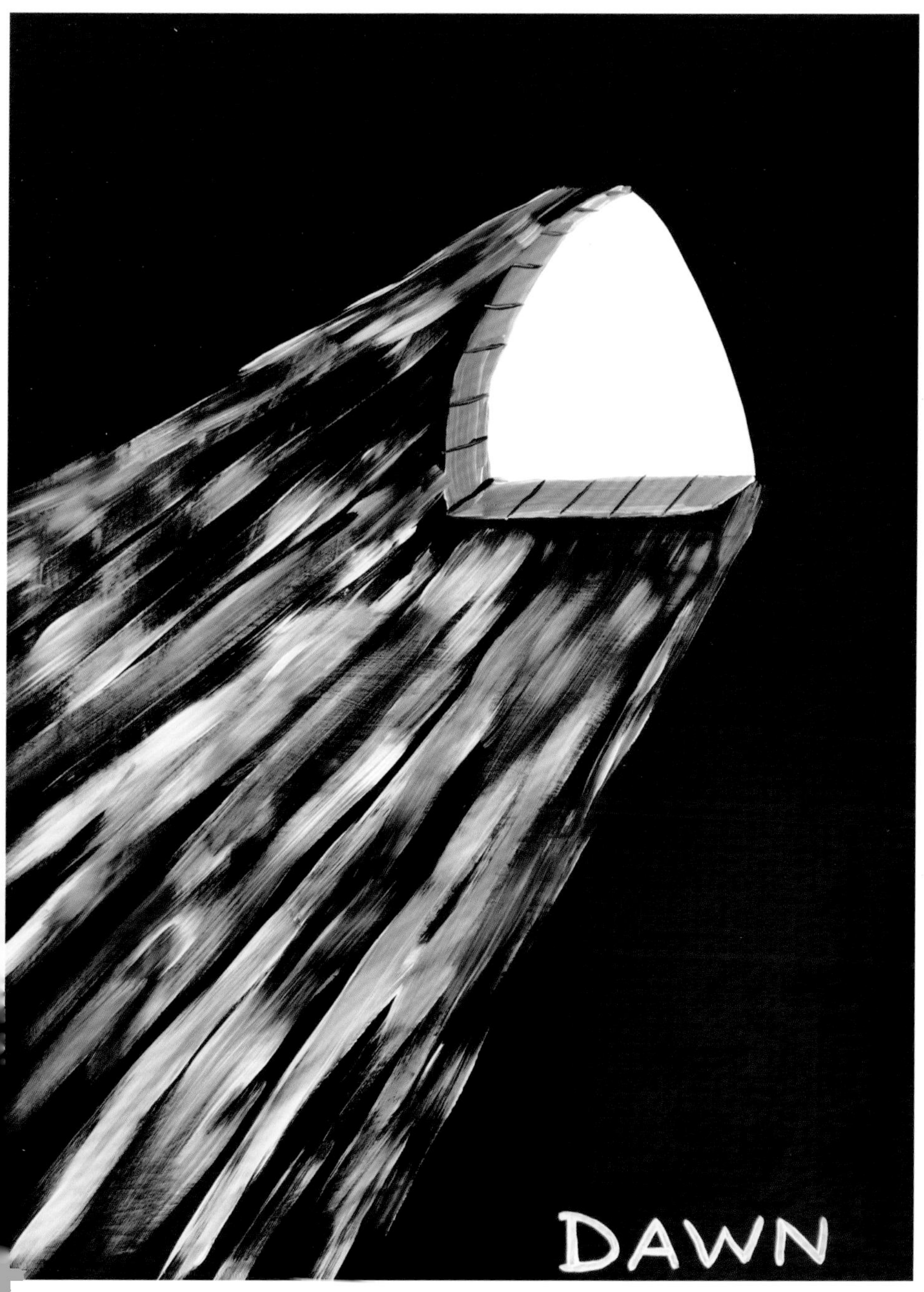
DAWN

UNCOMMON

I DON'T NORMALLY DO THIS
SHARING MY INTIMATE THOUGHTS
WRITING THEM ALL DOWN
FOR OTHERS TO READ
I WOULD NOT NORMALLY DO IT
BUT I FELT A NEED
AND I AM IMPULSIVE
AND CANNOT RESIST MY URGES
PLEASE FORGIVE ME

I AM NOT DROWNING
I AM ENJOYING SOME PEACE AND QUIET AT THE BOTTOM OF THE LAKE

VERY LITTLE SPACE TO EXPRESS YOURSELF

BUT YOU WILL NOT BE STOPPED FROM
EXPESSIING YOURSELF
SO BRAVO TO YOU!
BRAVO! BRAVO INDEED!

HOPE

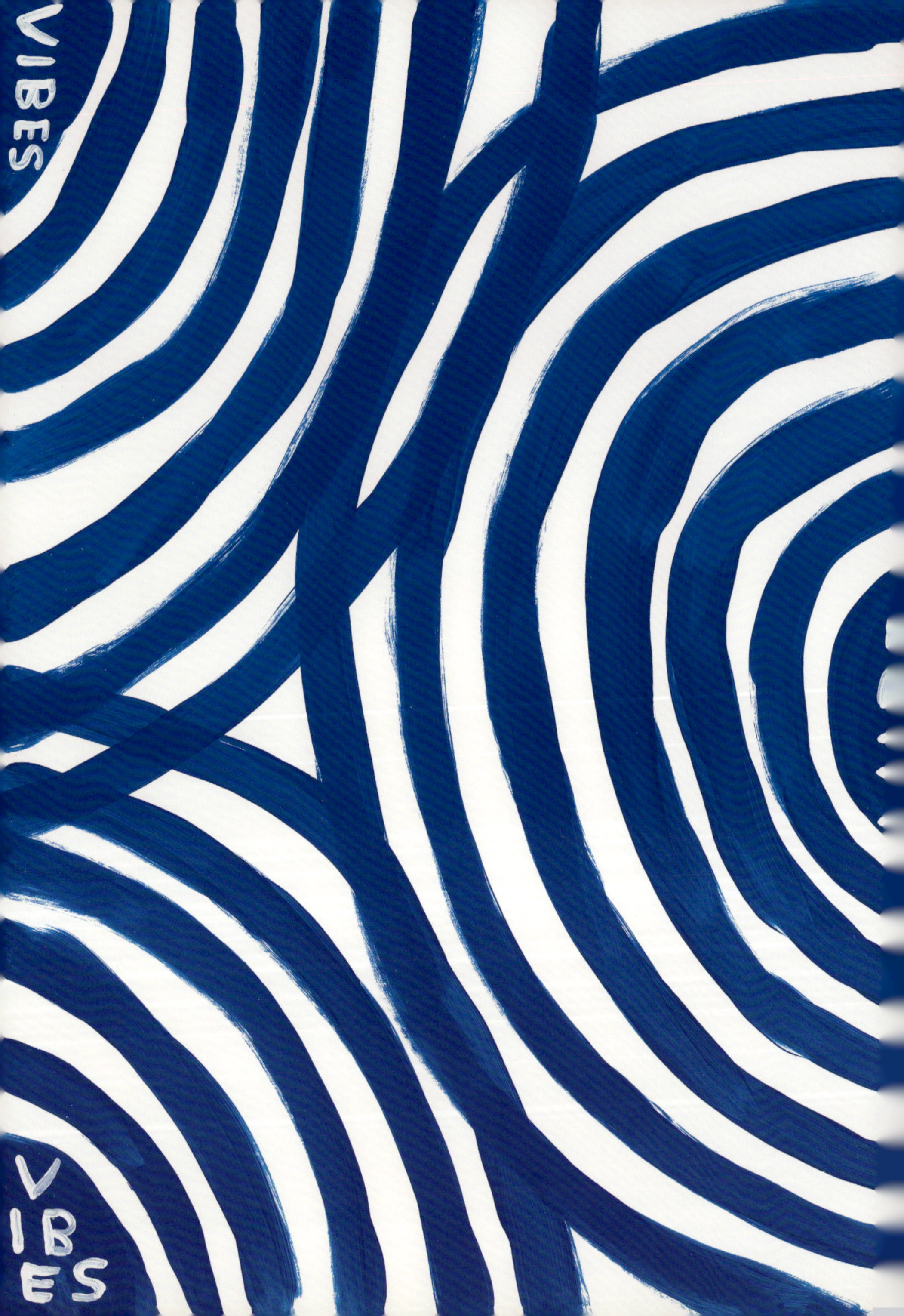
VIBES
VIBES

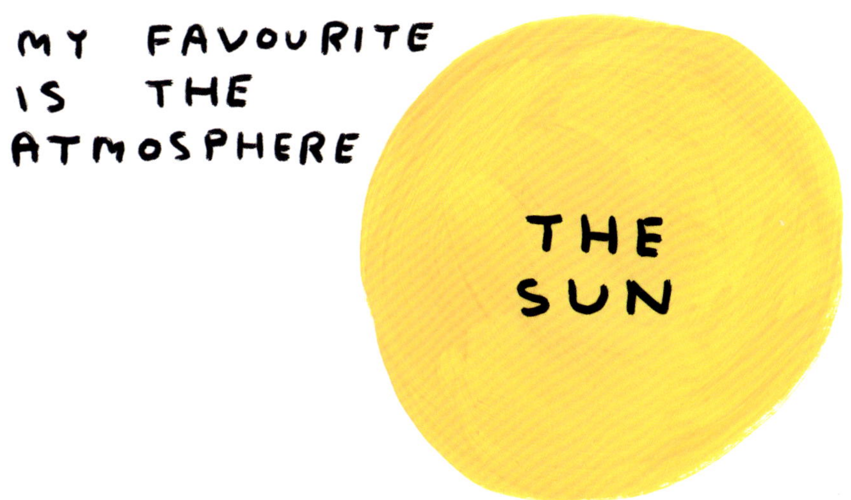

THE
ATMOSPHERE

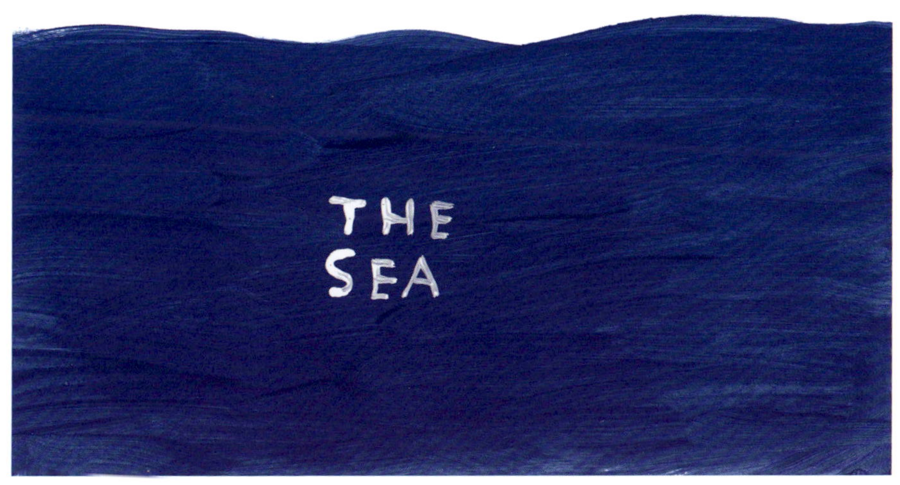

I TRIED TO RE-CREATE THE MOMENT

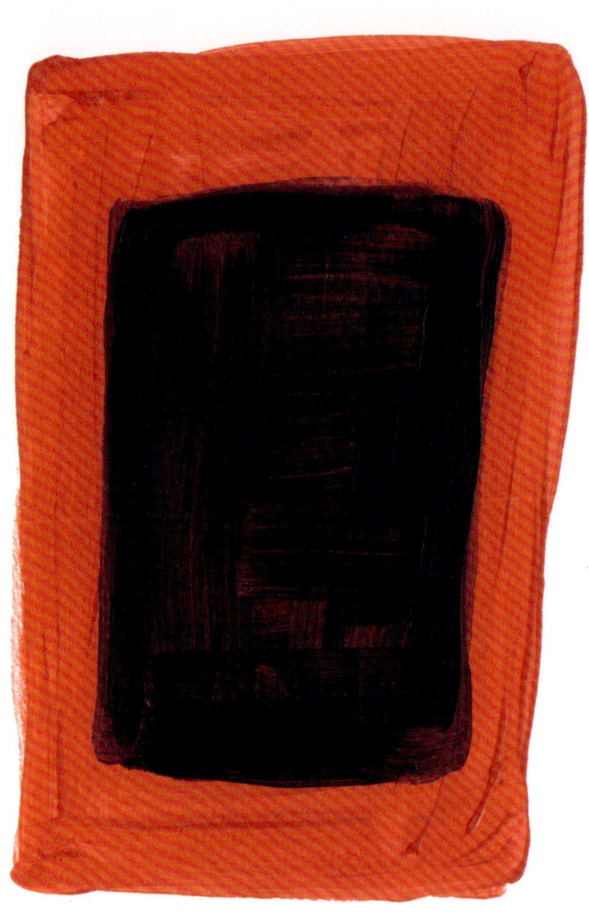

BUT I FAILED

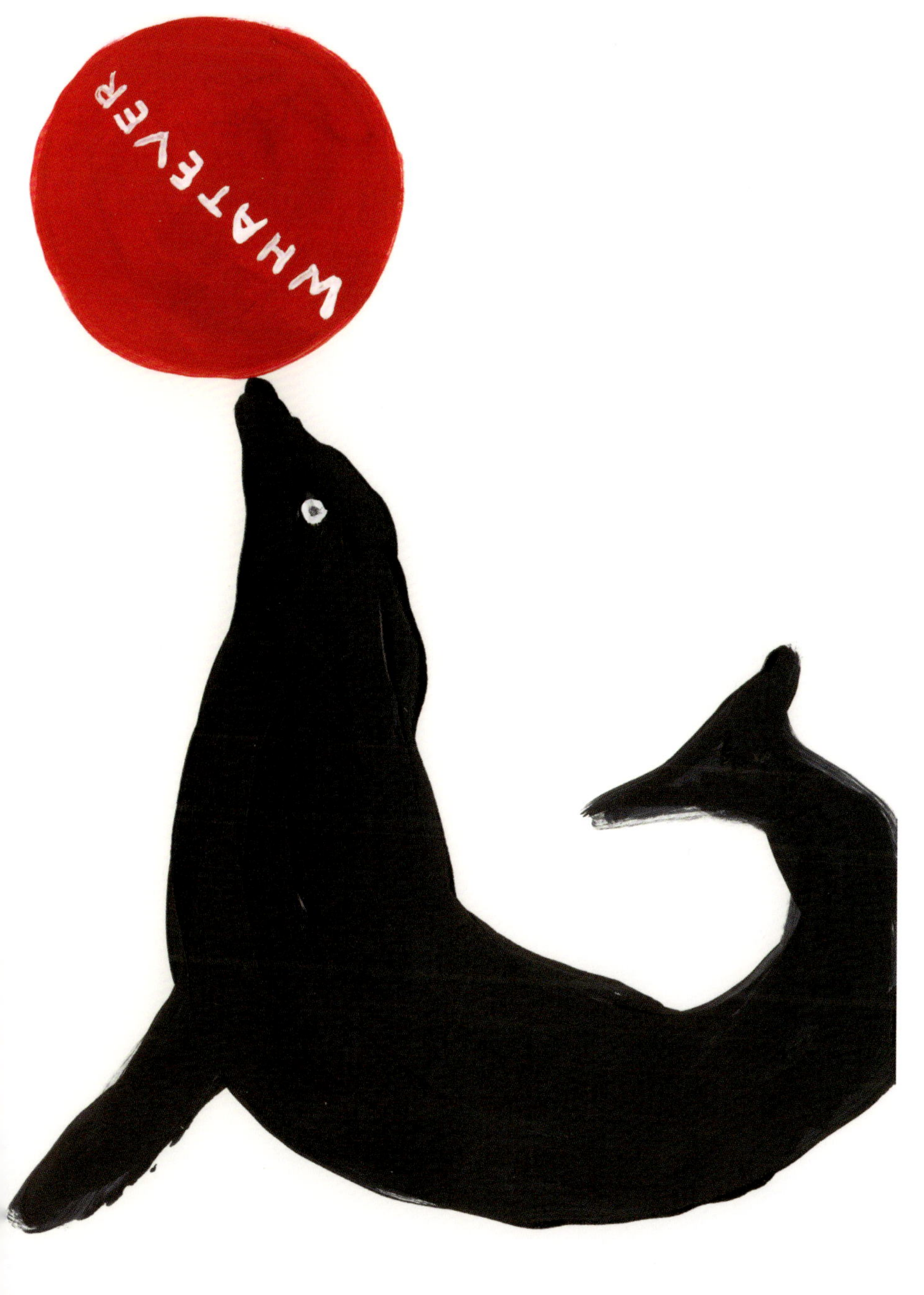
WHATEVER

THE WORLD

GIVE ME A WORLD
THAT IS HORRIBLE AND BORING
AND I WILL MAKE IT NICE AND
INTERESTING
I WILL PAINT IT BRIGHT COLOURS
FOR I AM AN ARTIST
AND THAT IS WHAT I DO
NOW SHUT UP
AND LET ME GET ON WITH MY WORK
YOU IDIOT

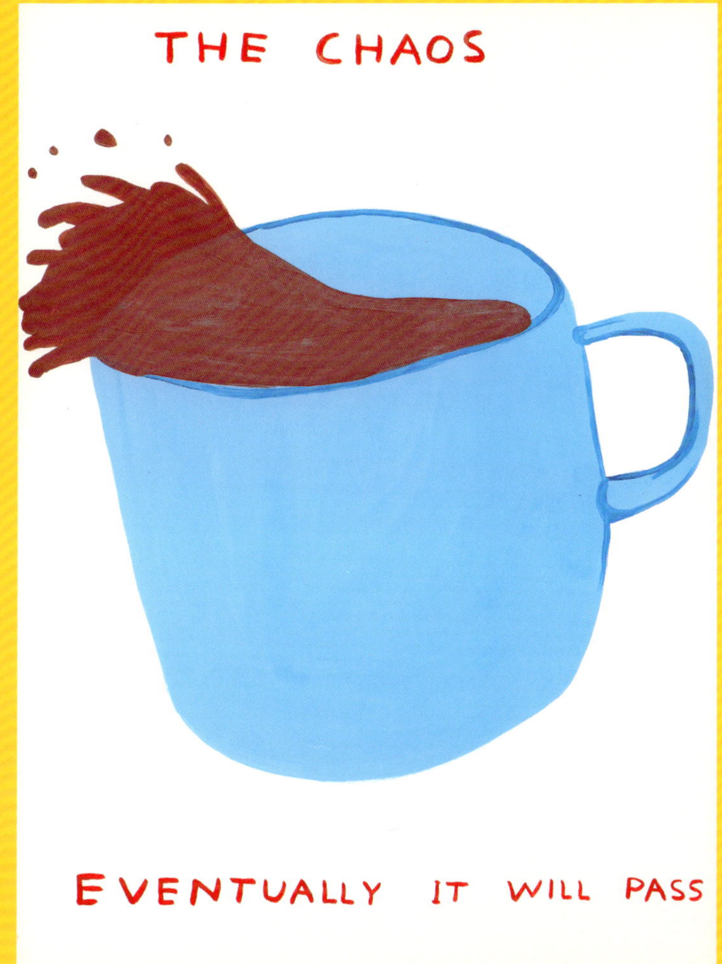
THE CHAOS
EVENTUALLY IT WILL PASS

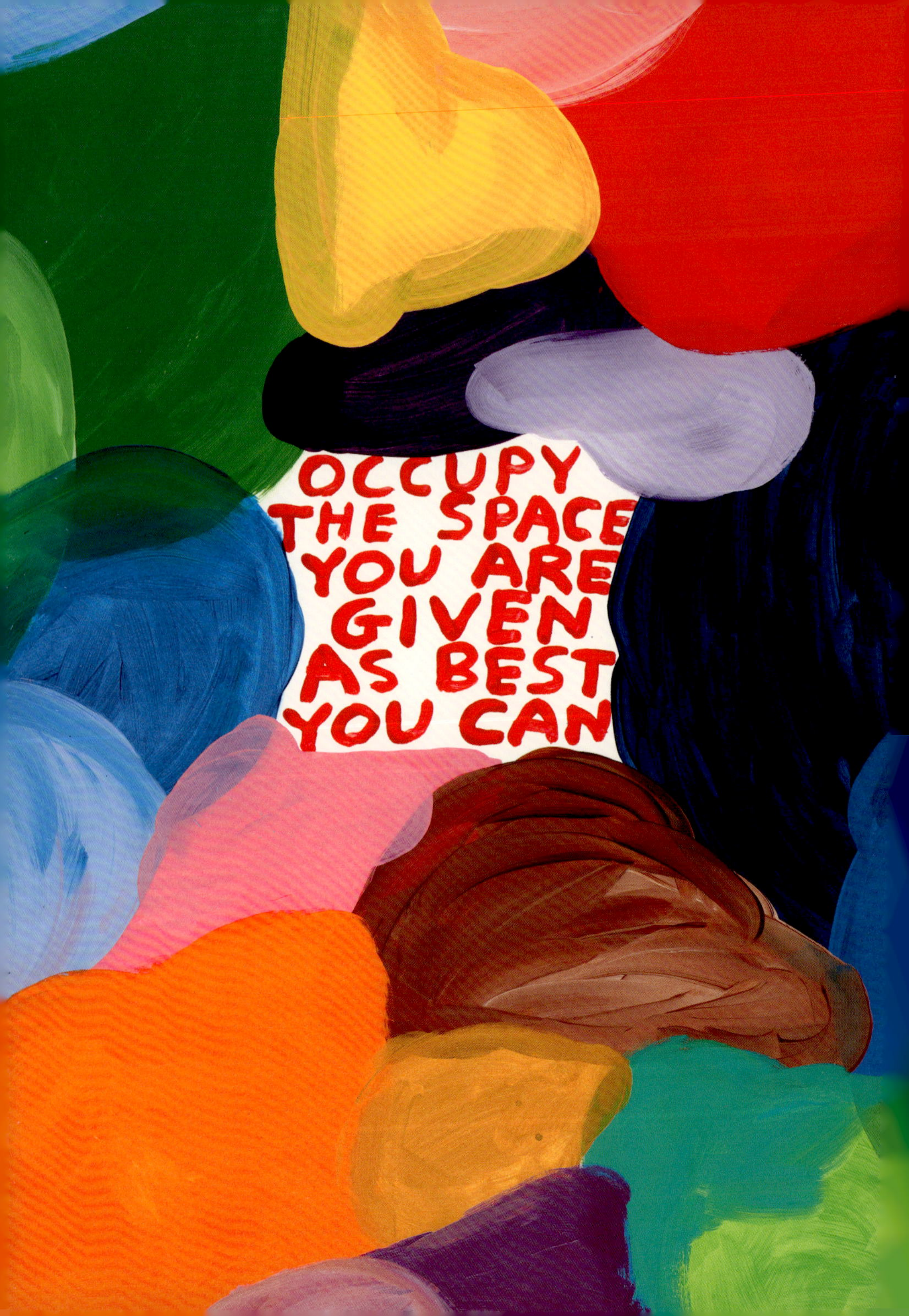
OCCUPY
THE SPACE
YOU ARE
GIVEN
AS BEST
YOU CAN

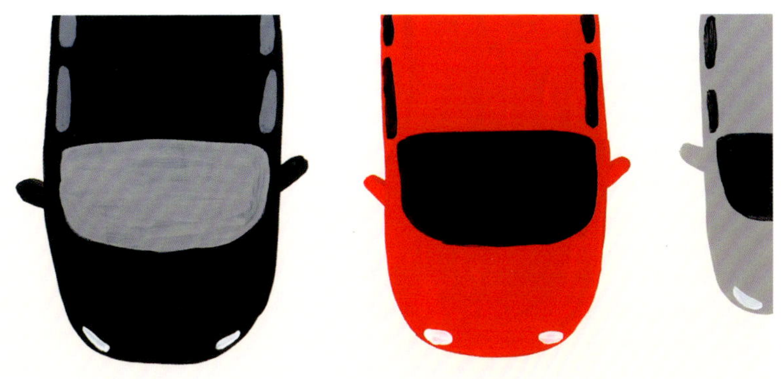

PARK CORRECTLY

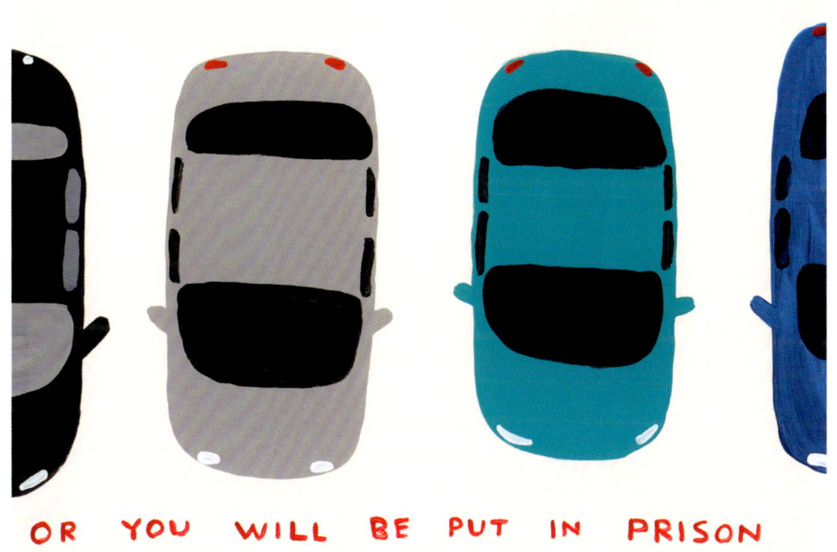

OR YOU WILL BE PUT IN PRISON

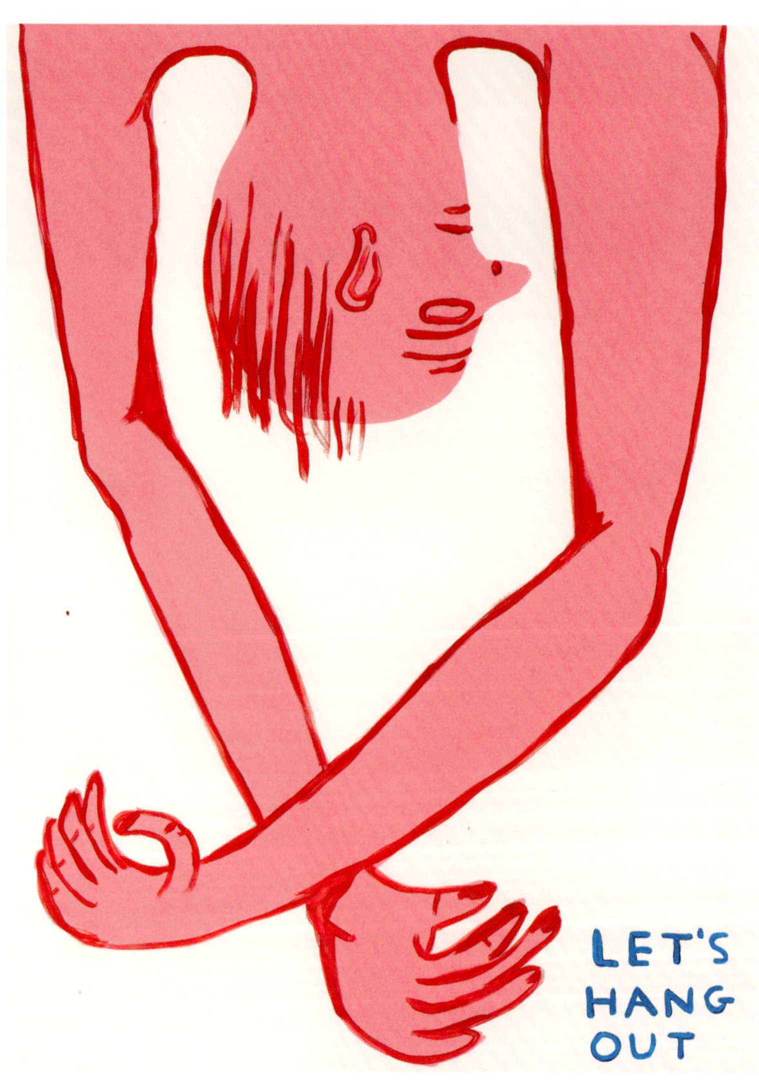
LET'S
HANG
OUT

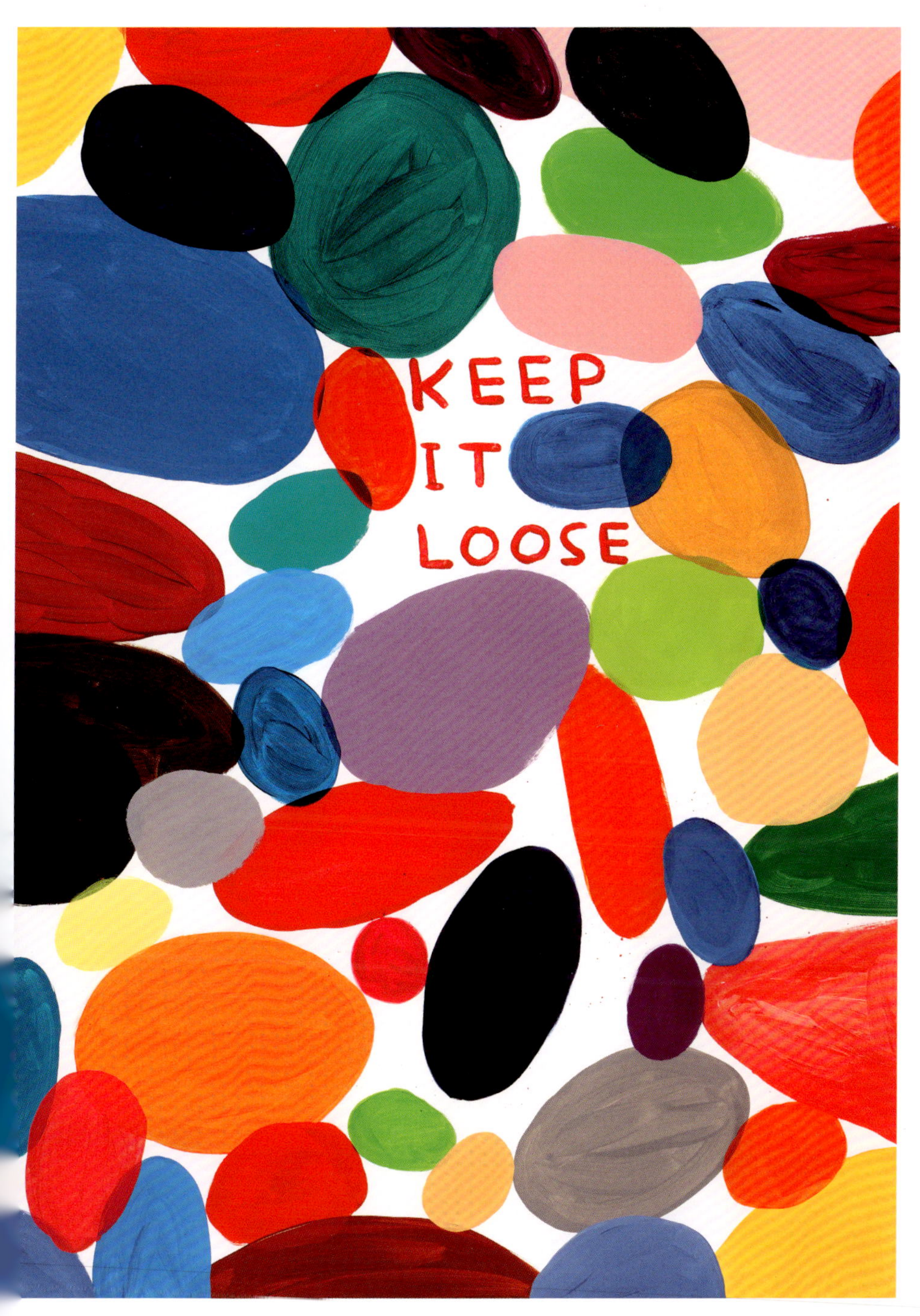
KEEP
IT
LOOSE

THE END

MY BATTERY IS RUNNING OUT
AND I DON'T HAVE THE MEANS TO
RE-CHARGE IT
THIS IS NOT AN EXCUSE
IT IS A VALID REASON
FOR ME TO STOP

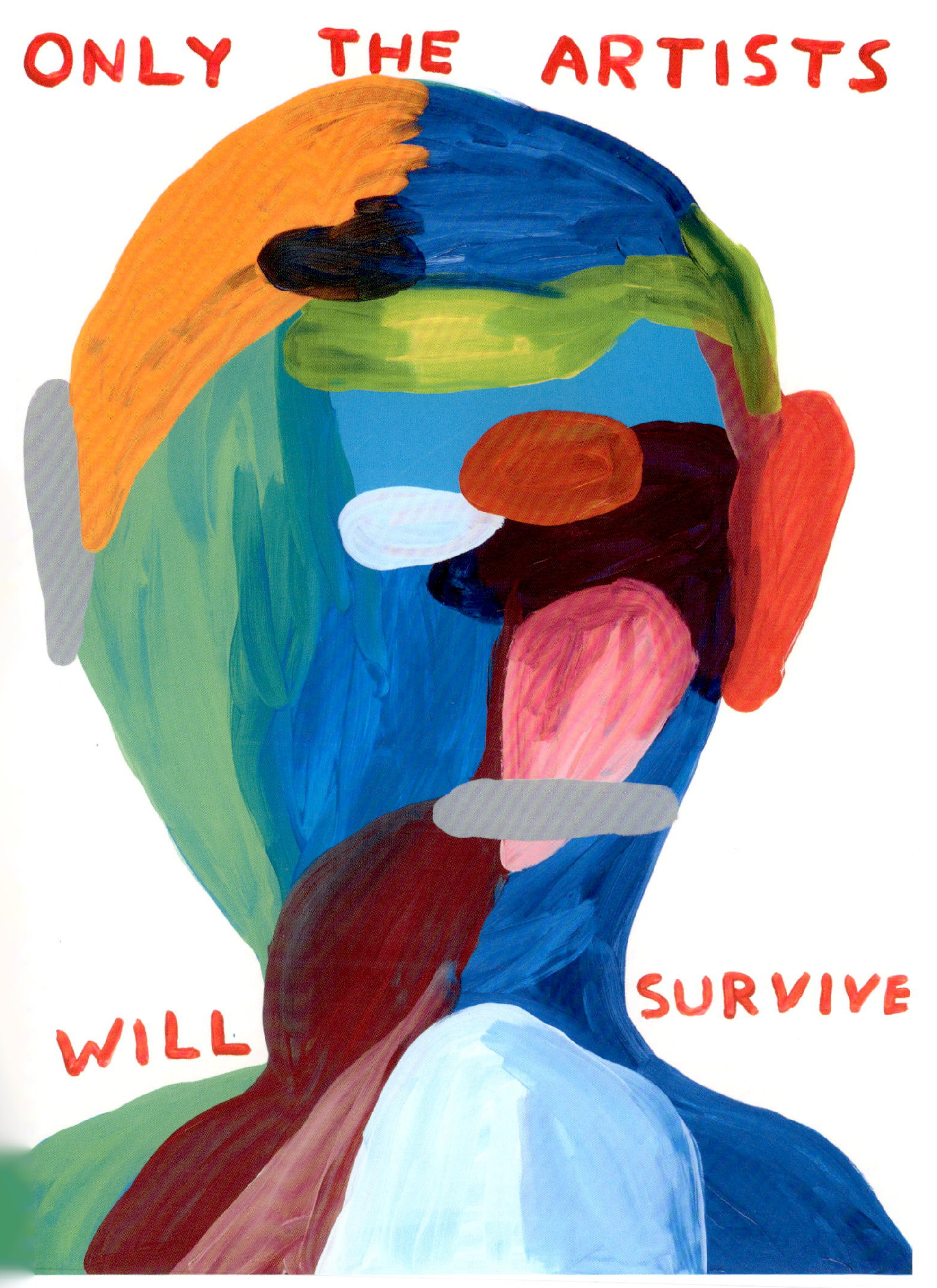
ONLY THE ARTISTS
WILL
SURVIVE

GET YOUR SHIT TOGETHER
BY DAVID SHRIGLEY

PUBLISHED BY CHRONICLE CHROMA:
STEVE CRIST AND GLORIA FOWLER
EDITOR AND ART DIRECTOR:
GLORIA FOWLER
DESIGN AND PRODUCTION:
ALEXANDRIA MARTINEZ
PRODUCTION: FREESIA BLIZARD

THANKS: BECKY BICK AND HAYLEY GIBSON

FIRST CHRONICLE CHROMA PAPERBACK
EDITION PUBLISHED IN 2025.

ORIGINALLY PUBLISHED IN HARDCOVER
IN 2022 BY CHRONICLE CHROMA.

ISBN 978-1-7972-3474-8
THE LIBRARY OF CONGRESS HAS CATALOGED THE
PREVIOUS EDITION UNDER ISBN 978-1-7972-2002-4.

SECOND PRINTING

PRINTED IN CHINA

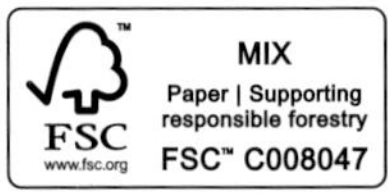

CHRONICLE CHROMA

CHRONICLE CHROMA IS AN
IMPRINT OF CHRONICLE BOOKS
LOS ANGELES, CALIFORNIA
CHRONICLECHROMA.COM

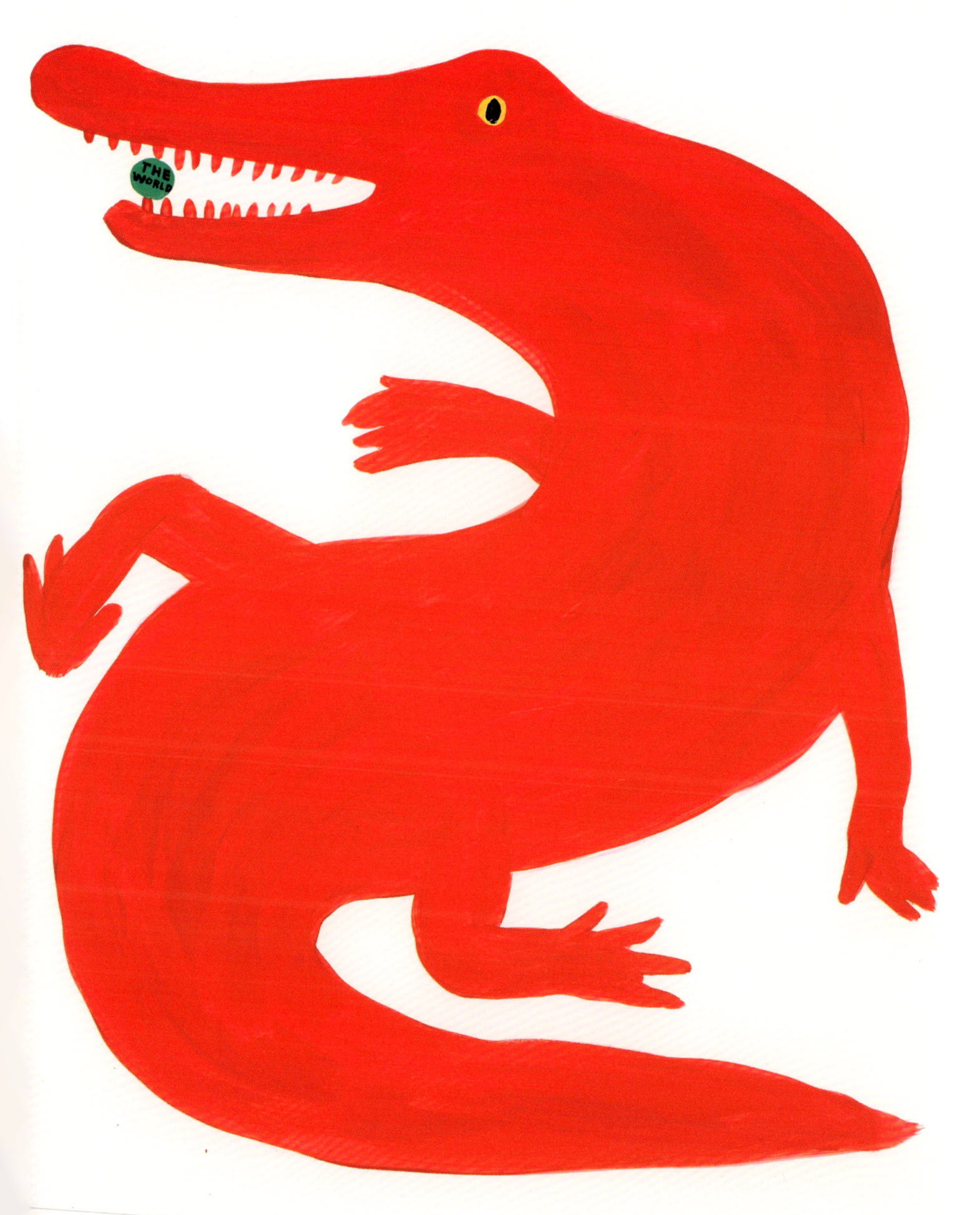
THE WORLD

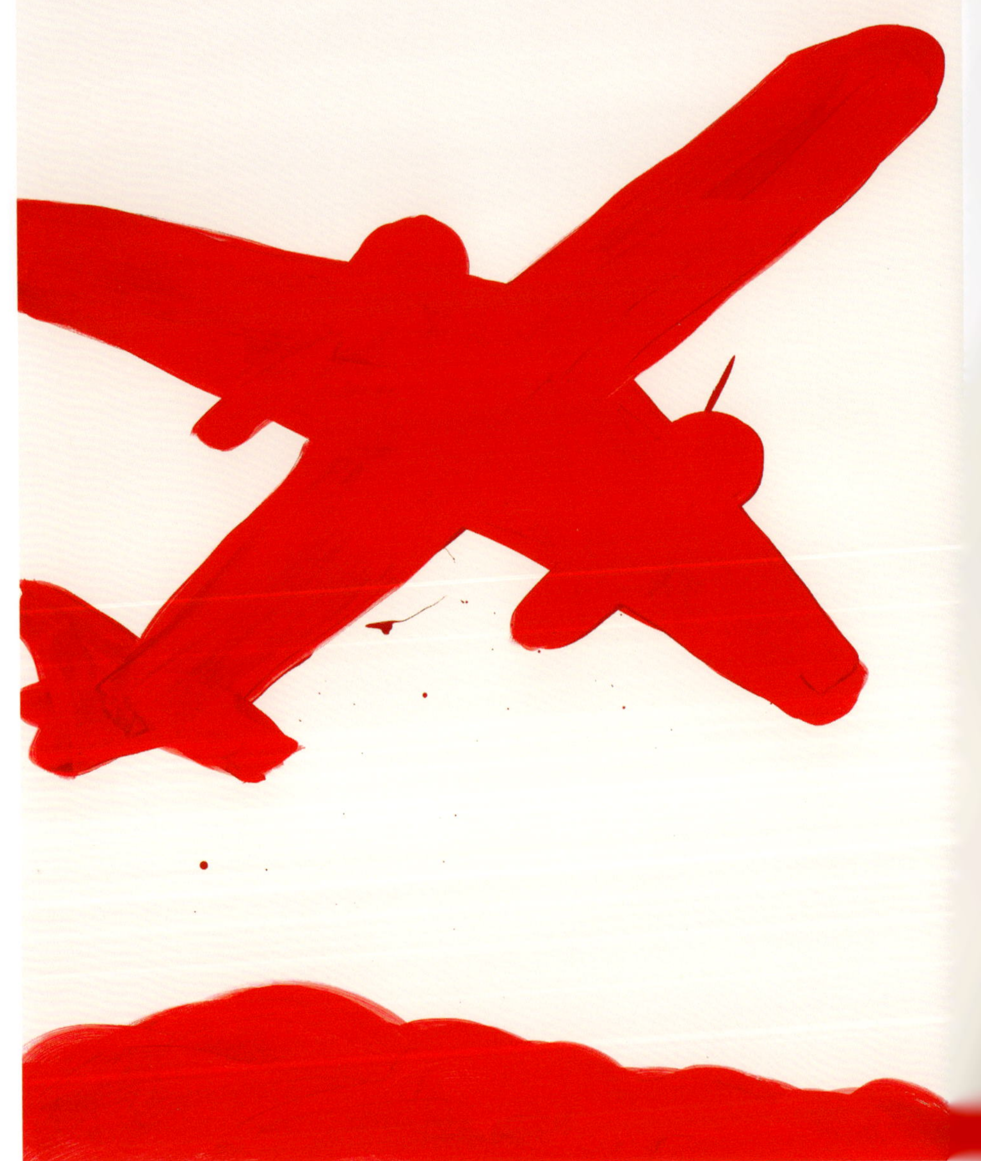
FLY HIGH TO AVOID
DEGENERATES ON THE GROUND

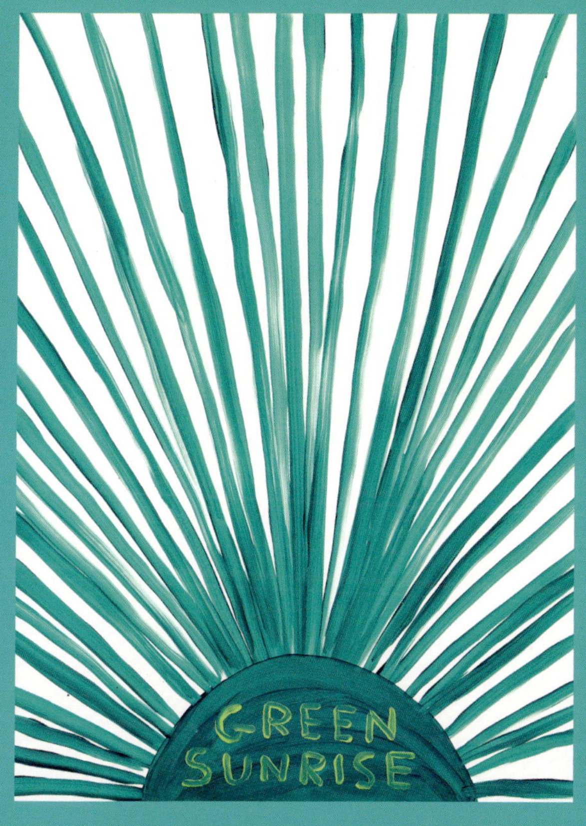
GREEN
SUNRISE

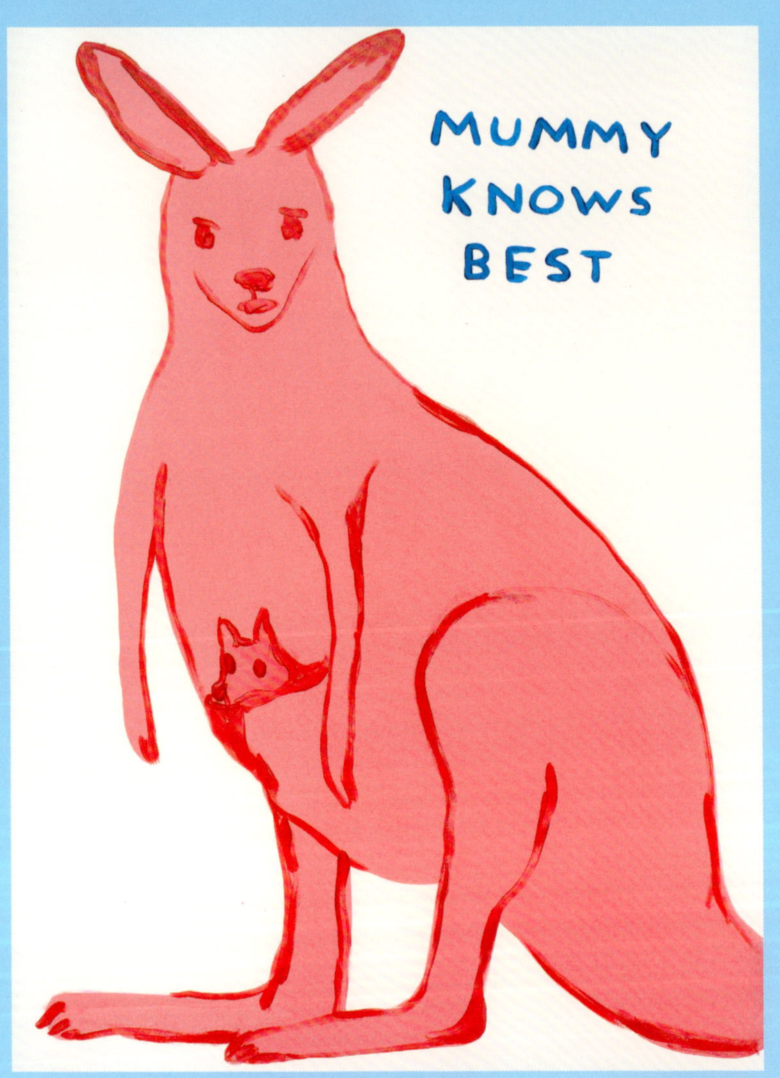
MUMMY
KNOWS
BEST

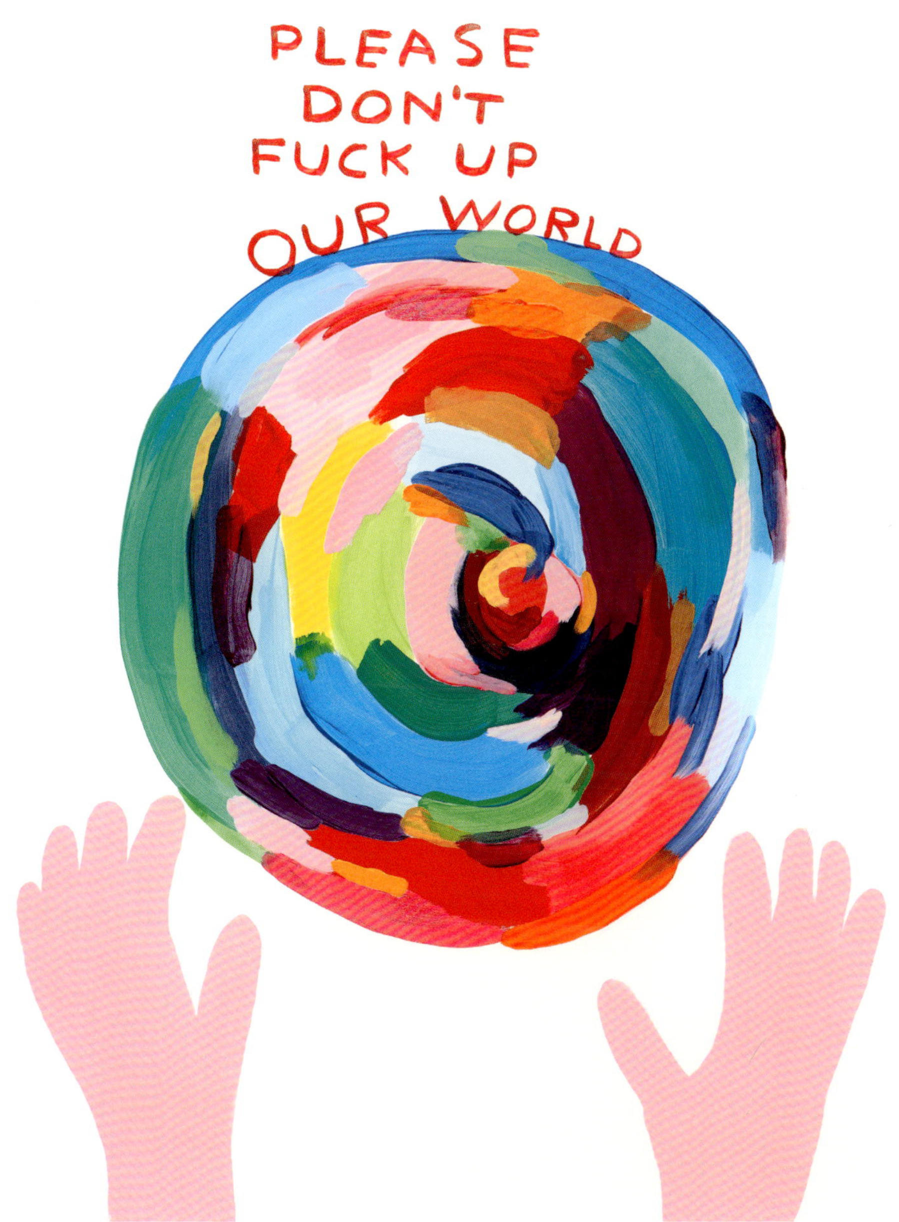
PLEASE
DON'T
FUCK UP
OUR WORLD

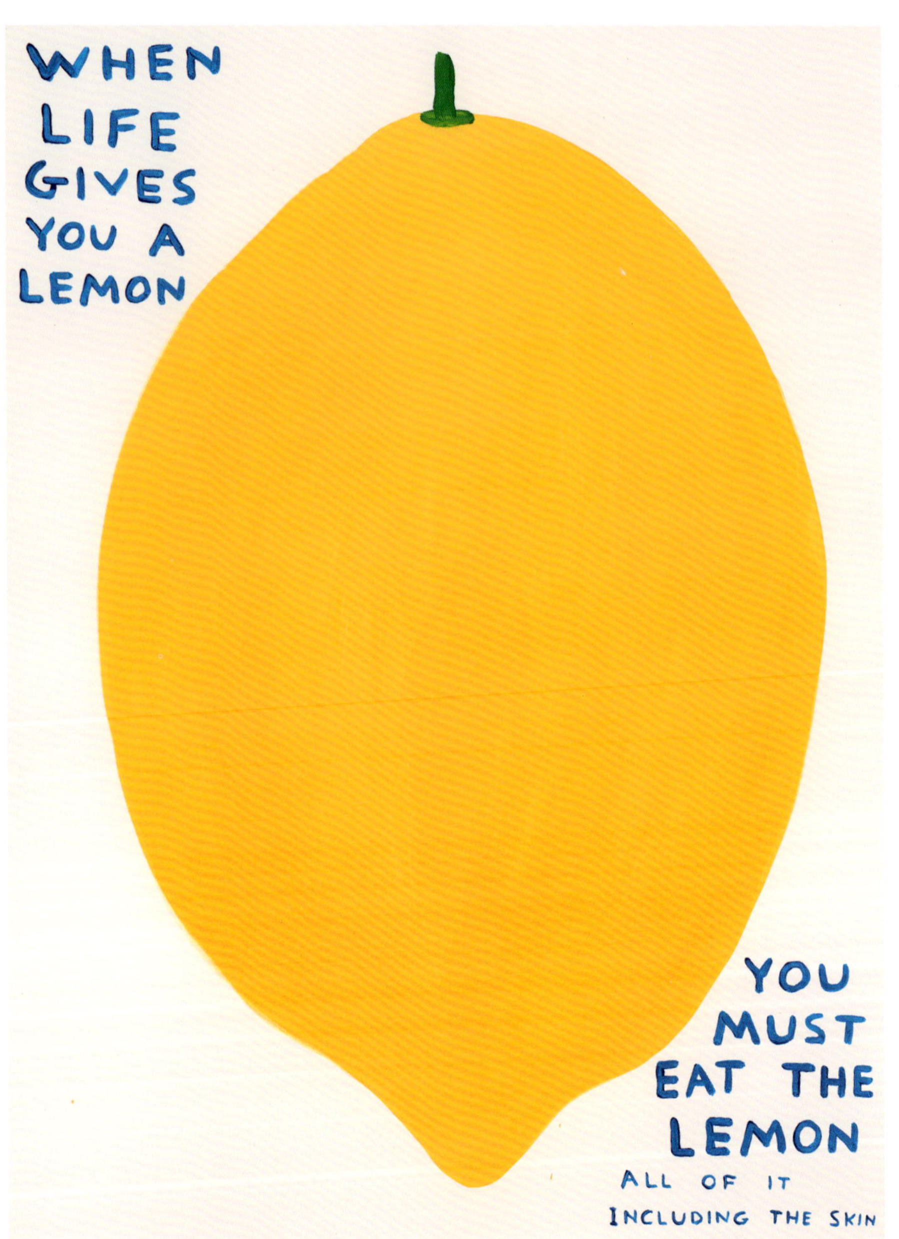
WHEN LIFE GIVES YOU A LEMON
YOU MUST EAT THE LEMON
ALL OF IT
INCLUDING THE SKIN